CEDAR MILL & BETHANY
COMMUNITY LIBRARIES

D1097673

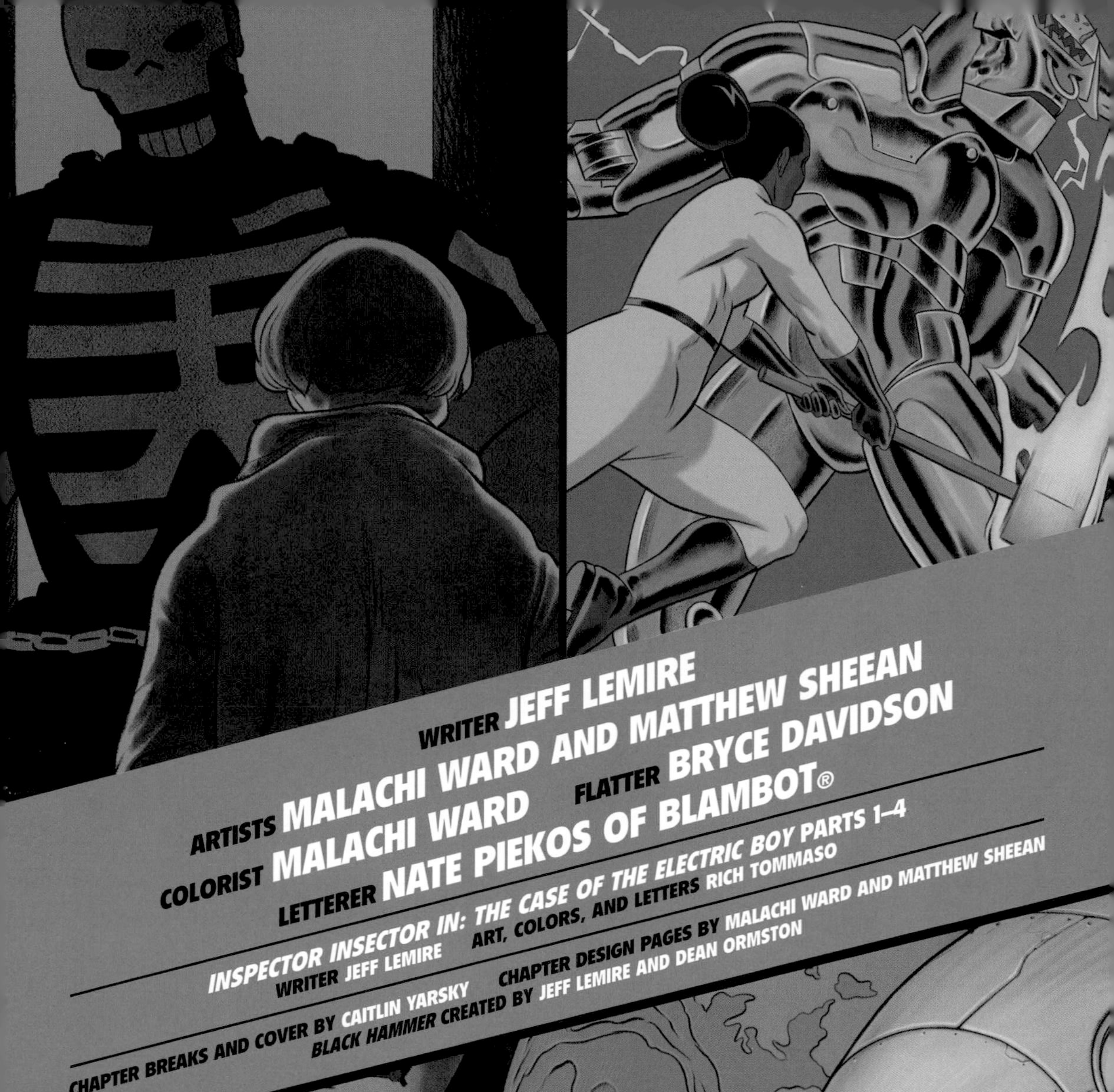

WRITER **JEFF LEMIRE**

ARTISTS **MALACHI WARD AND MATTHEW SHEEAN**

COLORIST **MALACHI WARD** FLATTER **BRYCE DAVIDSON**

LETTERER **NATE PIEKOS OF BLAMBOT®**

INSPECTOR INSECTOR IN: THE CASE OF THE ELECTRIC BOY PARTS 1–4
WRITER JEFF LEMIRE ART, COLORS, AND LETTERS RICH TOMMASO

CHAPTER BREAKS AND COVER BY CAITLIN YARSKY CHAPTER DESIGN PAGES BY MALACHI WARD AND MATTHEW SHEEAN
BLACK HAMMER CREATED BY JEFF LEMIRE AND DEAN ORMSTON

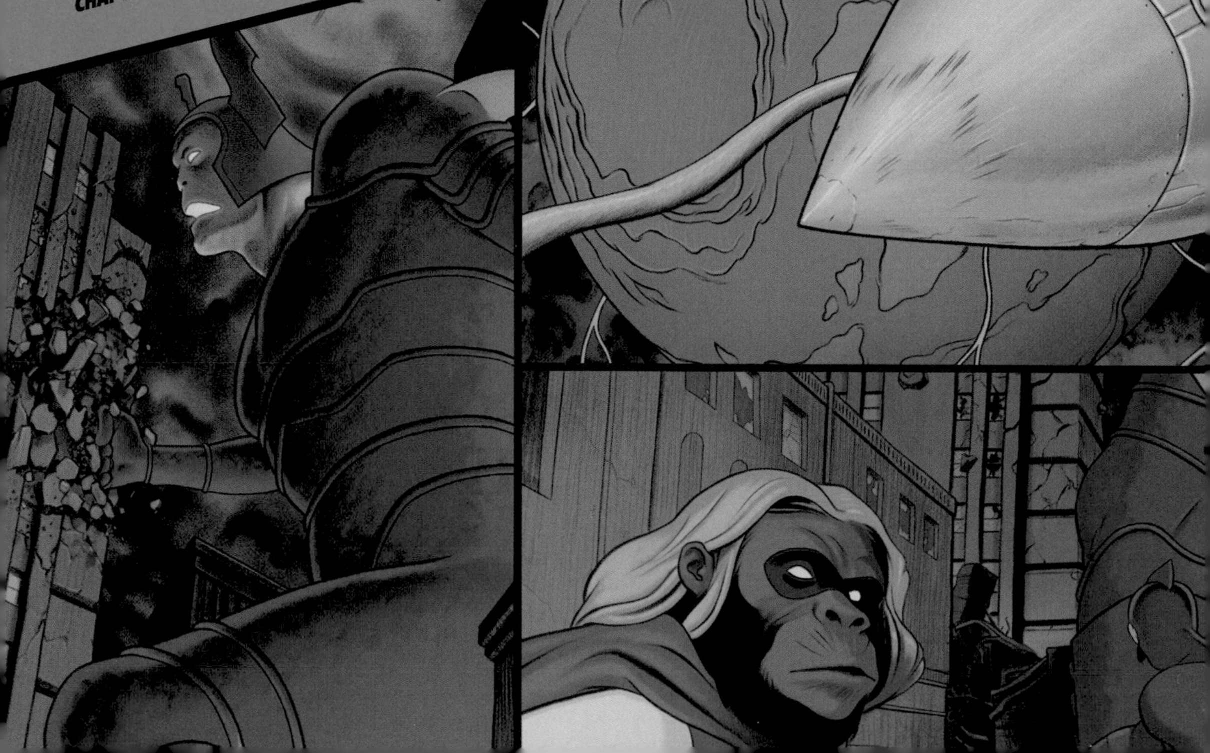

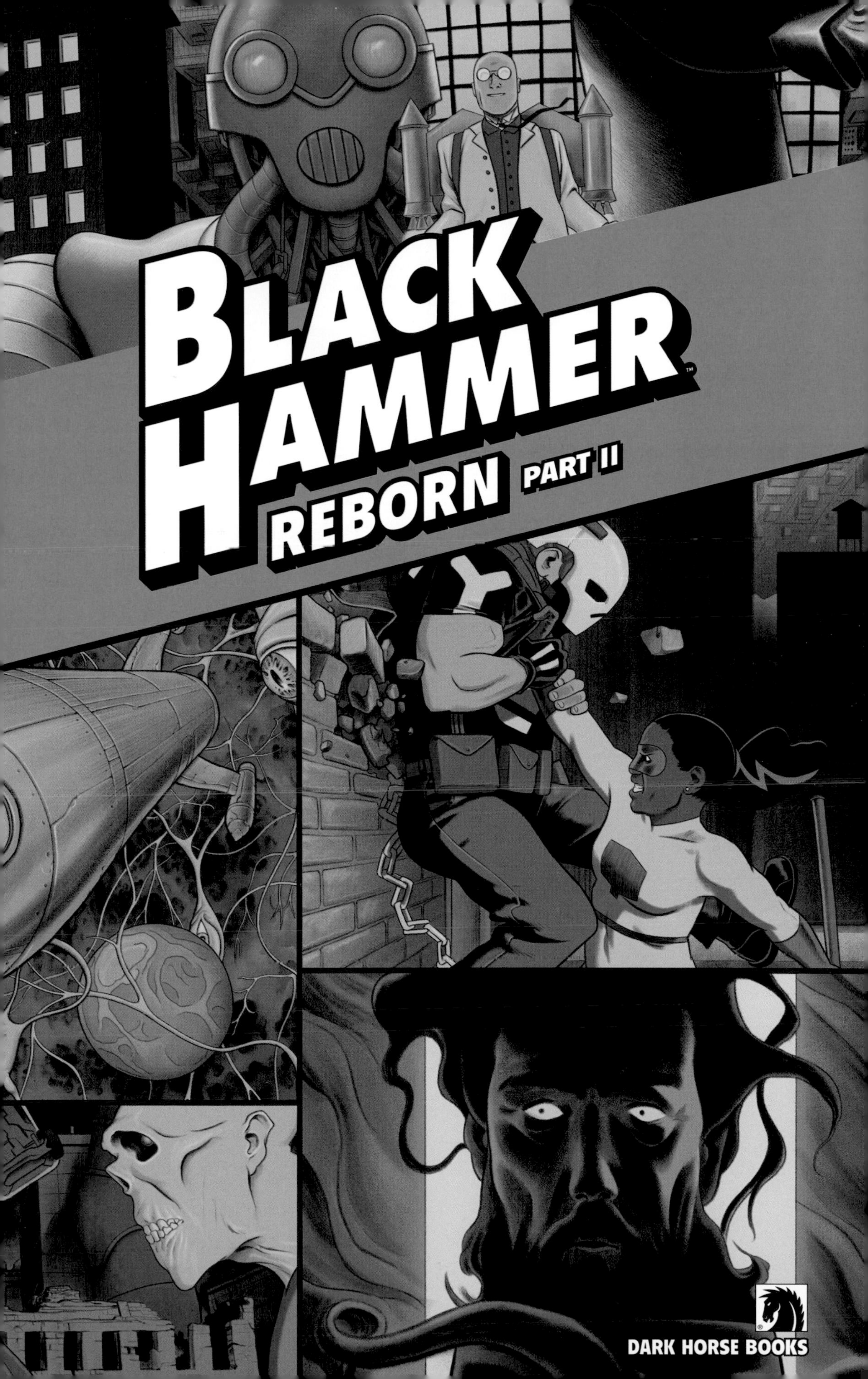
BLACK HAMMER
REBORN PART II
DARK HORSE BOOKS

PRESIDENT & PUBLISHER
MIKE RICHARDSON

EDITOR
DANIEL CHABON

ASSISTANT EDITORS
CHUCK HOWITT,
KONNER KNUDSEN,
AND MISHA GEHR

DESIGNER
ETHAN KIMBERLING

DIGITAL ART TECHNICIAN
JOSIE CHRISTENSEN

BLACK HAMMER VOLUME 6: REBORN PART II

Black Hammer Reborn™ © 2021, 2022 171 Studios, Inc., and Dean Ormston. Dark Horse Books® and the Dark Horse logo are registered trademarks of Dark Horse Comics LLC. All rights reserved. No portion of this publication may be reproduced or transmitted, in any form or by any means, without the express written permission of Dark Horse Comics LLC. Names, characters, places, and incidents featured in this publication either are the product of the author's imagination or are used fictitiously. Any resemblance to actual persons (living or dead), events, institutions, or locales, without satiric intent, is coincidental.

Collects issues #5–#8 of the Dark Horse Comics series *Black Hammer Reborn*.

Published by
Dark Horse Books
A division of Dark Horse Comics LLC
10956 SE Main Street
Milwaukie, OR 97222

DarkHorse.com

To find a comics shop in your area, visit comicshoplocator.com

First edition: June 2022
Ebook ISBN 978-1-50671-512-4
Trade Paperback ISBN 978-1-50671-515-5

10 9 8 7 6 5 4 3 2 1
Printed in China

NEIL HANKERSON Executive Vice President TOM WEDDLE Chief Financial Officer DALE LaFOUNTAIN Chief Information Officer TIM WIESCH Vice President of Licensing MATT PARKINSON Vice President of Marketing VANESSA TODD-HOLMES Vice President of Production and Scheduling MARK BERNARDI Vice President of Book Trade and Digital Sales RANDY LAHRMAN Vice President of Product Development KEN LIZZI General Counsel DAVE MARSHALL Editor in Chief DAVEY ESTRADA Editorial Director CHRIS WARNER Senior Books Editor CARY GRAZZINI Director of Specialty Projects LIA RIBACCHI Art Director MATT DRYER Director of Digital Art and Prepress MICHAEL GOMBOS Senior Director of Licensed Publications KARI YADRO Director of Custom Programs KARI TORSON Director of International Licensing

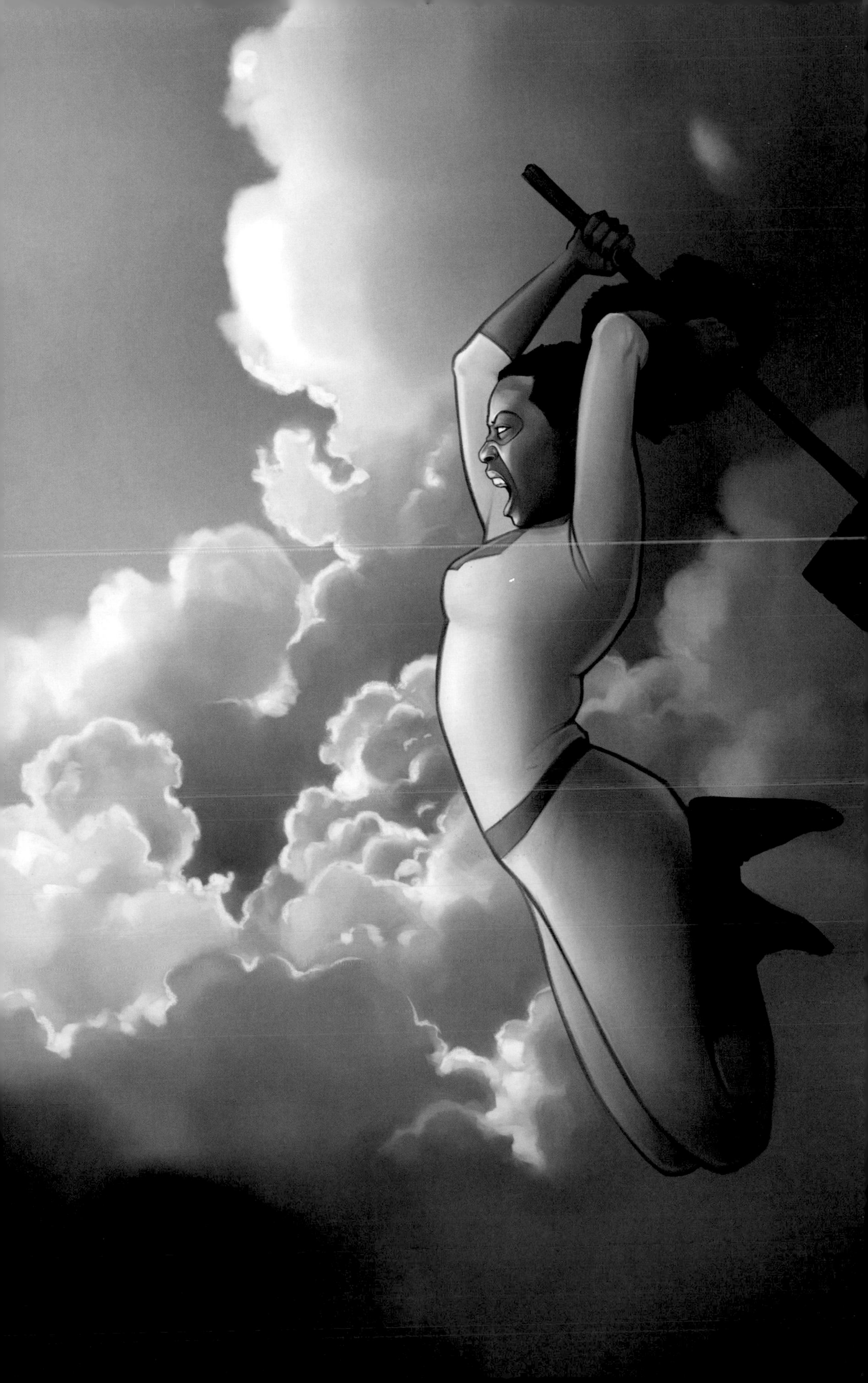

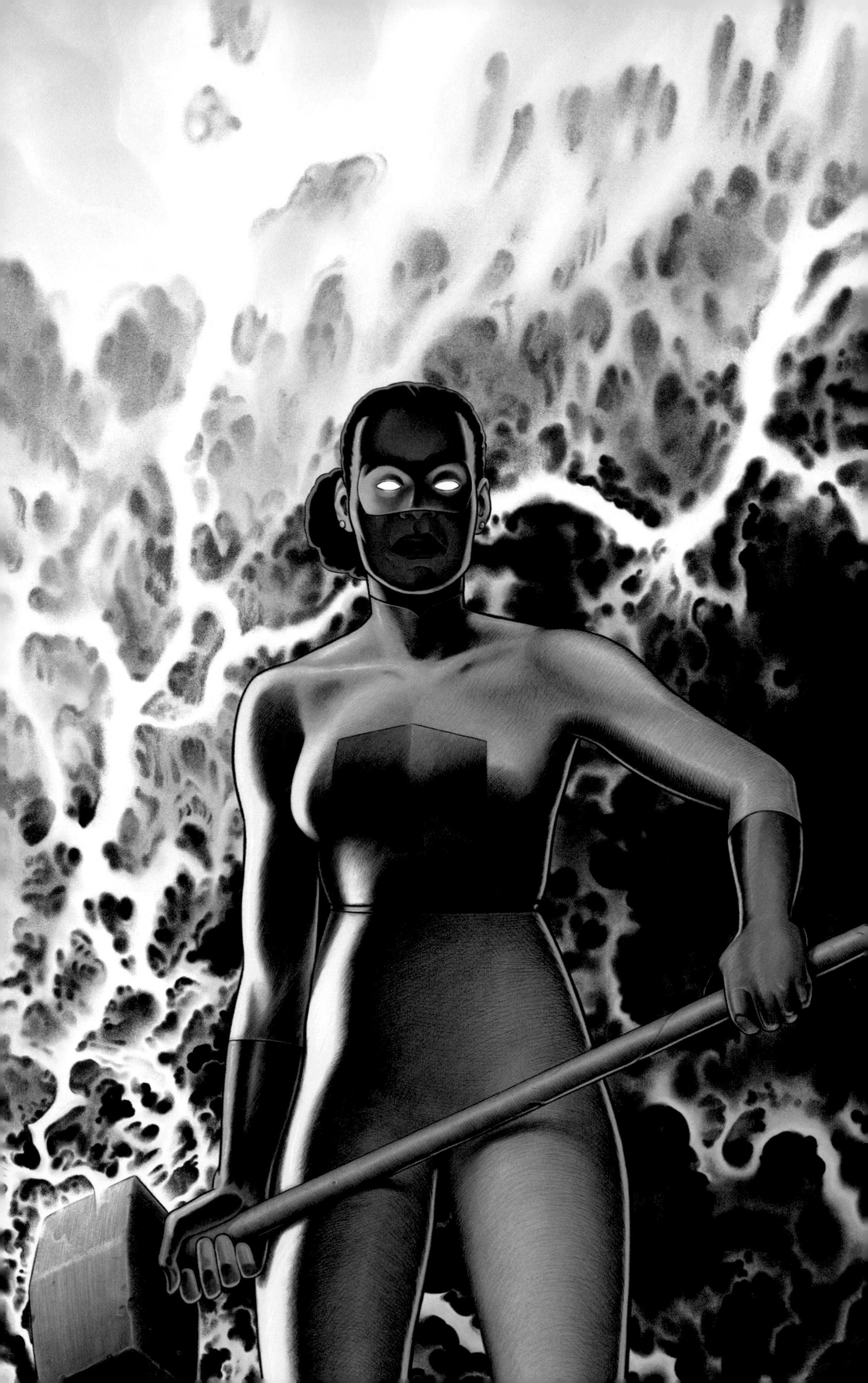

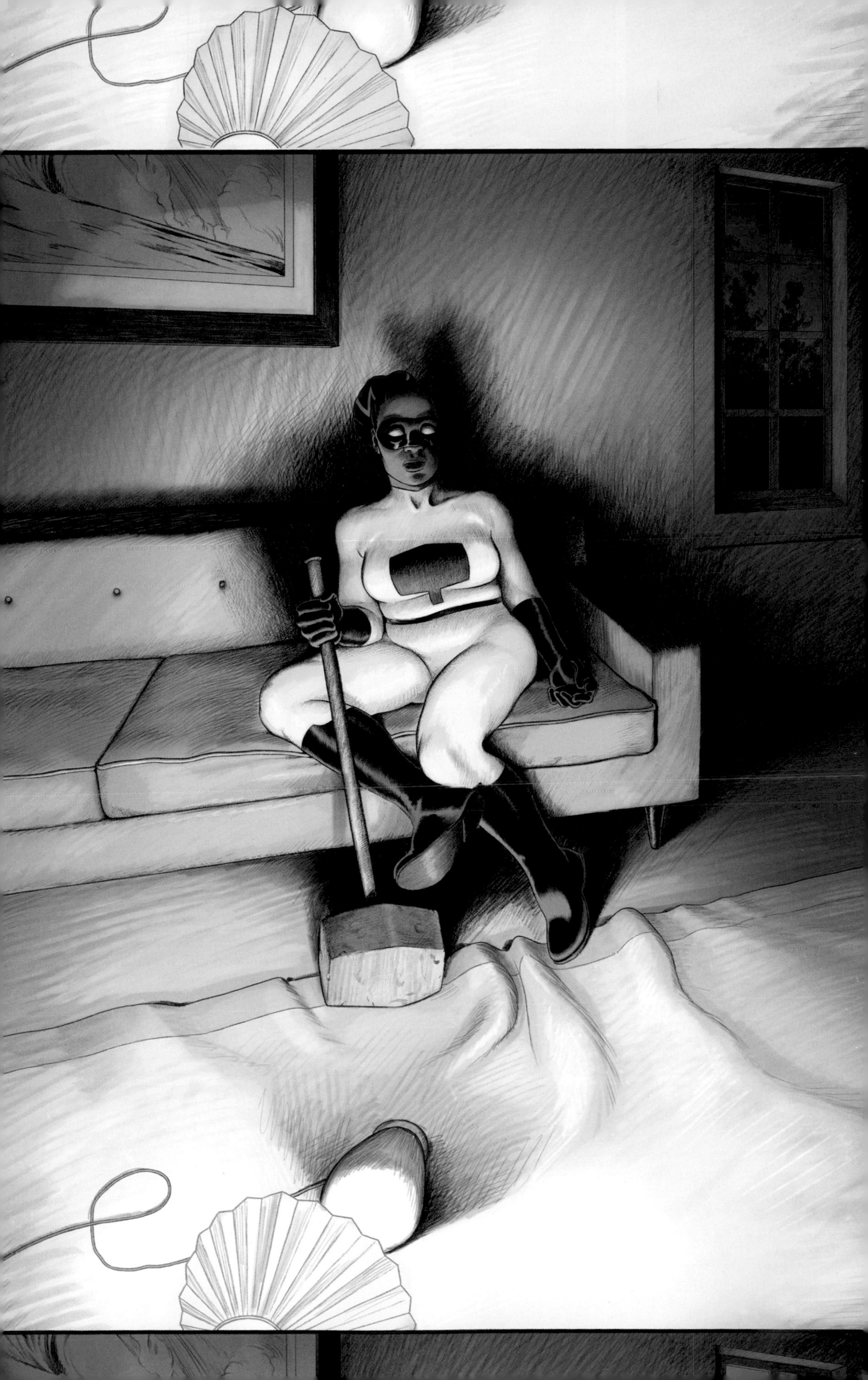

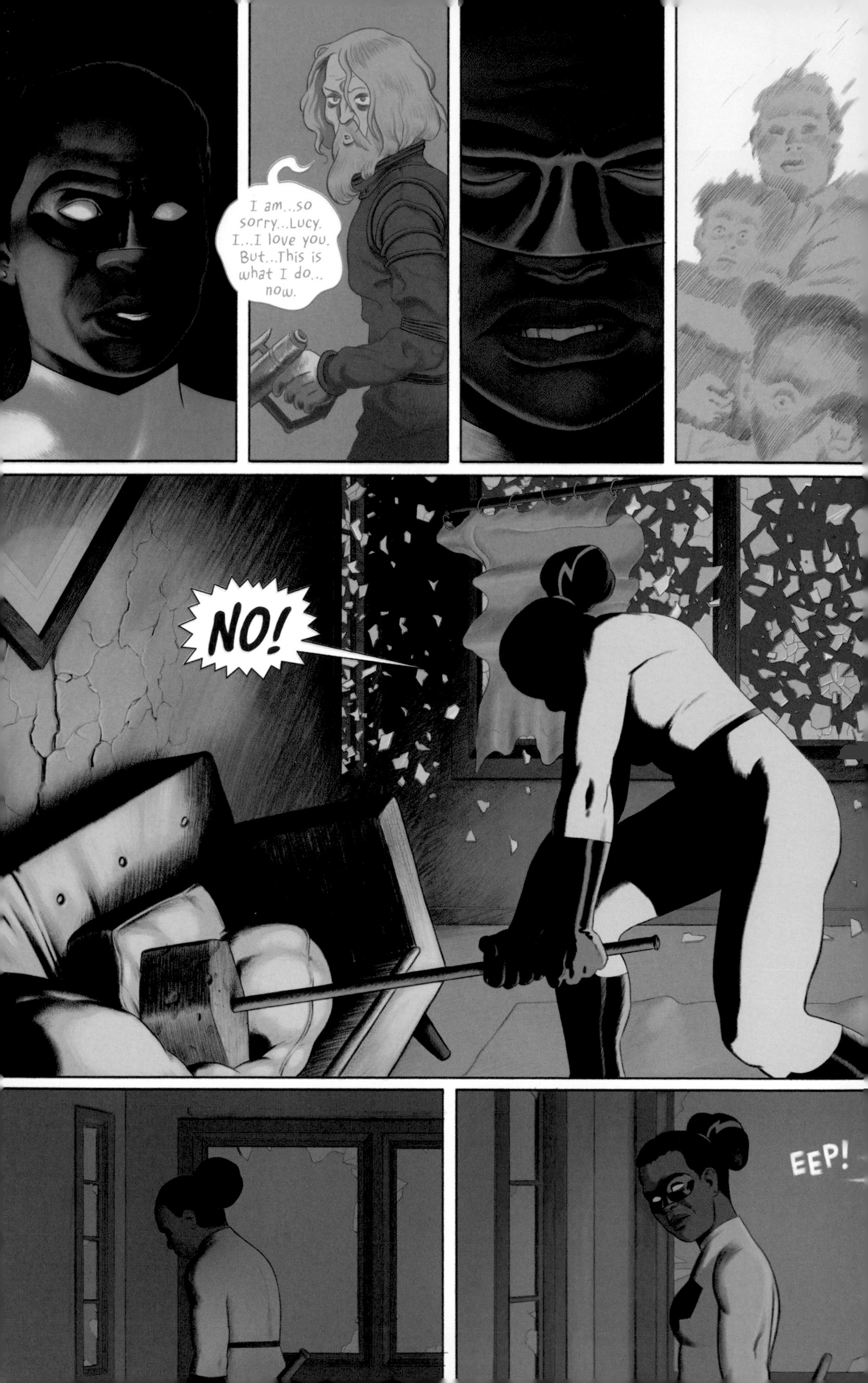
I am...so sorry...Lucy. I...I love you. But...This is what I do... now.
NO!
EEP!

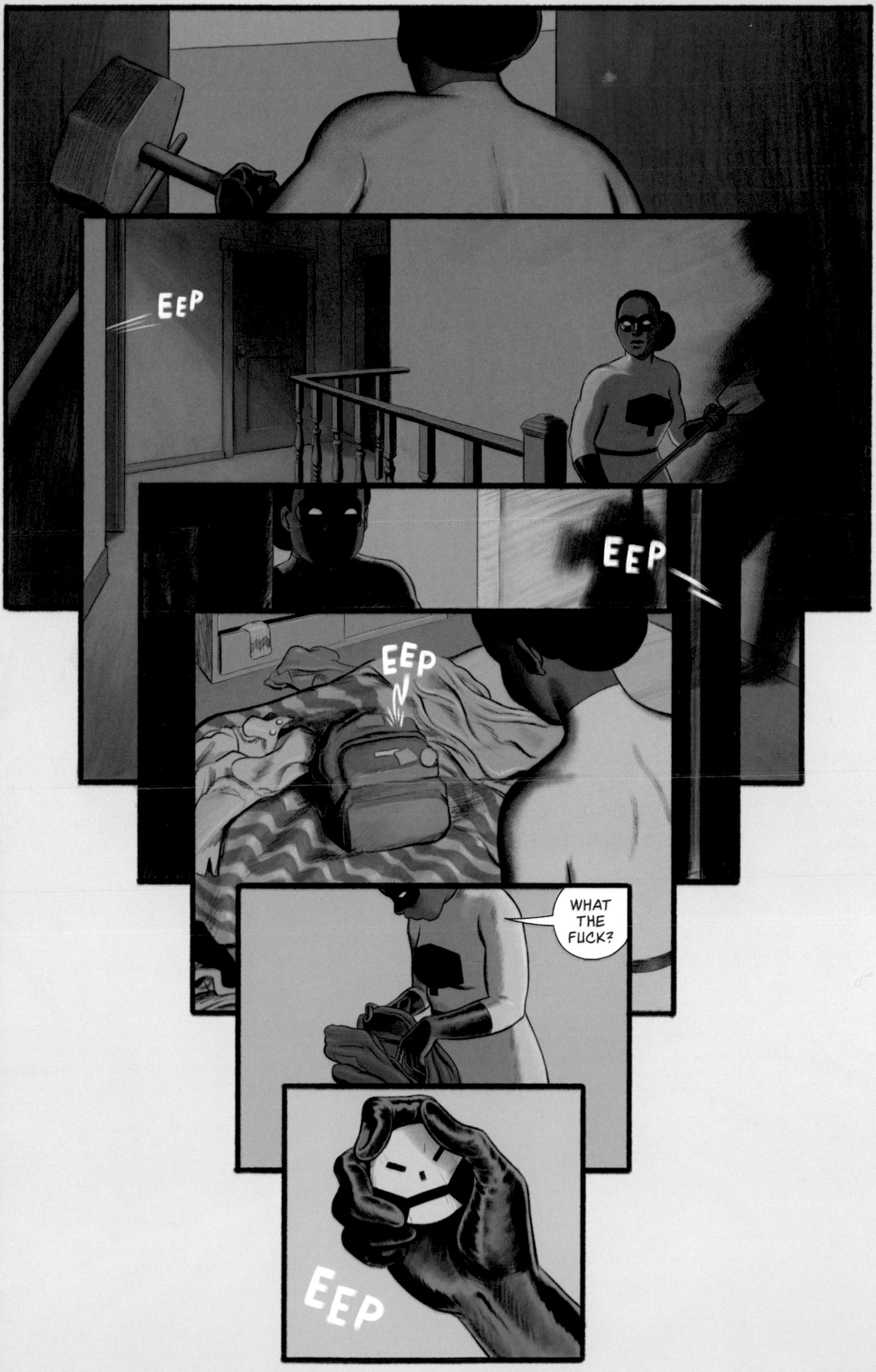
EEP
EEP
EEP
WHAT THE FUCK?
EEP

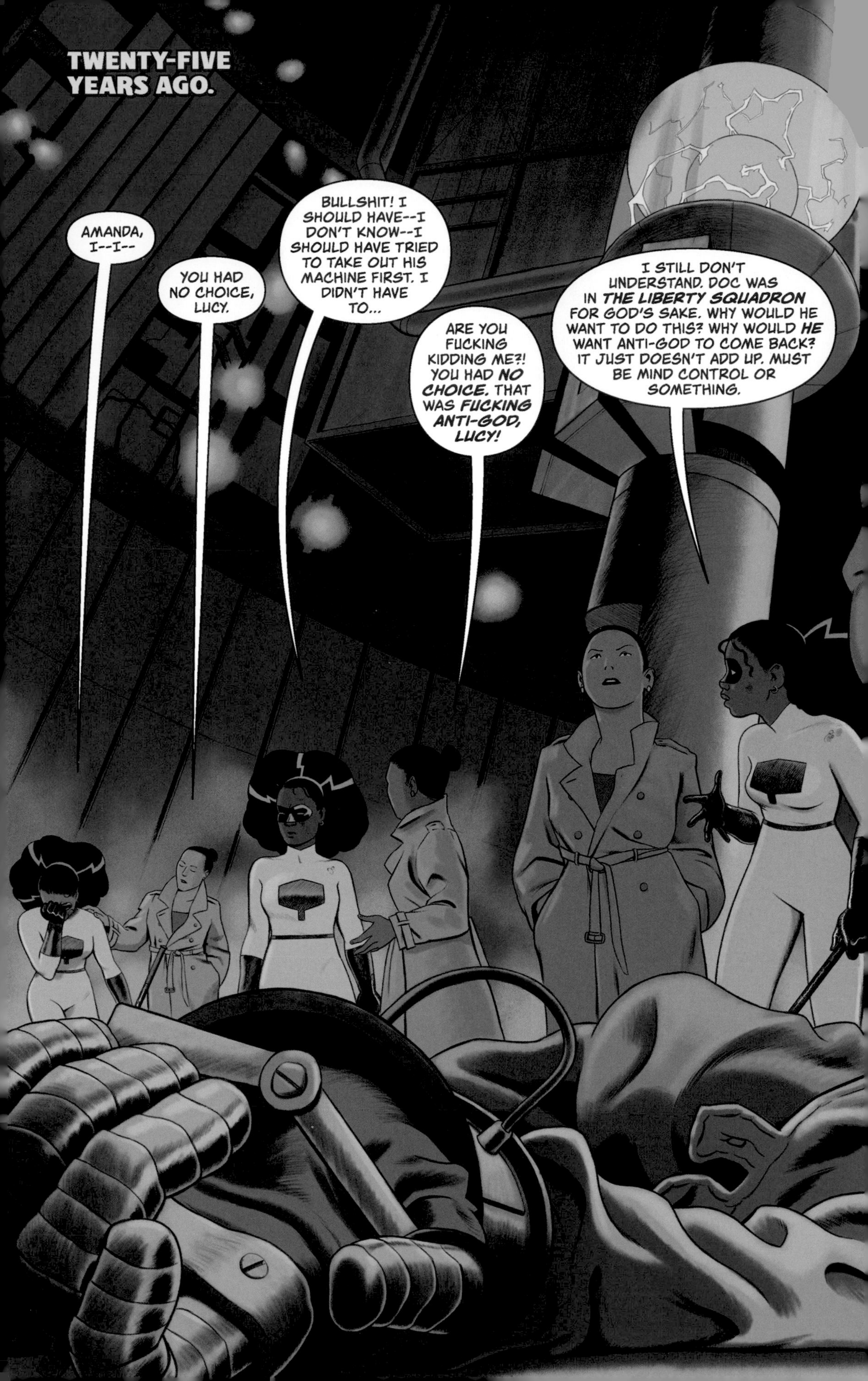
TWENTY-FIVE YEARS AGO.
AMANDA, I--I--
YOU HAD NO CHOICE, LUCY.
BULLSHIT! I SHOULD HAVE--I DON'T KNOW--I SHOULD HAVE TRIED TO TAKE OUT HIS MACHINE FIRST. I DIDN'T HAVE TO...
ARE YOU FUCKING KIDDING ME?! YOU HAD NO CHOICE. THAT WAS FUCKING ANTI-GOD, LUCY!
I STILL DON'T UNDERSTAND. DOC WAS IN THE LIBERTY SQUADRON FOR GOD'S SAKE. WHY WOULD HE WANT TO DO THIS? WHY WOULD HE WANT ANTI-GOD TO COME BACK? IT JUST DOESN'T ADD UP. MUST BE MIND CONTROL OR SOMETHING.

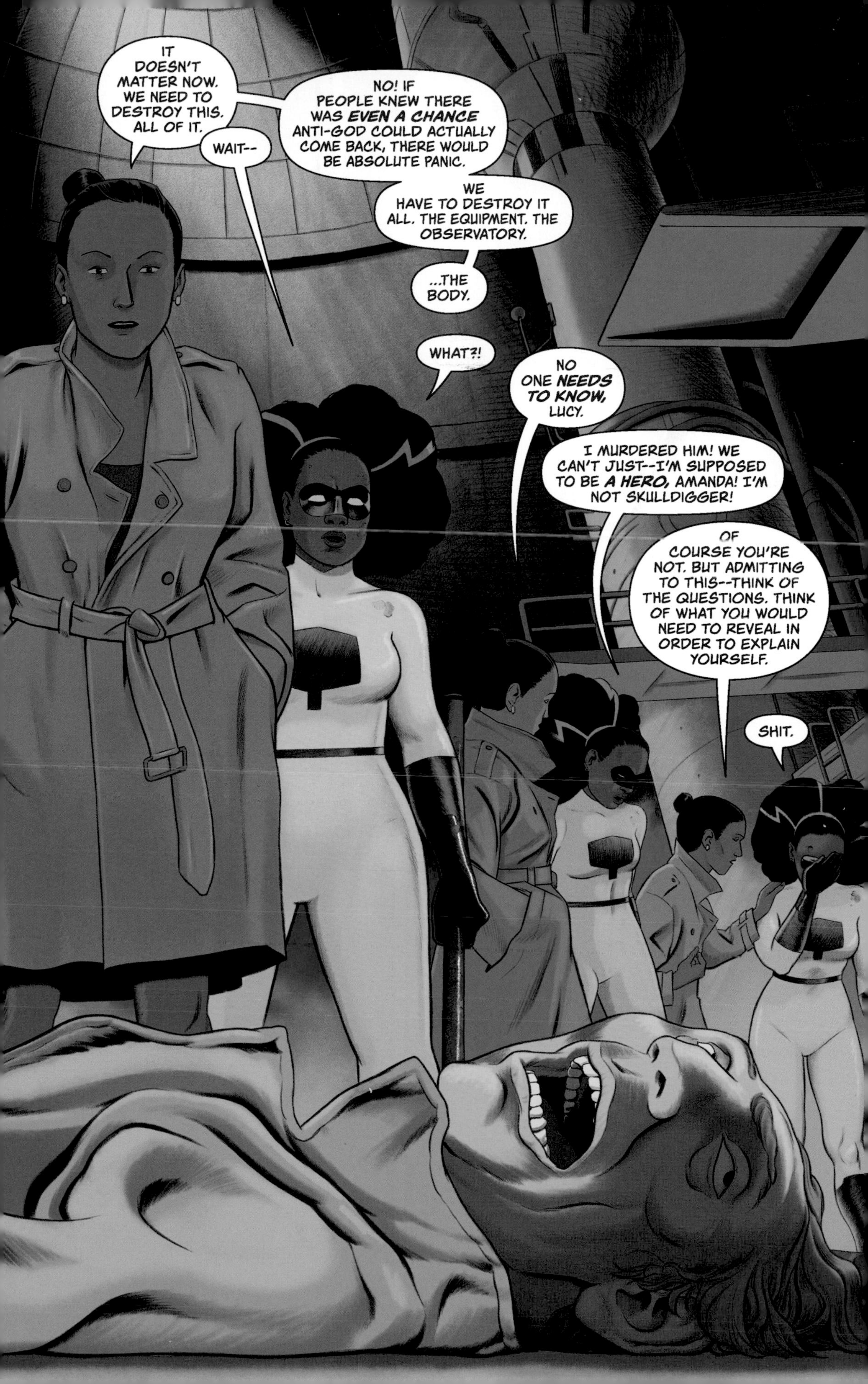
IT DOESN'T MATTER NOW. WE NEED TO DESTROY THIS. ALL OF IT.
WAIT--
NO! IF PEOPLE KNEW THERE WAS EVEN A CHANCE ANTI-GOD COULD ACTUALLY COME BACK, THERE WOULD BE ABSOLUTE PANIC.
WE HAVE TO DESTROY IT ALL. THE EQUIPMENT. THE OBSERVATORY.
...THE BODY.
WHAT?!
NO ONE NEEDS TO KNOW, LUCY.
I MURDERED HIM! WE CAN'T JUST--I'M SUPPOSED TO BE A HERO, AMANDA! I'M NOT SKULLDIGGER!
OF COURSE YOU'RE NOT. BUT ADMITTING TO THIS--THINK OF THE QUESTIONS. THINK OF WHAT YOU WOULD NEED TO REVEAL IN ORDER TO EXPLAIN YOURSELF.
SHIT.

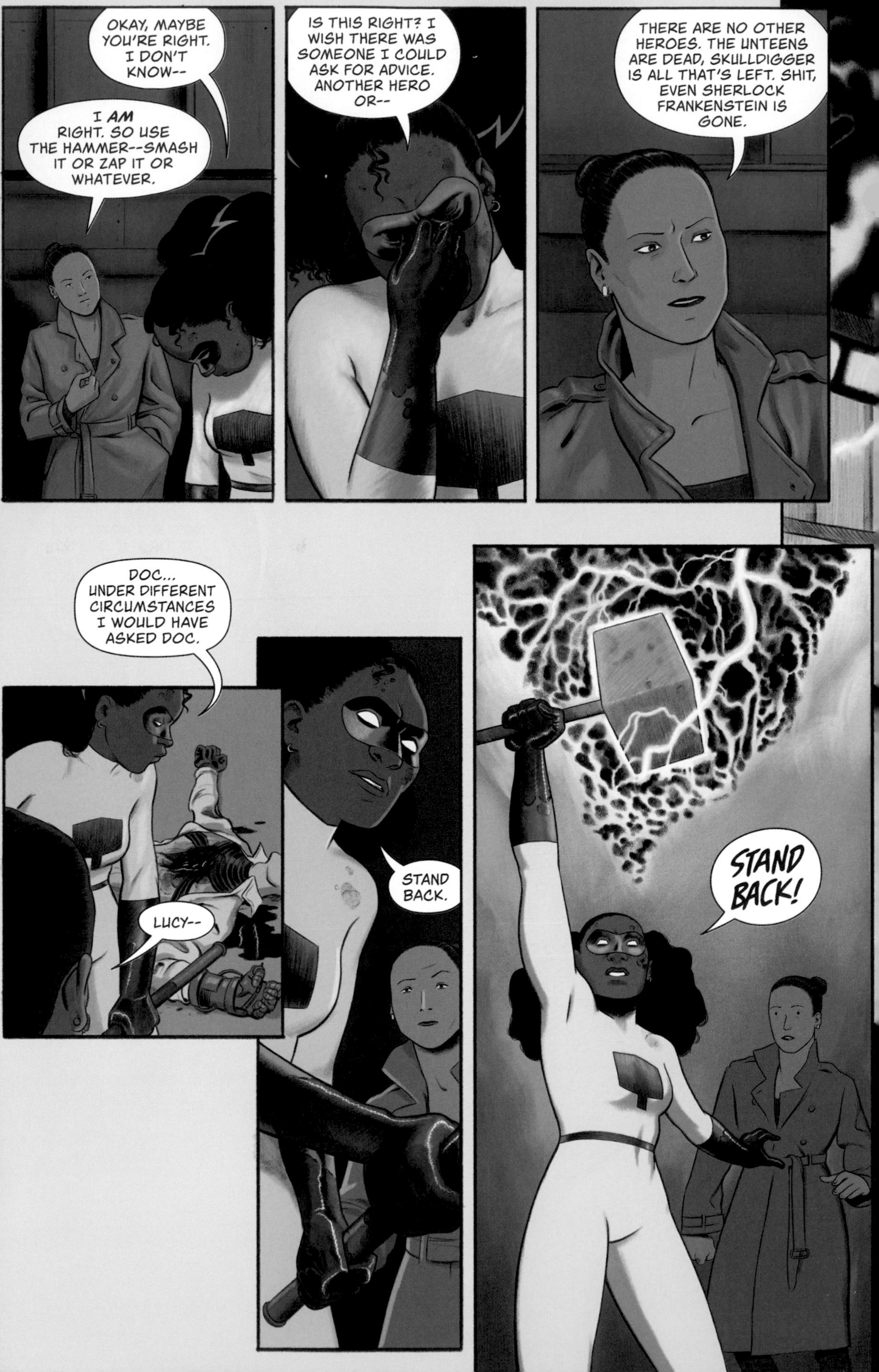
OKAY, MAYBE YOU'RE RIGHT. I DON'T KNOW--
I *AM* RIGHT. SO USE THE HAMMER--SMASH IT OR ZAP IT OR WHATEVER.
IS THIS RIGHT? I WISH THERE WAS SOMEONE I COULD ASK FOR ADVICE. ANOTHER HERO OR--
THERE ARE NO OTHER HEROES. THE UNTEENS ARE DEAD, SKULLDIGGER IS ALL THAT'S LEFT. SHIT, EVEN SHERLOCK FRANKENSTEIN IS GONE.
DOC... UNDER DIFFERENT CIRCUMSTANCES I WOULD HAVE ASKED DOC.
LUCY--
STAND BACK.
STAND BACK!

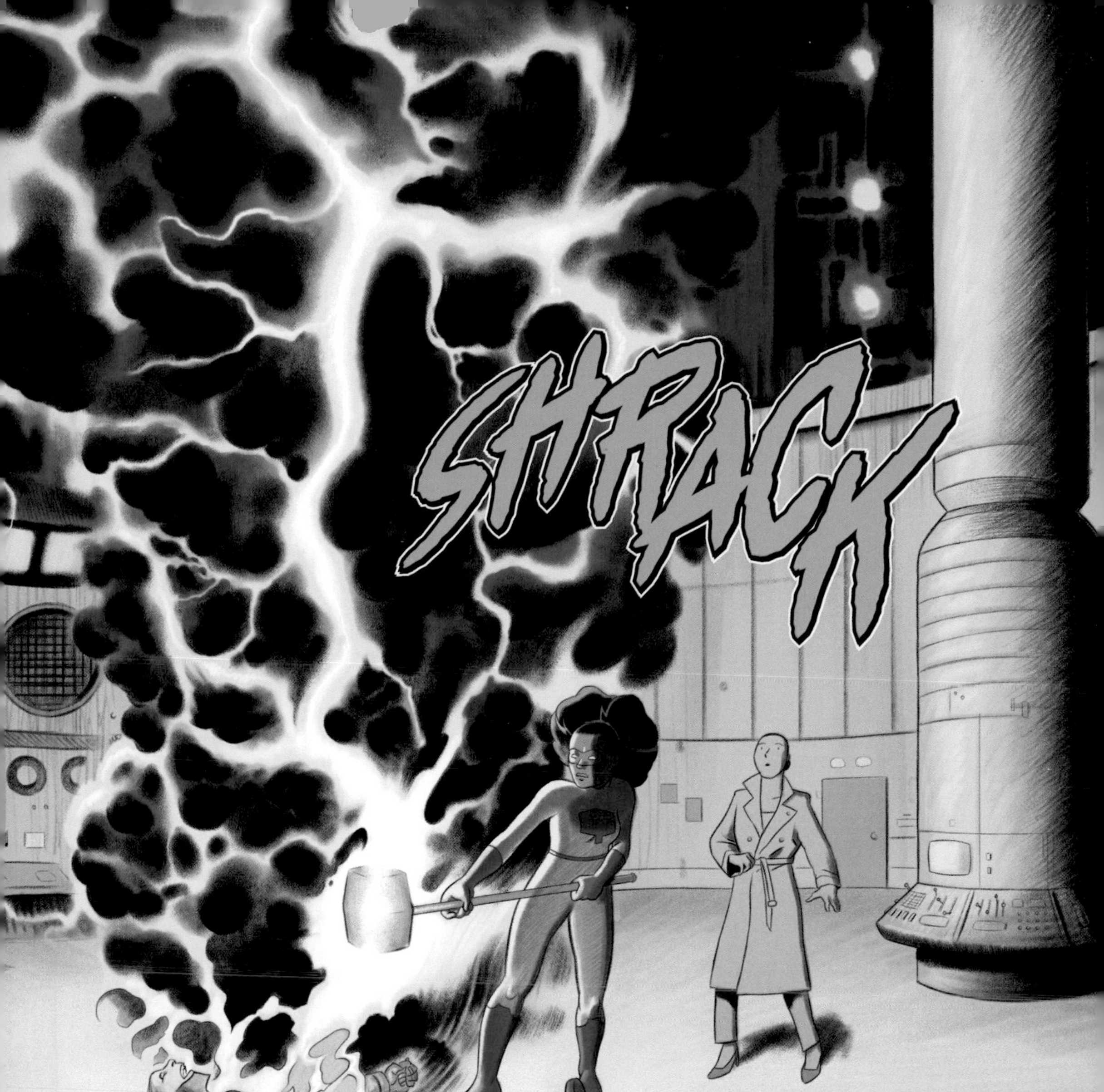
SHRACK
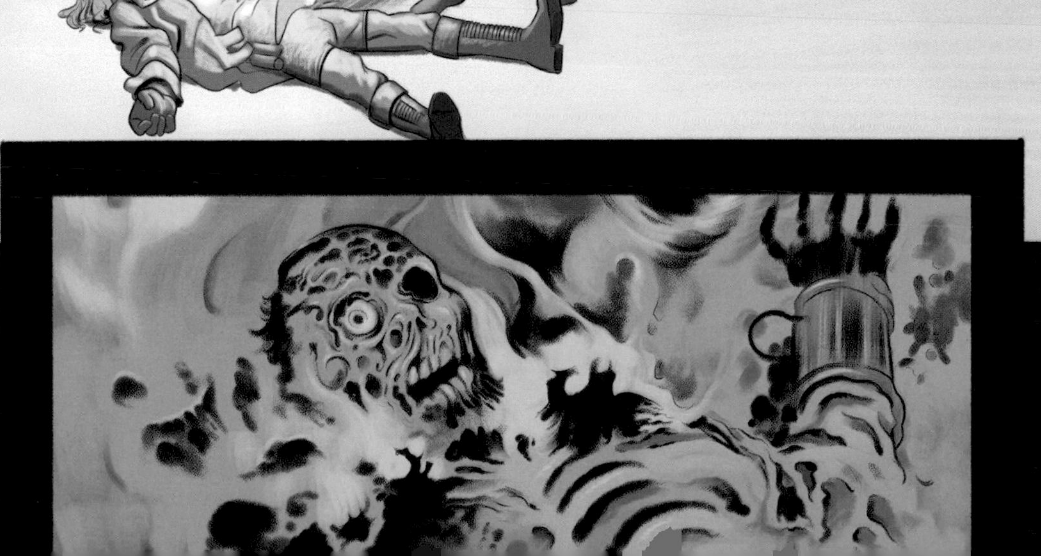

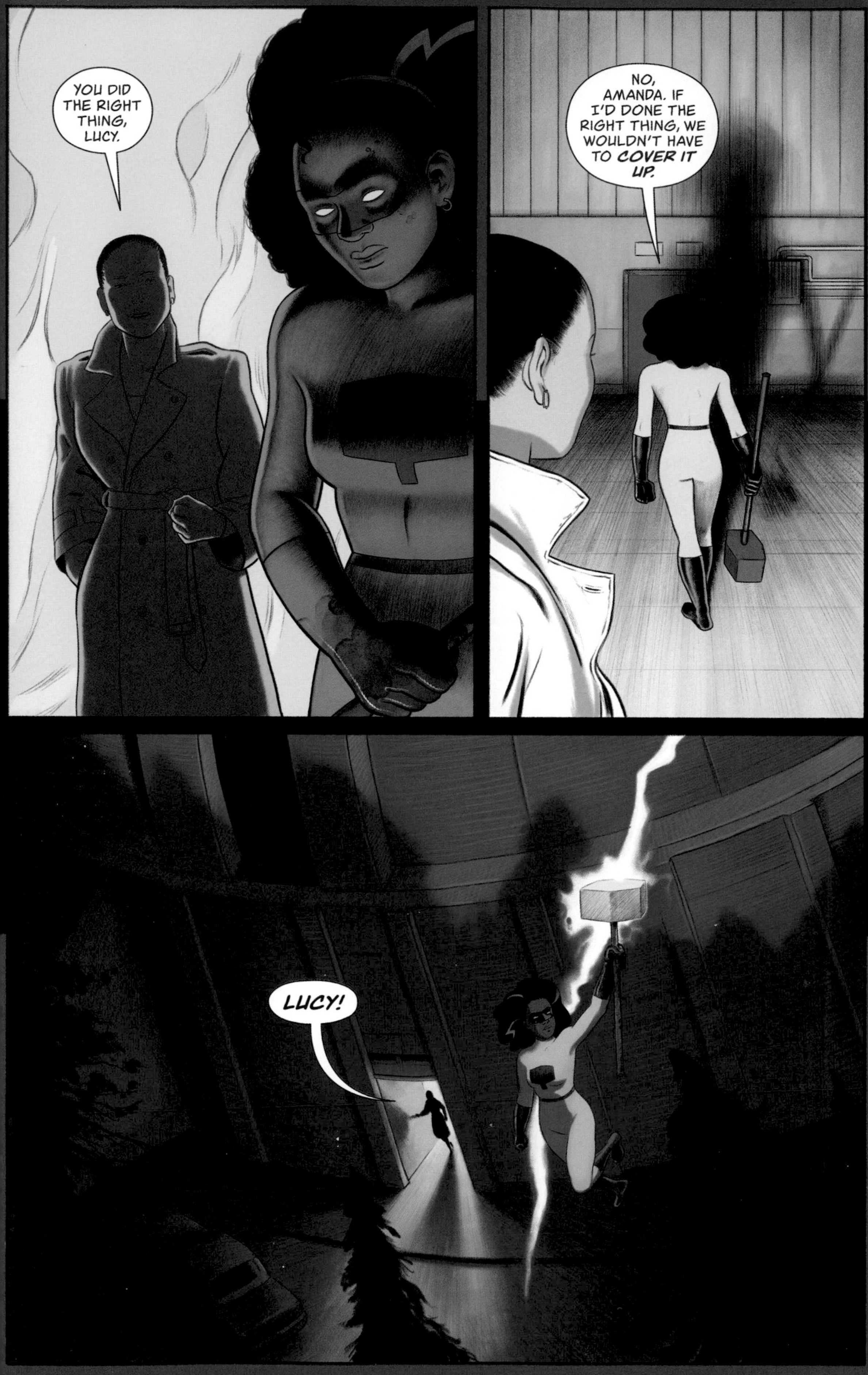
YOU DID THE RIGHT THING, LUCY.
NO, AMANDA. IF I'D DONE THE RIGHT THING, WE WOULDN'T HAVE TO **COVER IT UP.**
LUCY!

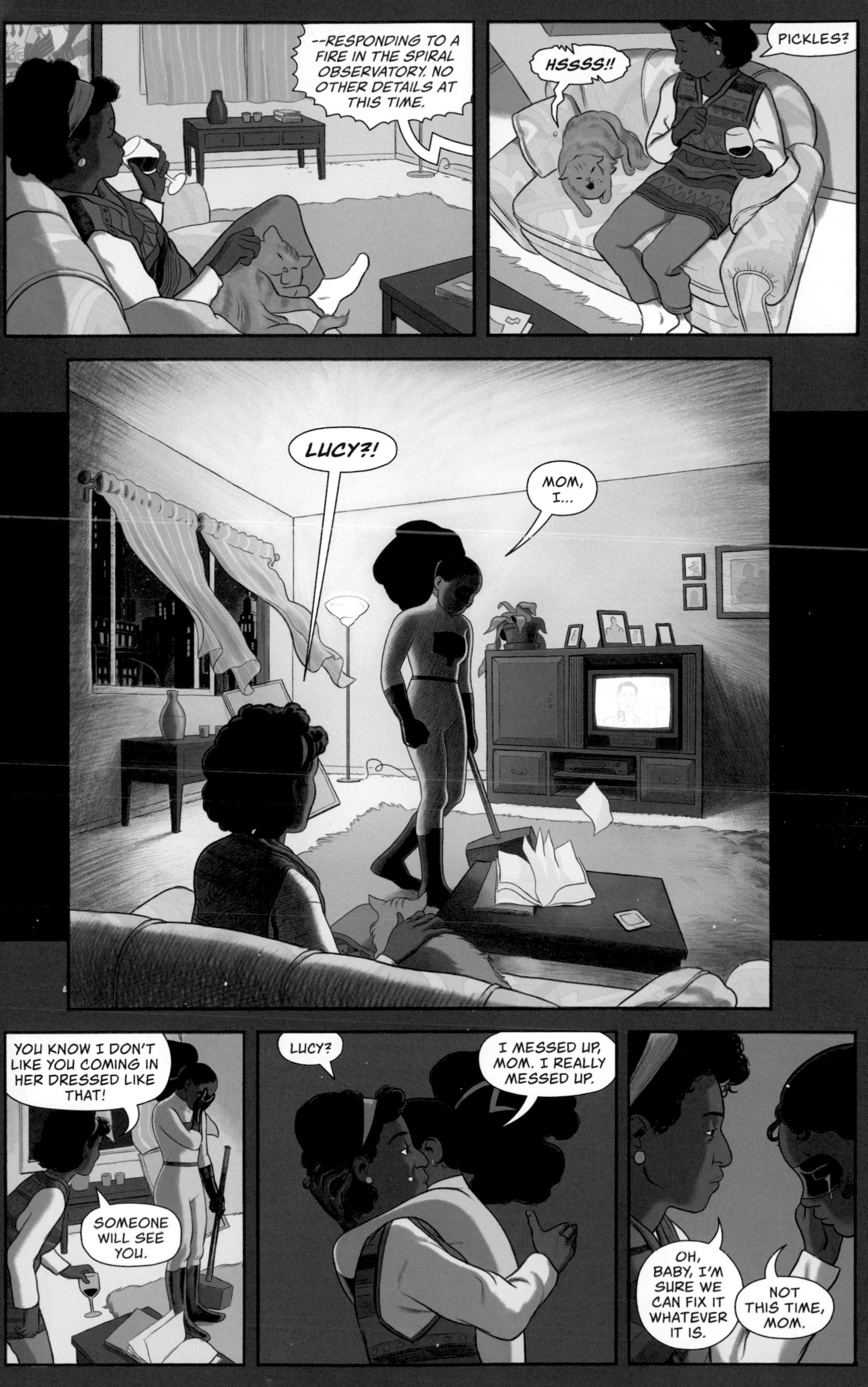
--RESPONDING TO A FIRE IN THE SPIRAL OBSERVATORY. NO OTHER DETAILS AT THIS TIME.
HSSSS!!
PICKLES?
LUCY?!
MOM, I...
YOU KNOW I DON'T LIKE YOU COMING IN HER DRESSED LIKE THAT!
SOMEONE WILL SEE YOU.
LUCY?
I MESSED UP, MOM. I REALLY MESSED UP.
OH, BABY, I'M SURE WE CAN FIX IT WHATEVER IT IS.
NOT THIS TIME, MOM.

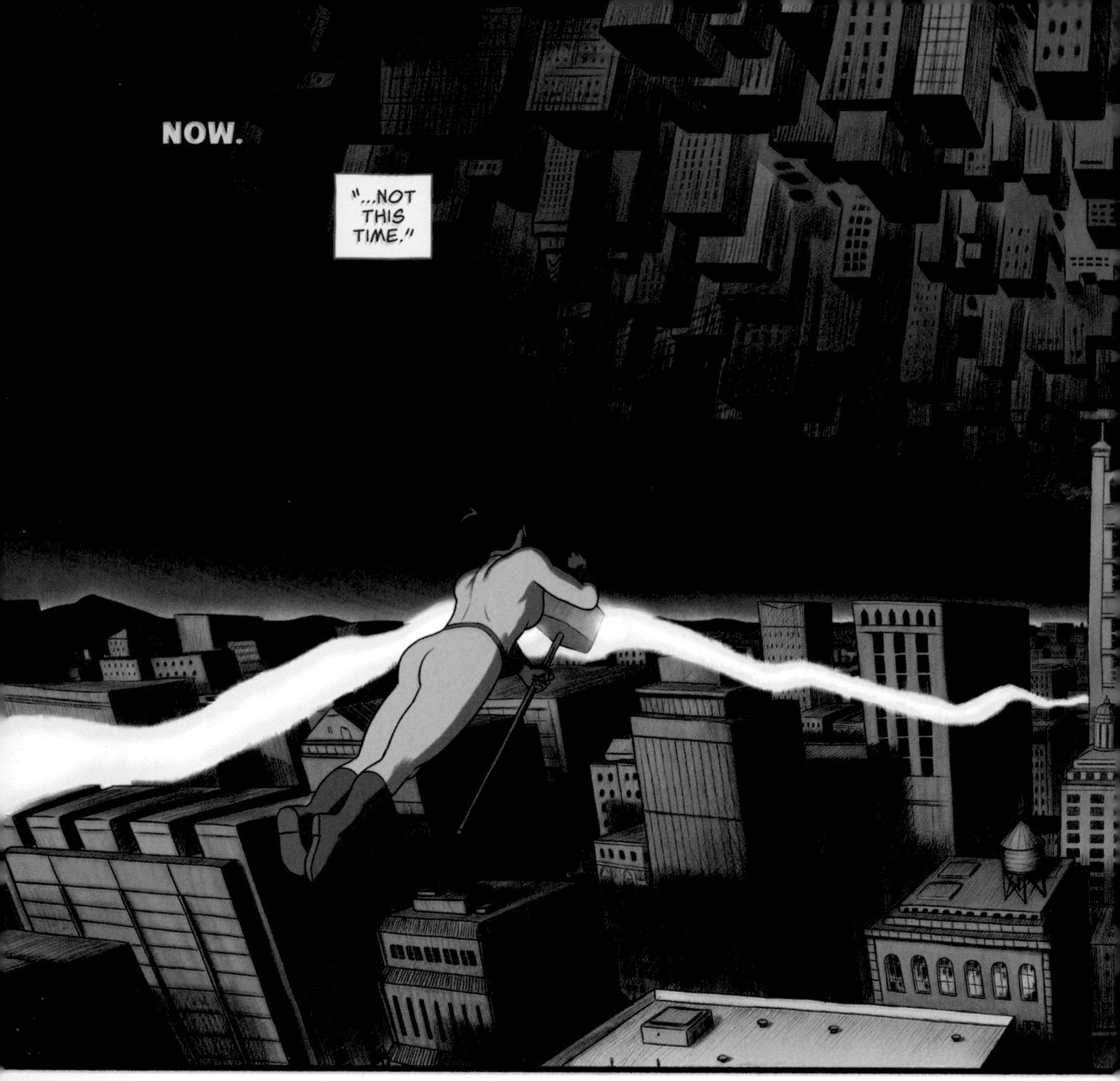
NOW.
"...NOT THIS TIME."

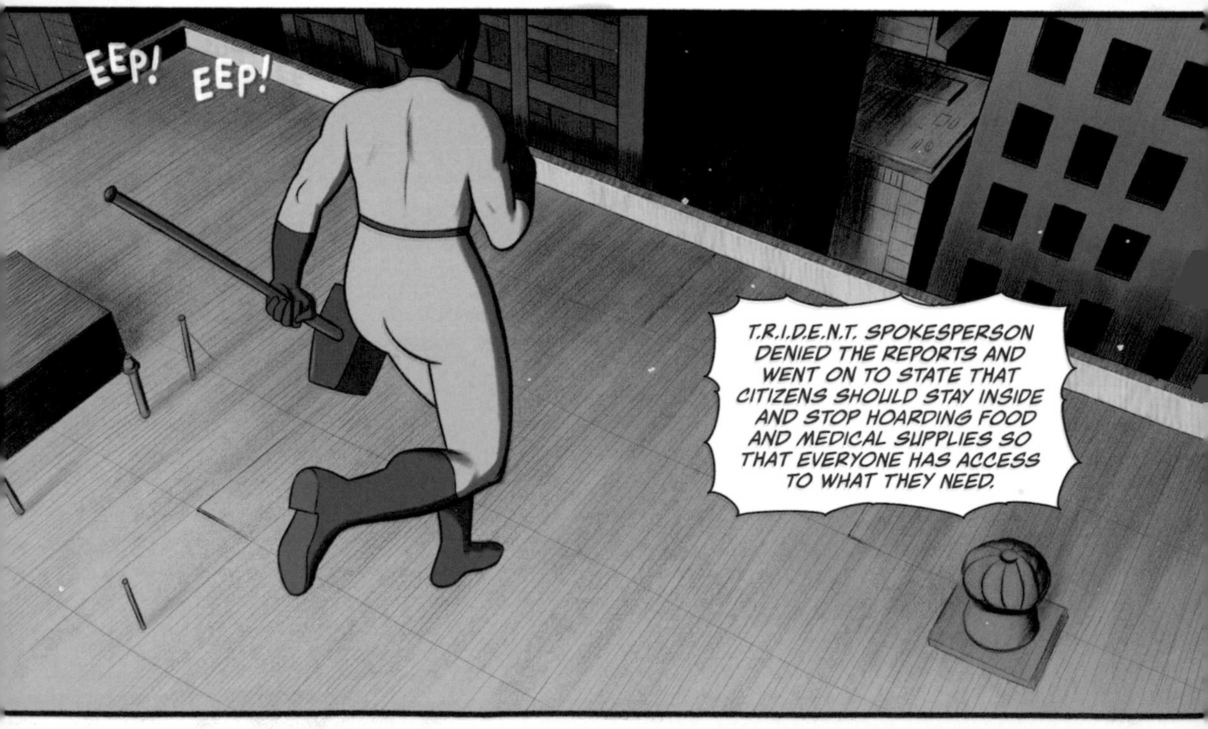
EEP! EEP!
T.R.I.D.E.N.T. SPOKESPERSON DENIED THE REPORTS AND WENT ON TO STATE THAT CITIZENS SHOULD STAY INSIDE AND STOP HOARDING FOOD AND MEDICAL SUPPLIES SO THAT EVERYONE HAS ACCESS TO WHAT THEY NEED.

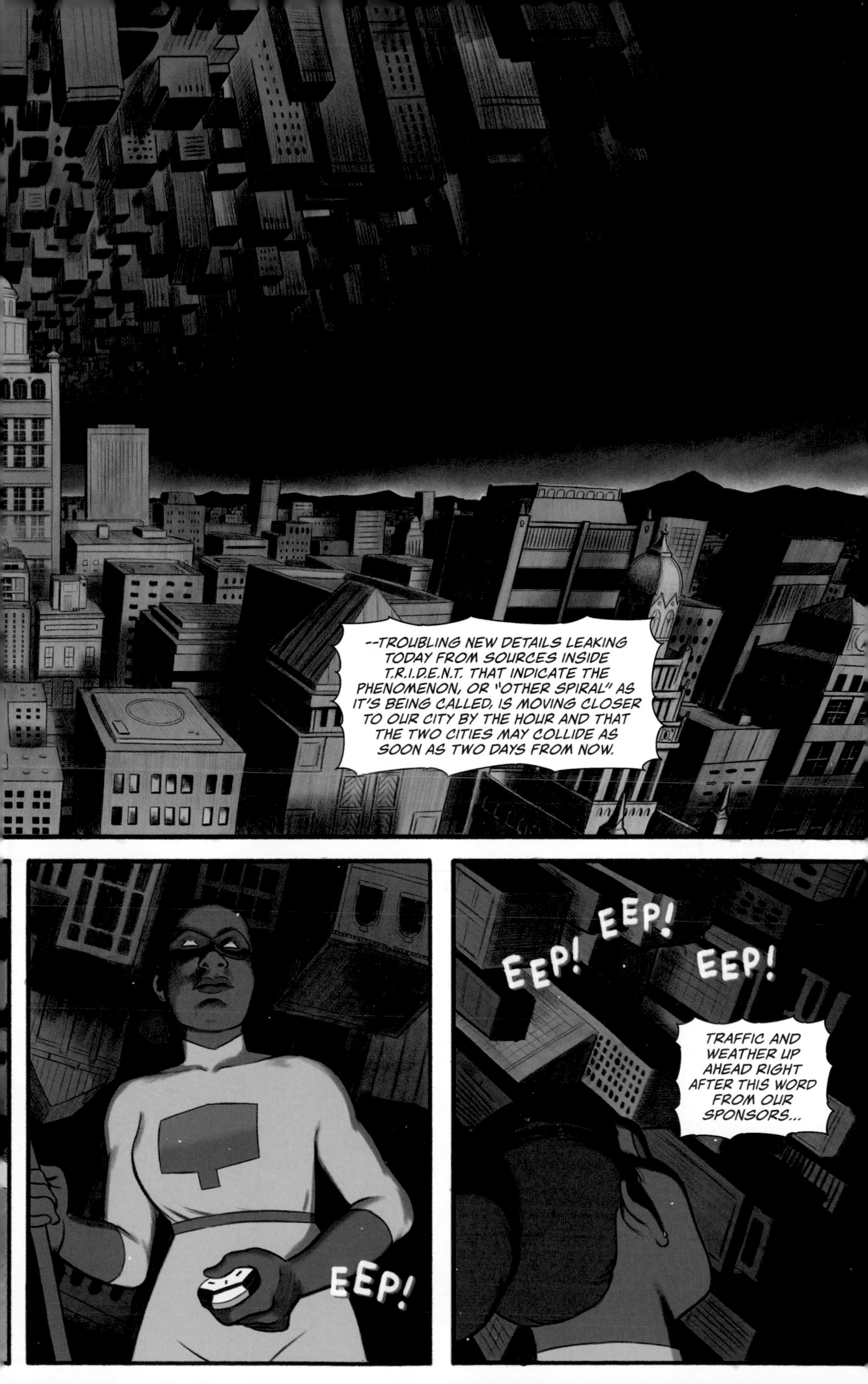
--TROUBLING NEW DETAILS LEAKING TODAY FROM SOURCES INSIDE T.R.I.D.E.N.T. THAT INDICATE THE PHENOMENON, OR "OTHER SPIRAL" AS IT'S BEING CALLED, IS MOVING CLOSER TO OUR CITY BY THE HOUR AND THAT THE TWO CITIES MAY COLLIDE AS SOON AS TWO DAYS FROM NOW.
EEP!
EEP!
EEP!
EEP!
TRAFFIC AND WEATHER UP AHEAD RIGHT AFTER THIS WORD FROM OUR SPONSORS...

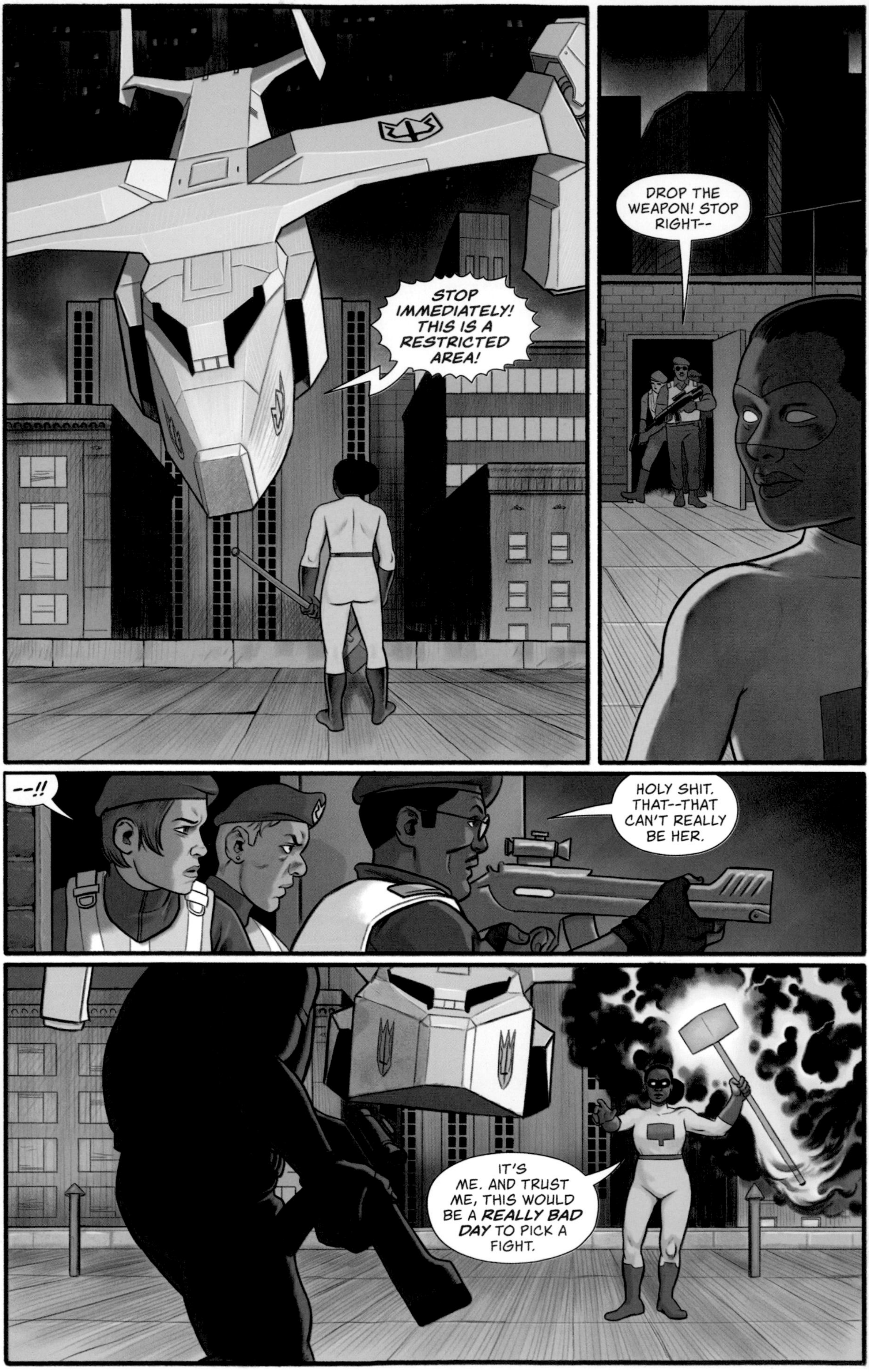
STOP IMMEDIATELY! THIS IS A RESTRICTED AREA!
DROP THE WEAPON! STOP RIGHT--
--!!
HOLY SHIT. THAT--THAT CAN'T REALLY BE HER.
IT'S ME. AND TRUST ME, THIS WOULD BE A **REALLY BAD DAY** TO PICK A FIGHT.

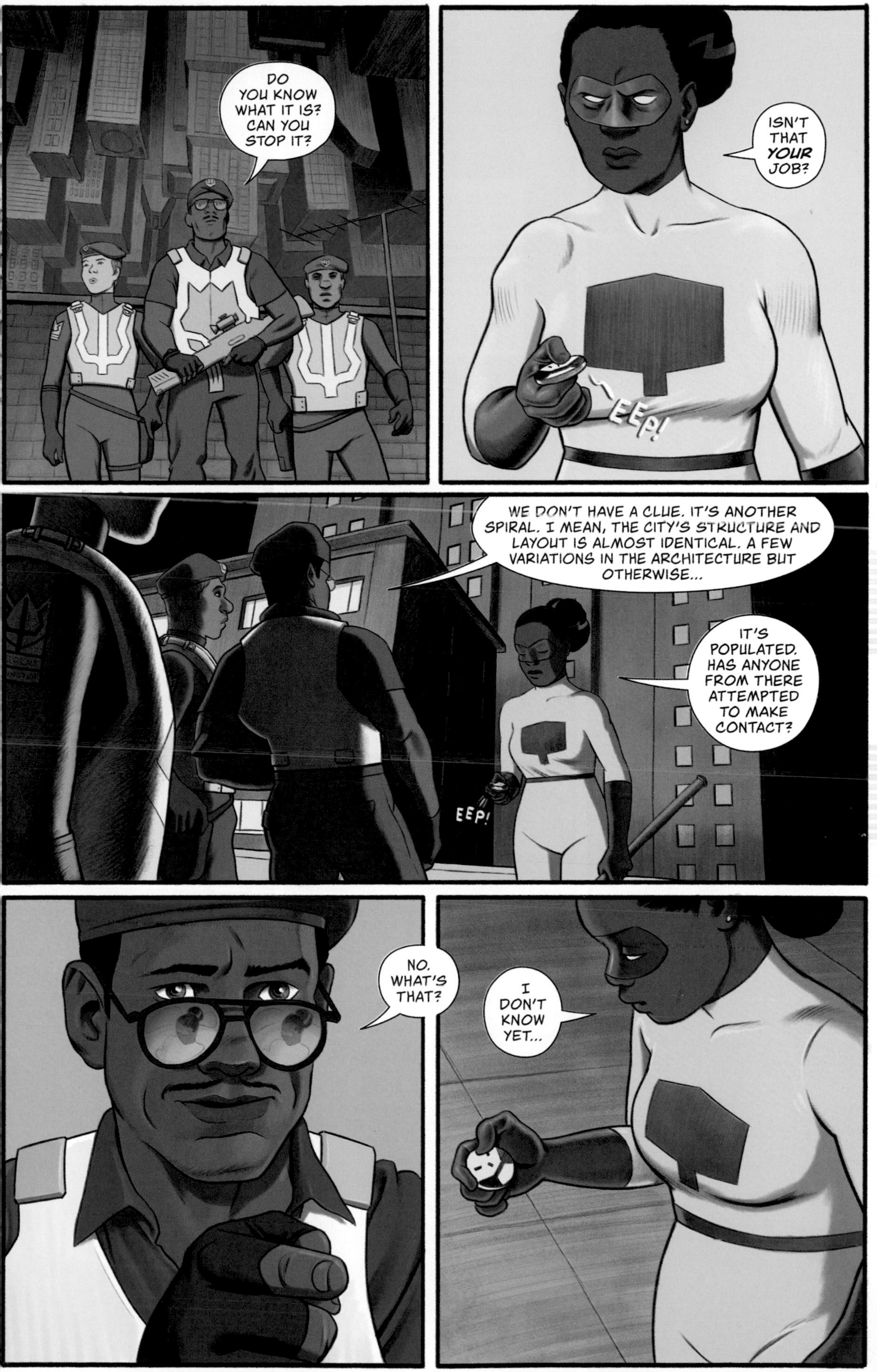
DO YOU KNOW WHAT IT IS? CAN YOU STOP IT?
ISN'T THAT ***YOUR*** JOB?
EEP!
WE DON'T HAVE A CLUE. IT'S ANOTHER SPIRAL. I MEAN, THE CITY'S STRUCTURE AND LAYOUT IS ALMOST IDENTICAL. A FEW VARIATIONS IN THE ARCHITECTURE BUT OTHERWISE...
IT'S POPULATED. HAS ANYONE FROM THERE ATTEMPTED TO MAKE CONTACT?
EEP!
NO. WHAT'S THAT?
I DON'T KNOW YET...

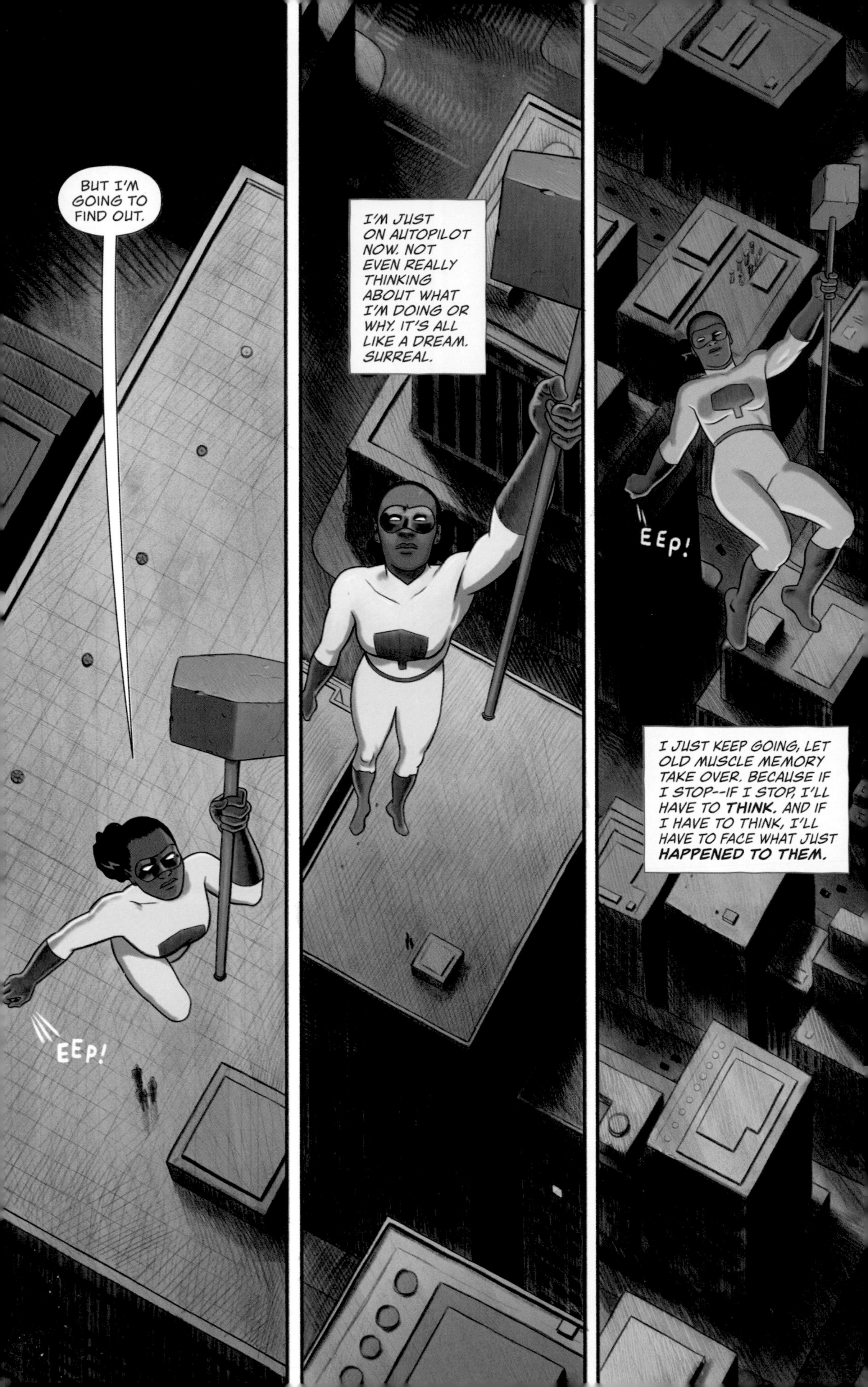
BUT I'M GOING TO FIND OUT.
EEP!
I'M JUST ON AUTOPILOT NOW. NOT EVEN REALLY THINKING ABOUT WHAT I'M DOING OR WHY. IT'S ALL LIKE A DREAM. SURREAL.
EEP!
I JUST KEEP GOING, LET OLD MUSCLE MEMORY TAKE OVER. BECAUSE IF I STOP--IF I STOP, I'LL HAVE TO THINK. AND IF I HAVE TO THINK, I'LL HAVE TO FACE WHAT JUST HAPPENED TO THEM.

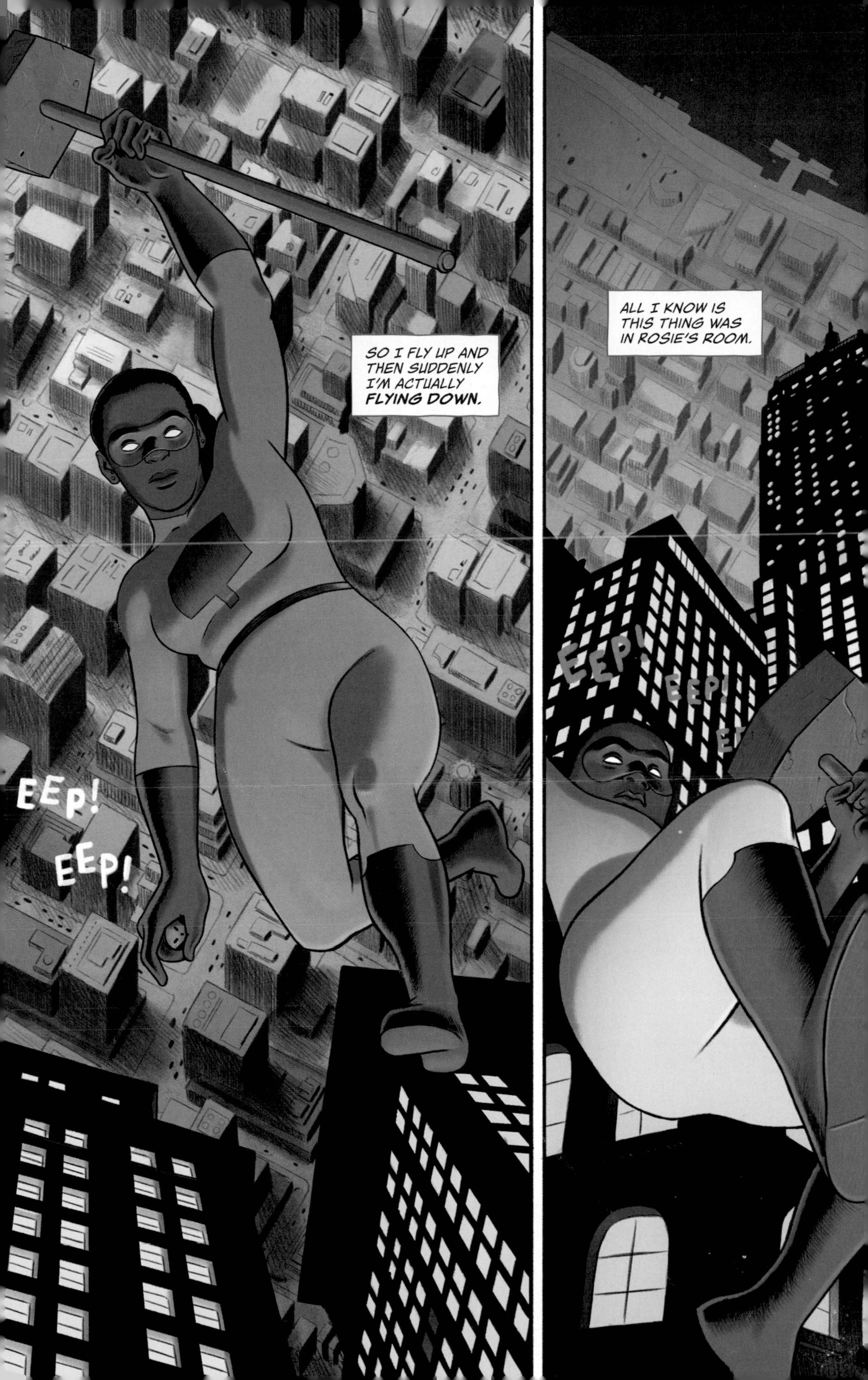
SO I FLY UP AND
THEN SUDDENLY
I'M ACTUALLY
FLYING DOWN.
EEP!
EEP!
ALL I KNOW IS
THIS THING WAS
IN ROSIE'S ROOM.
EEP!
EEP!

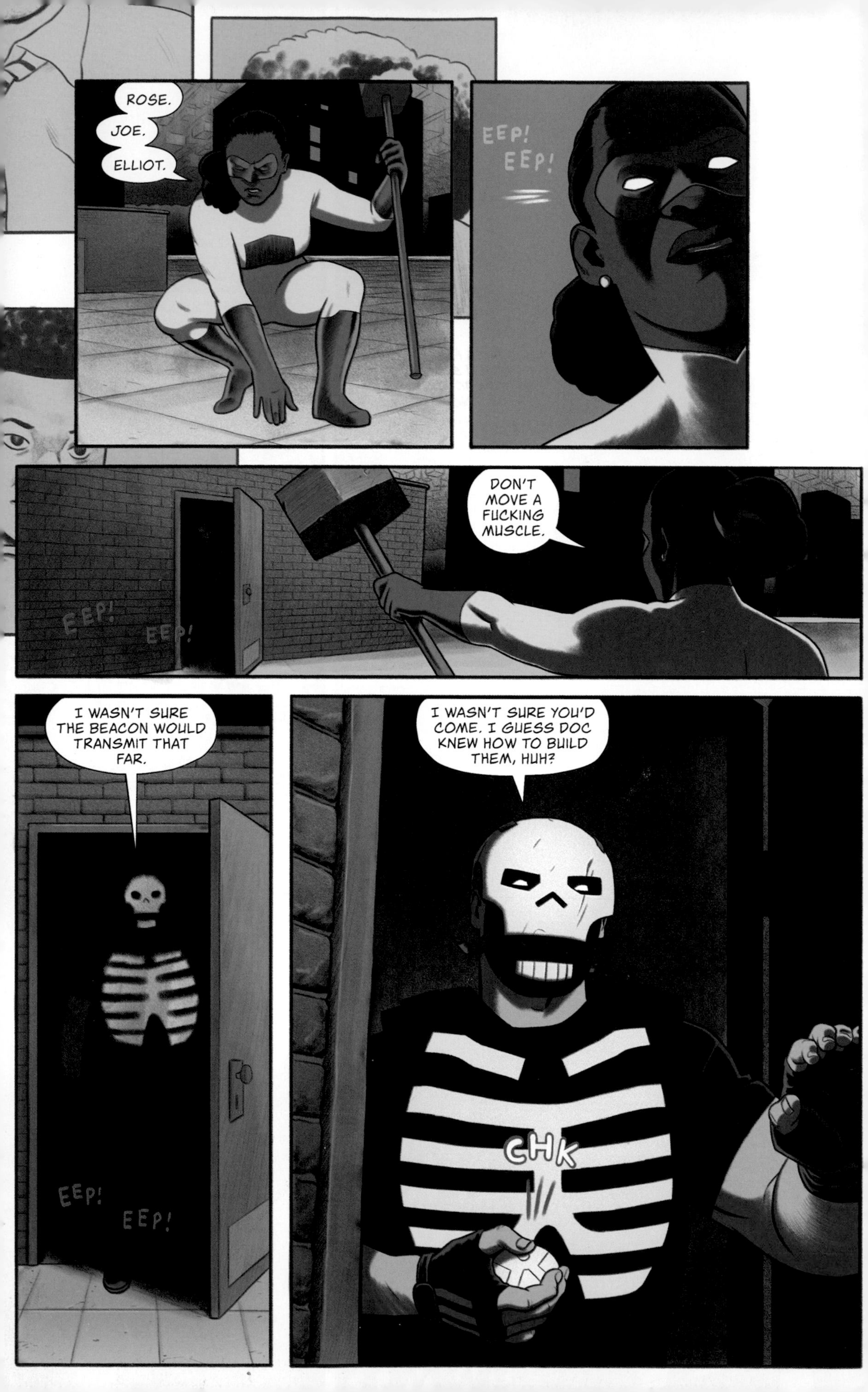
ROSE.
JOE.
ELLIOT.
EEP!
EEP!
DON'T MOVE A FUCKING MUSCLE.
EEP!
EEP!
I WASN'T SURE THE BEACON WOULD TRANSMIT THAT FAR.
EEP!
EEP!
I WASN'T SURE YOU'D COME. I GUESS DOC KNEW HOW TO BUILD THEM, HUH?
CHK

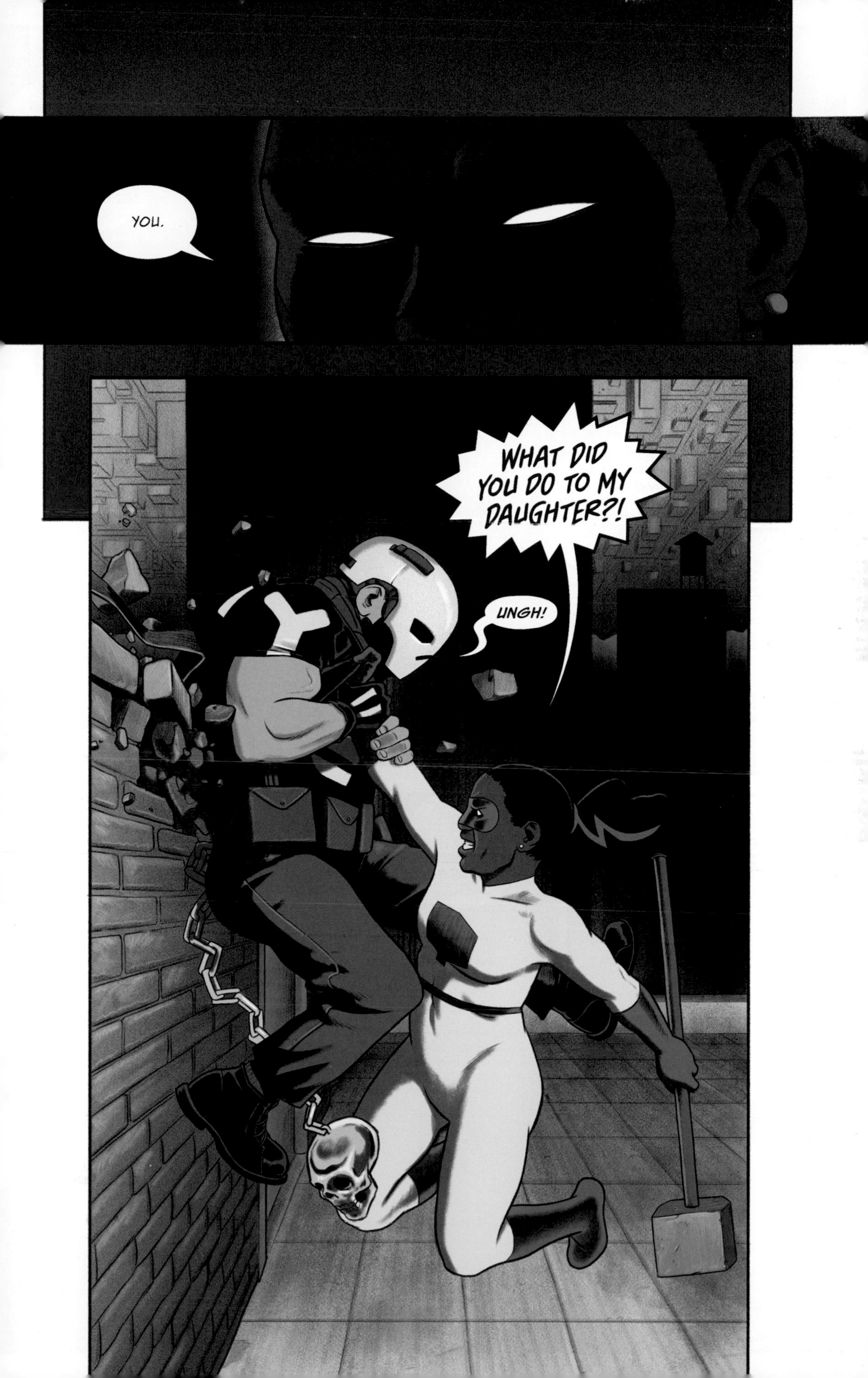
YOU.
WHAT DID YOU DO TO MY DAUGHTER?!
UNGH!

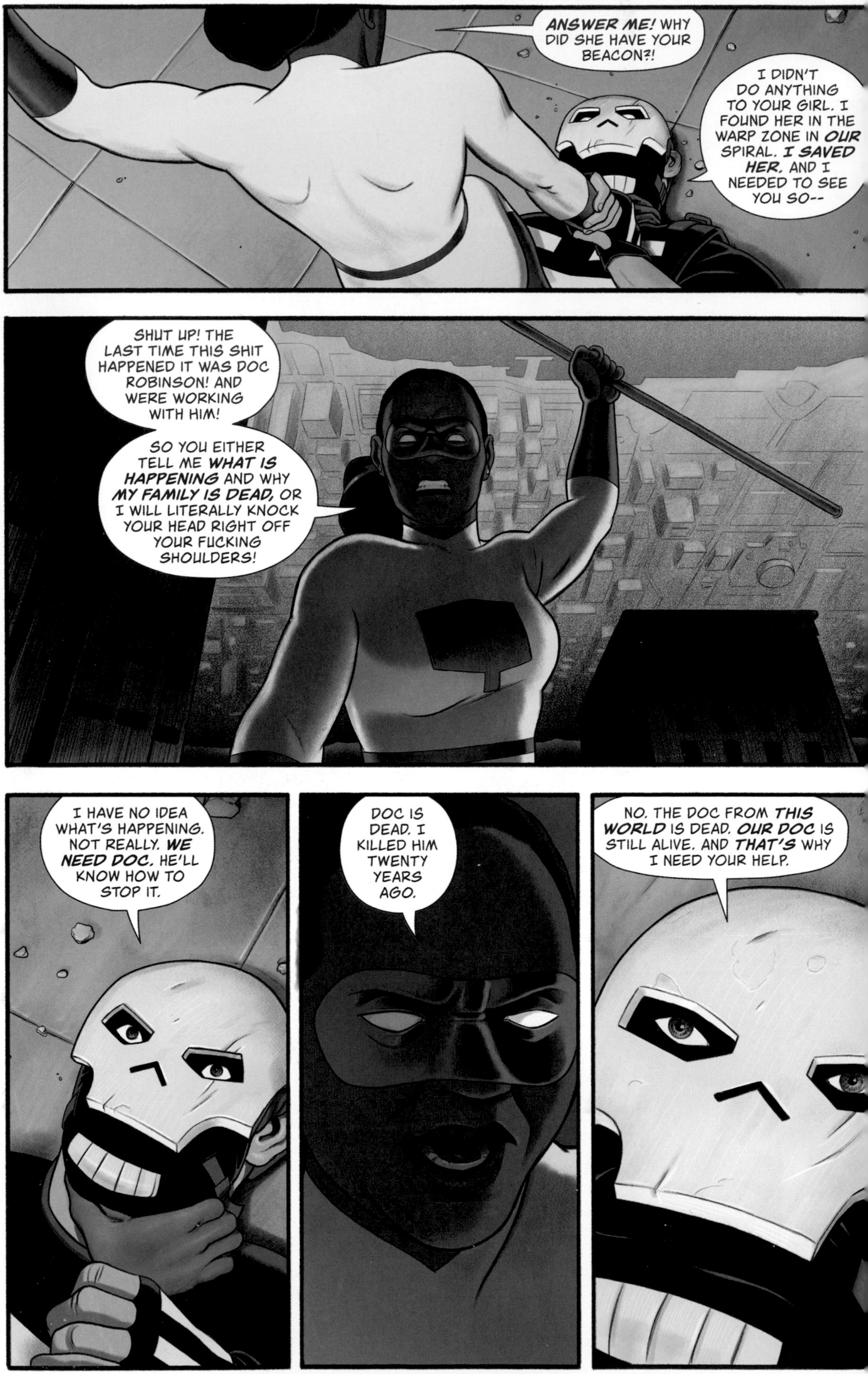
ANSWER ME! WHY DID SHE HAVE YOUR BEACON?!
I DIDN'T DO ANYTHING TO YOUR GIRL. I FOUND HER IN THE WARP ZONE IN OUR SPIRAL. I SAVED HER. AND I NEEDED TO SEE YOU SO--
SHUT UP! THE LAST TIME THIS SHIT HAPPENED IT WAS DOC ROBINSON! AND WERE WORKING WITH HIM!
SO YOU EITHER TELL ME WHAT IS HAPPENING AND WHY MY FAMILY IS DEAD, OR I WILL LITERALLY KNOCK YOUR HEAD RIGHT OFF YOUR FUCKING SHOULDERS!
I HAVE NO IDEA WHAT'S HAPPENING. NOT REALLY. WE NEED DOC. HE'LL KNOW HOW TO STOP IT.
DOC IS DEAD. I KILLED HIM TWENTY YEARS AGO.
NO. THE DOC FROM THIS WORLD IS DEAD. OUR DOC IS STILL ALIVE. AND THAT'S WHY I NEED YOUR HELP.

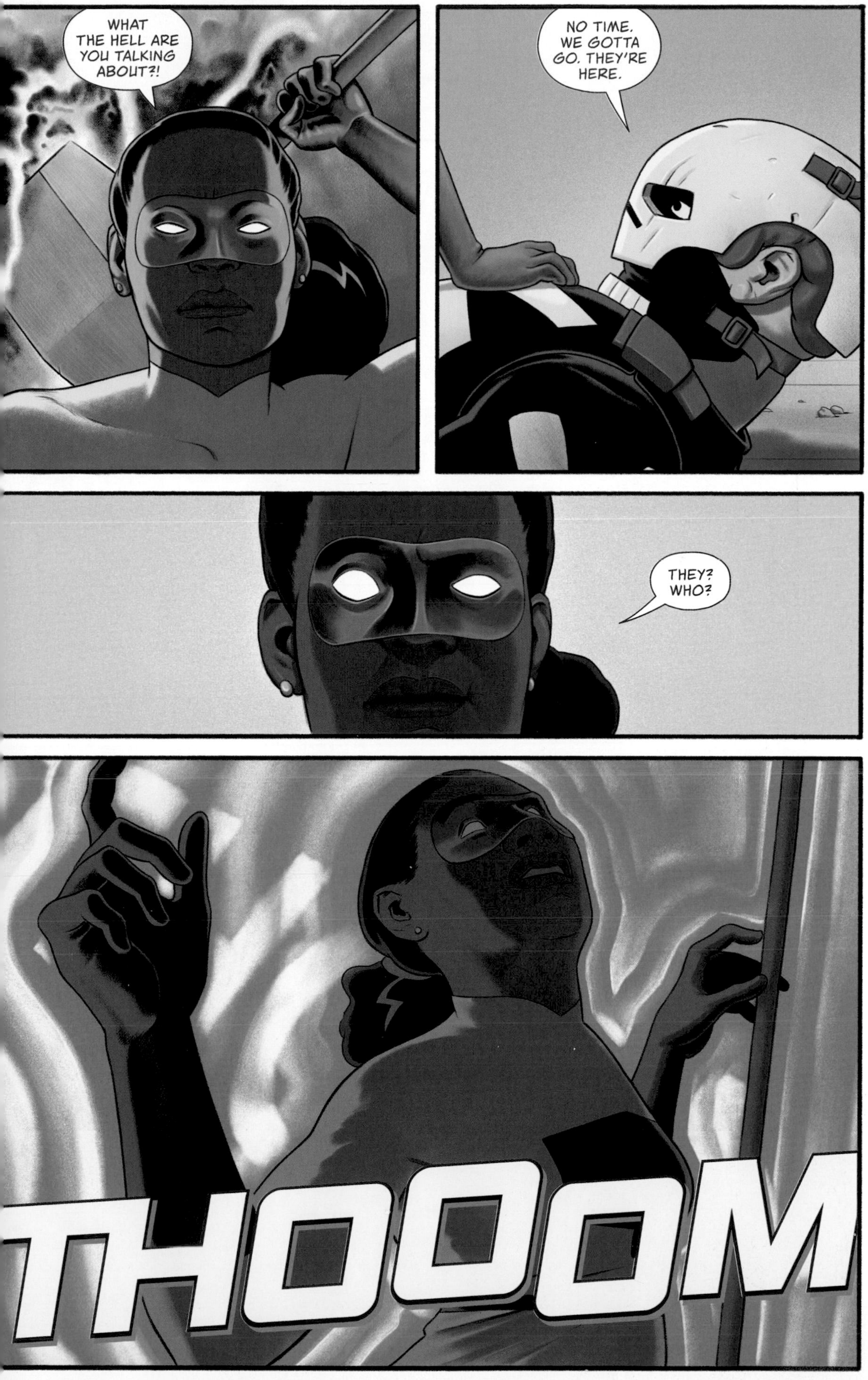
WHAT THE HELL ARE YOU TALKING ABOUT?!
NO TIME. WE GOTTA GO. THEY'RE HERE.
THEY? WHO?
THOOOM

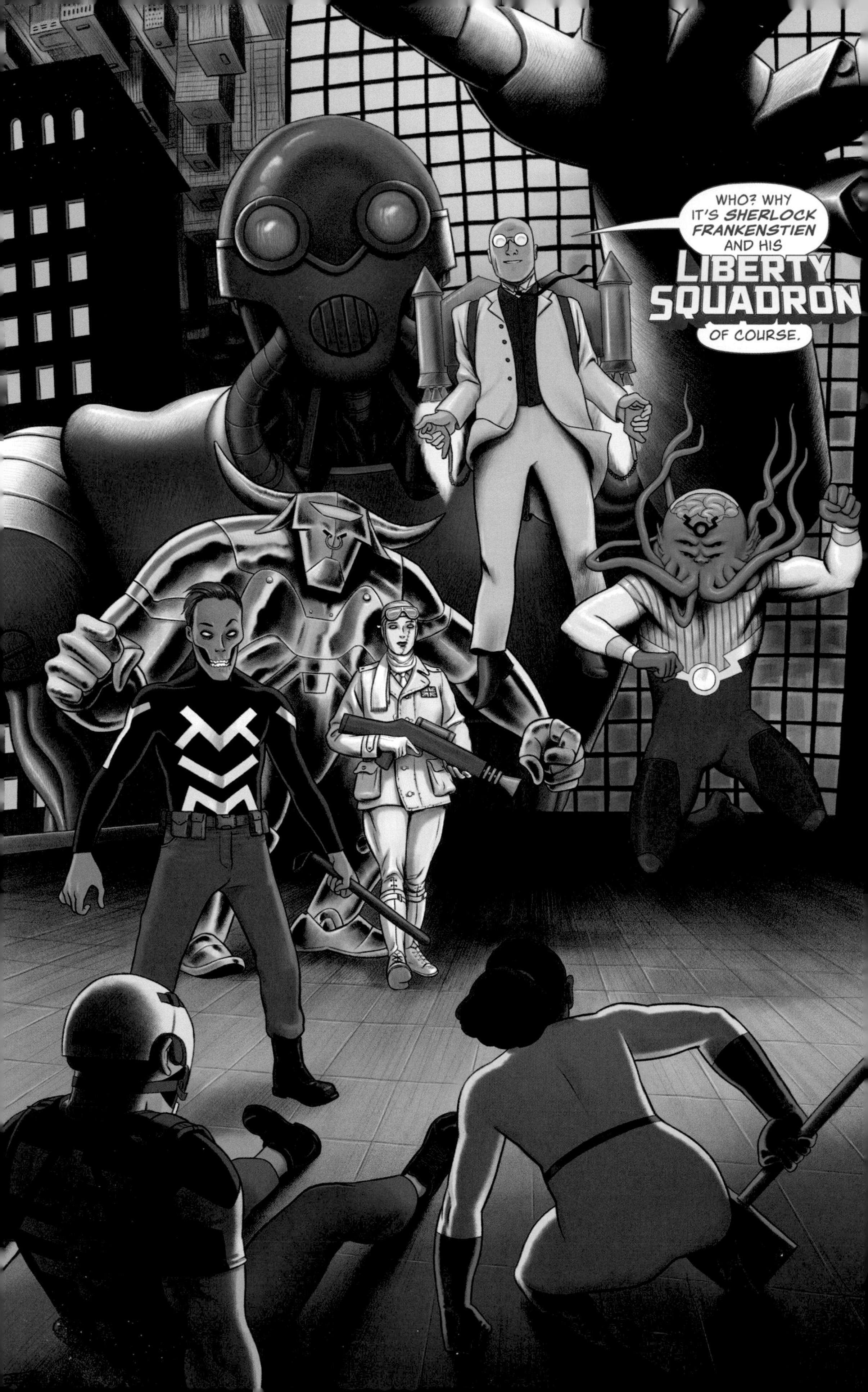
WHO? WHY IT'S SHERLOCK FRANKENSTIEN AND HIS LIBERTY SQUADRON OF COURSE.

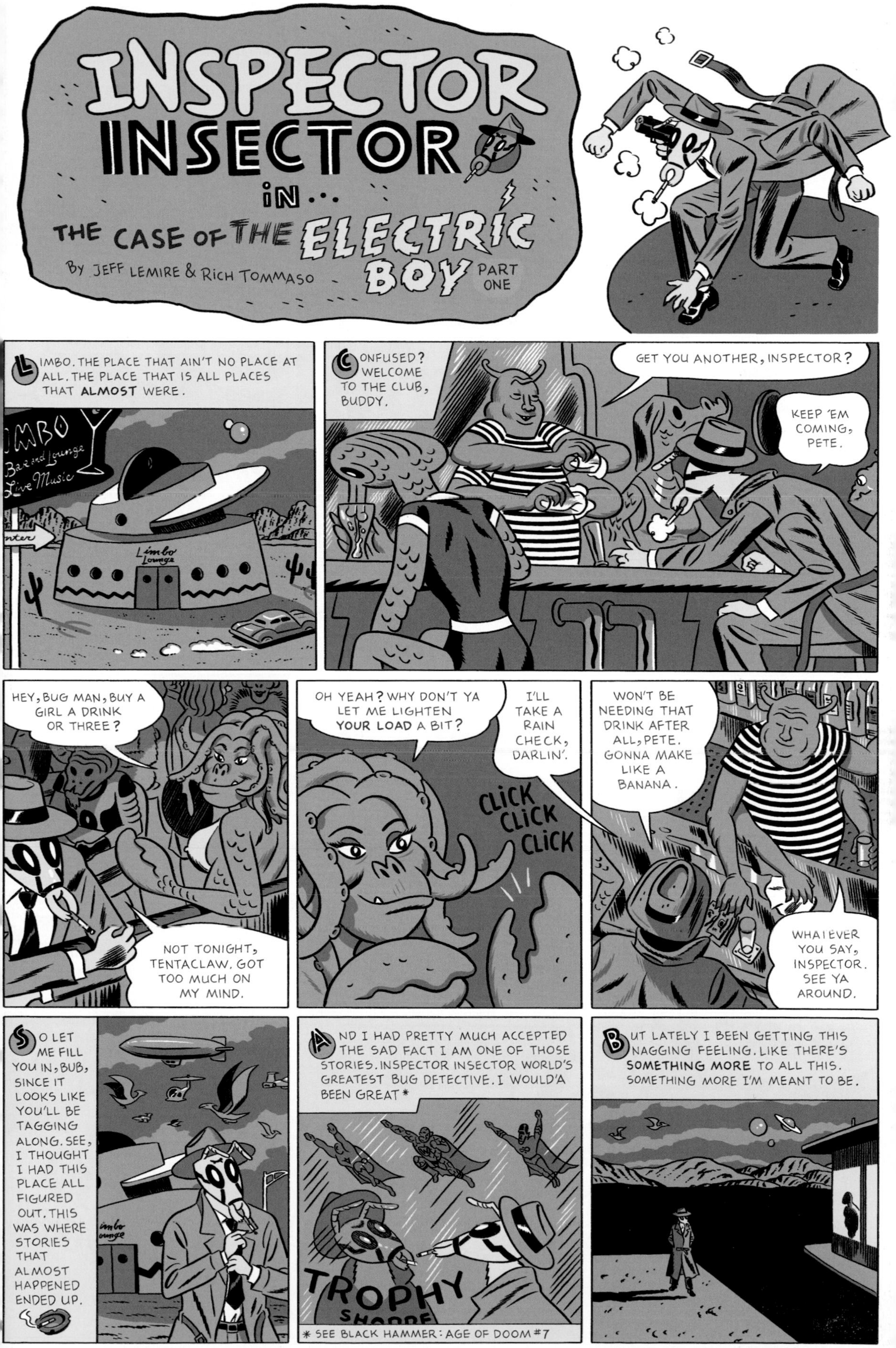
INSPECTOR INSECTOR
IN...
THE CASE OF THE ELECTRIC BOY
BY JEFF LEMIRE & RICH TOMMASO
PART ONE
LIMBO. THE PLACE THAT AIN'T NO PLACE AT ALL. THE PLACE THAT IS ALL PLACES THAT ALMOST WERE.
LIMBO Bar and Lounge Live Music
Limbo Lounge
CONFUSED? WELCOME TO THE CLUB, BUDDY.
GET YOU ANOTHER, INSPECTOR?
KEEP 'EM COMING, PETE.
HEY, BUG MAN, BUY A GIRL A DRINK OR THREE?
NOT TONIGHT, TENTACLAW. GOT TOO MUCH ON MY MIND.
OH YEAH? WHY DON'T YA LET ME LIGHTEN YOUR LOAD A BIT?
I'LL TAKE A RAIN CHECK, DARLIN'.
CLICK CLICK CLICK
WON'T BE NEEDING THAT DRINK AFTER ALL, PETE. GONNA MAKE LIKE A BANANA.
WHATEVER YOU SAY, INSPECTOR. SEE YA AROUND.
SO LET ME FILL YOU IN, BUB, SINCE IT LOOKS LIKE YOU'LL BE TAGGING ALONG. SEE, I THOUGHT I HAD THIS PLACE ALL FIGURED OUT. THIS WAS WHERE STORIES THAT ALMOST HAPPENED ENDED UP.
AND I HAD PRETTY MUCH ACCEPTED THE SAD FACT I AM ONE OF THOSE STORIES. INSPECTOR INSECTOR WORLD'S GREATEST BUG DETECTIVE. I WOULD'A BEEN GREAT*
TROPHY SHOPPE
* SEE BLACK HAMMER: AGE OF DOOM #7
BUT LATELY I BEEN GETTING THIS NAGGING FEELING. LIKE THERE'S SOMETHING MORE TO ALL THIS. SOMETHING MORE I'M MEANT TO BE.

SCHWAK!

JUMPIN' JUNE BUGS!

THAT WAS WEIRD EVEN FOR LIMBO. I SMELL TROUBLE...

STUFF COMES AND GOES IN LIMBO. STORIES ARE IMAGINED AND NEVER REALIZED, AND THEY POP UP HERE UNTIL THEY'RE FORGOTTEN AGAIN.

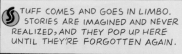

BUT I AIN'T NEVER SEEN A STORY POP UP LIKE **THAT** BEFORE...

HOLD IT RIGHT THERE, SHORT STUFF. DON'T TRY ANYTHING--

JUST A KID!

TAKE IT EASY, KIDDO. I AIN'T GONNA HURT YOU. YOU GOT A NAME?

MY NAME IS JOE... JOSEPH WEBER.

I THINK--I THINK I'M DEAD.

WEBER?

YEH, I SMELL TROUBLE ALL RIGHT. BUT EVEN MORE... I SMELL **A MYSTERY.**

TO BEE CONTINUED!

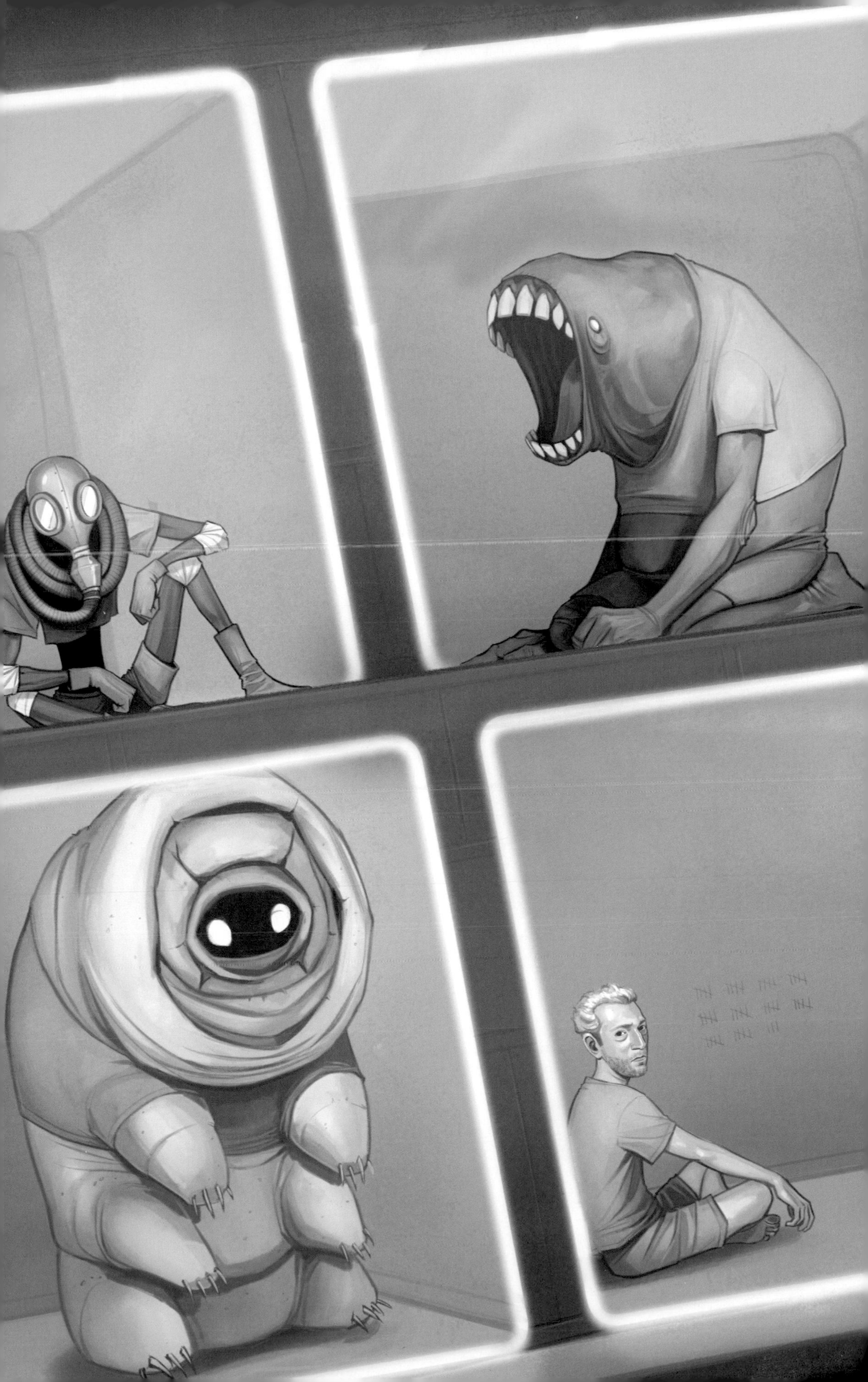

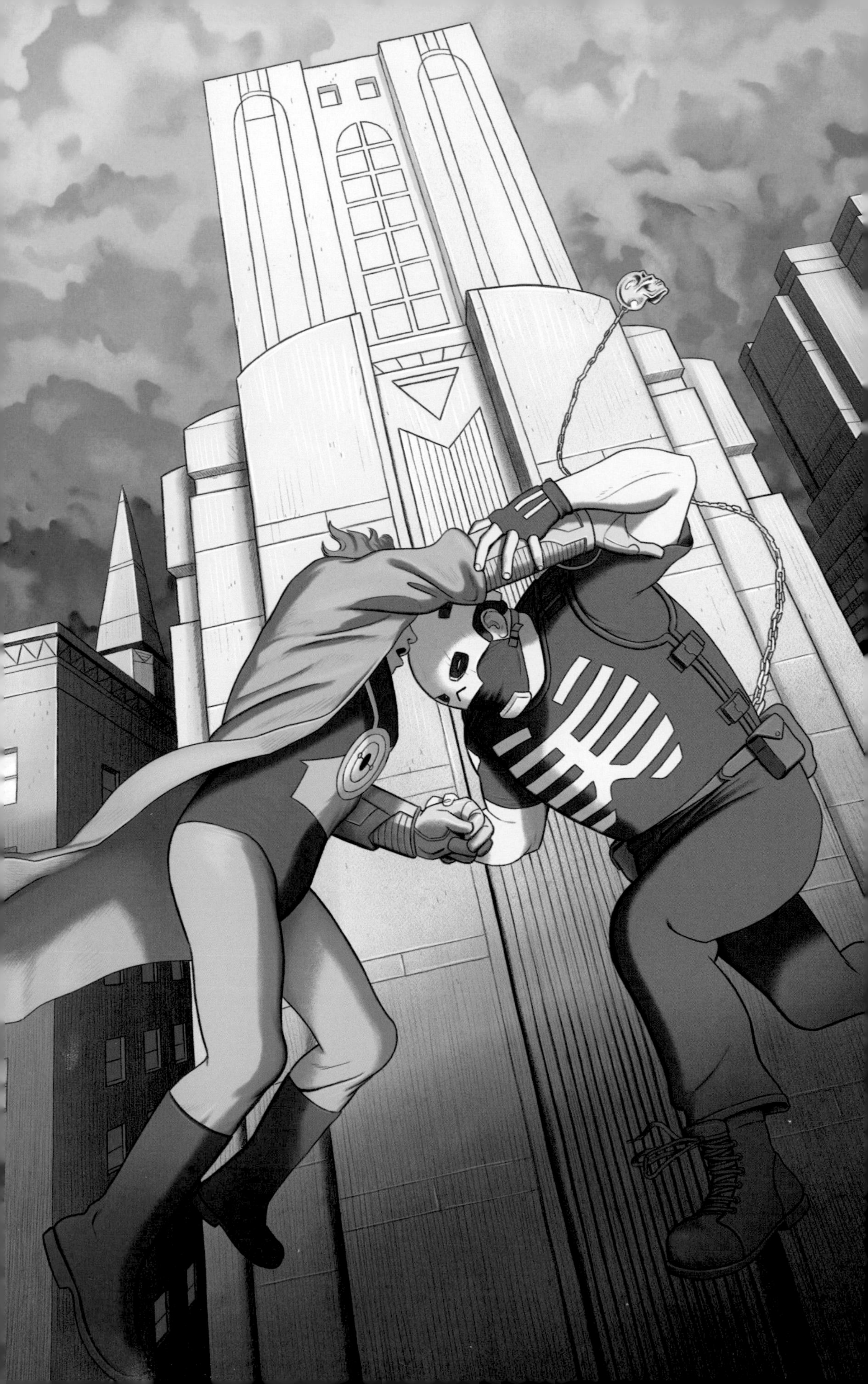

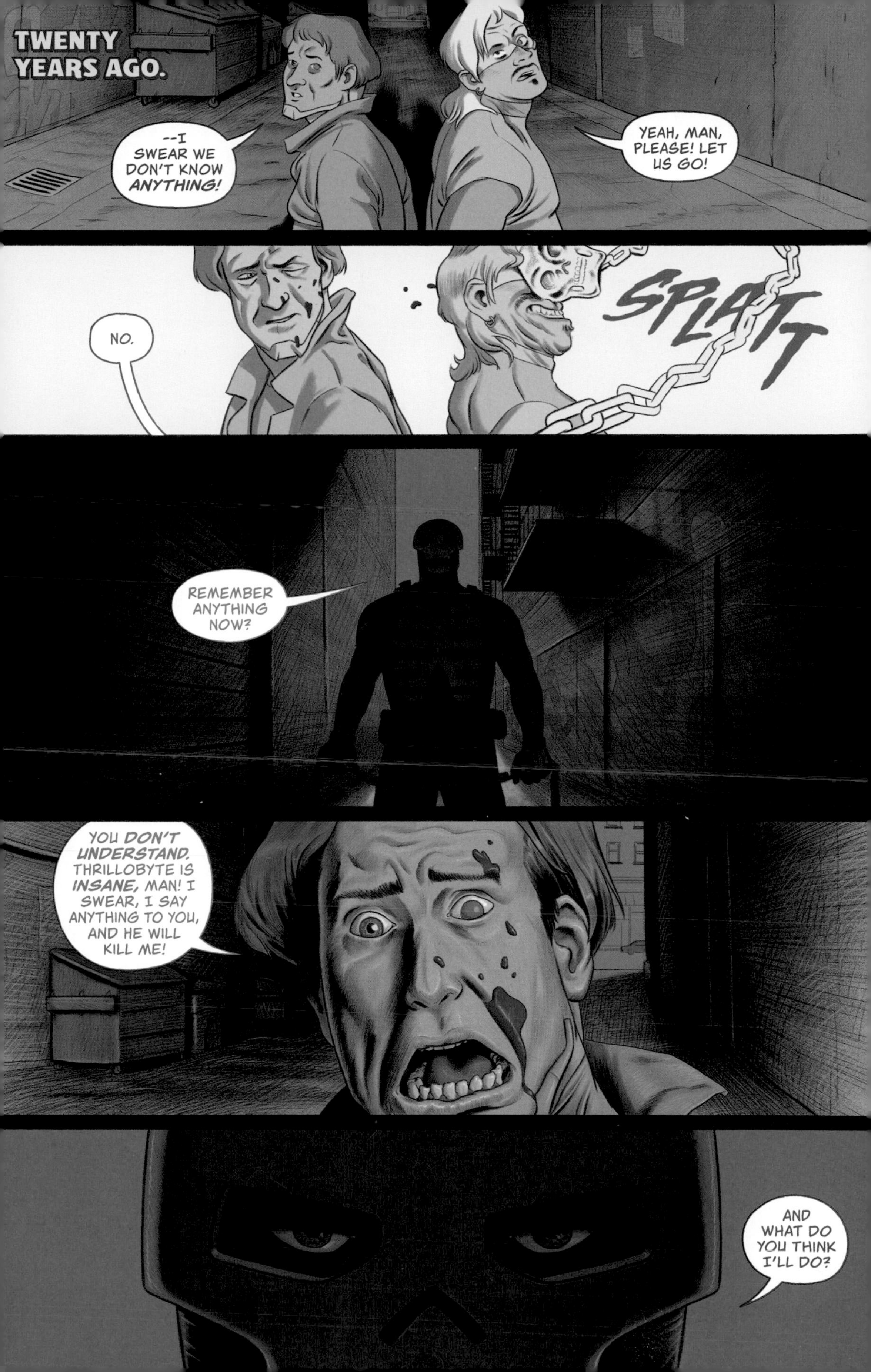
TWENTY YEARS AGO.
--I SWEAR WE DON'T KNOW ANYTHING!
YEAH, MAN, PLEASE! LET US GO!
NO.
SPLATT
REMEMBER ANYTHING NOW?
YOU DON'T UNDERSTAND. THRILLOBYTE IS INSANE, MAN! I SWEAR, I SAY ANYTHING TO YOU, AND HE WILL KILL ME!
AND WHAT DO YOU THINK I'LL DO?

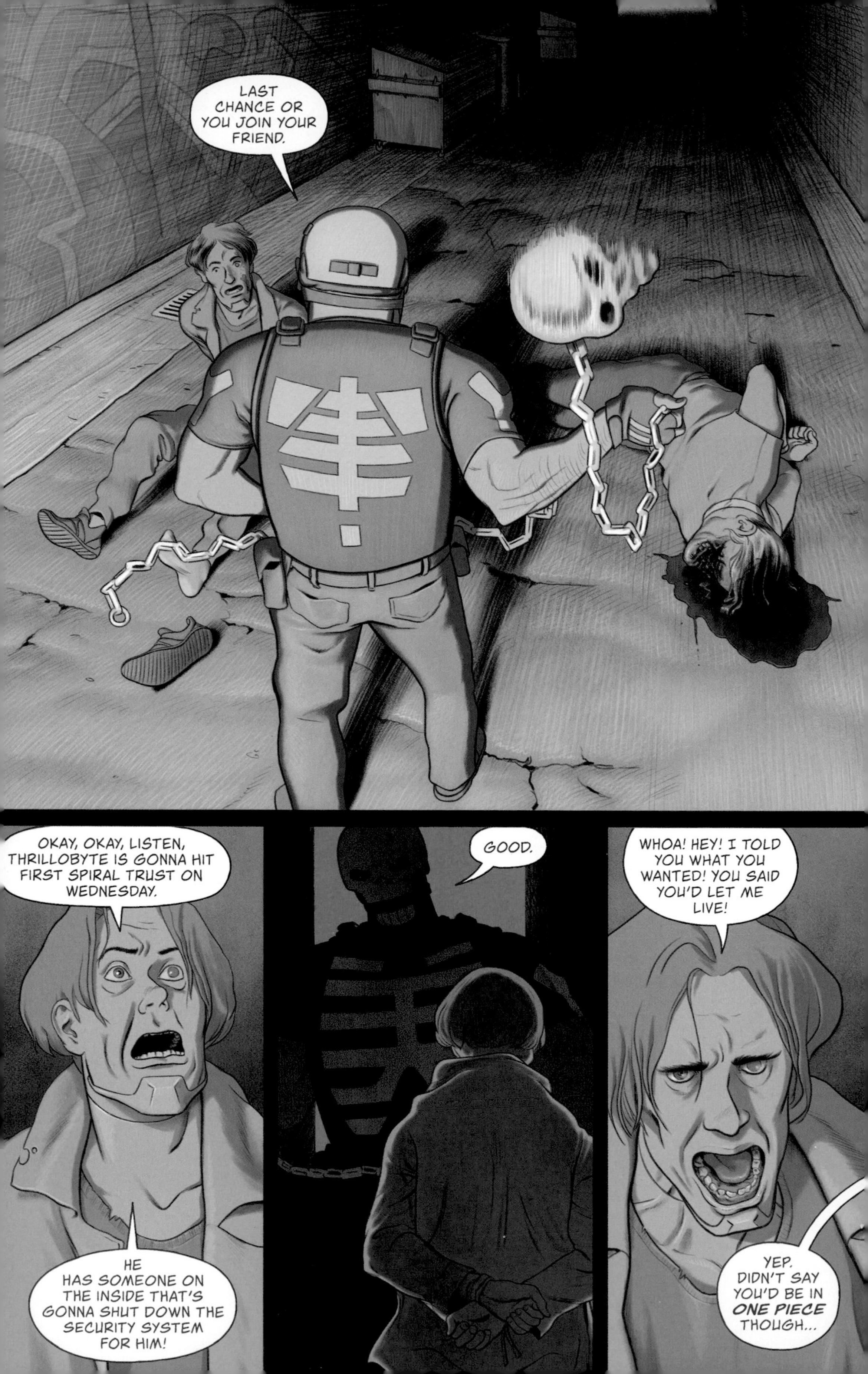
LAST CHANCE OR YOU JOIN YOUR FRIEND.
OKAY, OKAY, LISTEN, THRILLOBYTE IS GONNA HIT FIRST SPIRAL TRUST ON WEDNESDAY.
HE HAS SOMEONE ON THE INSIDE THAT'S GONNA SHUT DOWN THE SECURITY SYSTEM FOR HIM!
GOOD.
WHOA! HEY! I TOLD YOU WHAT YOU WANTED! YOU SAID YOU'D LET ME LIVE!
YEP. DIDN'T SAY YOU'D BE IN ONE PIECE THOUGH...

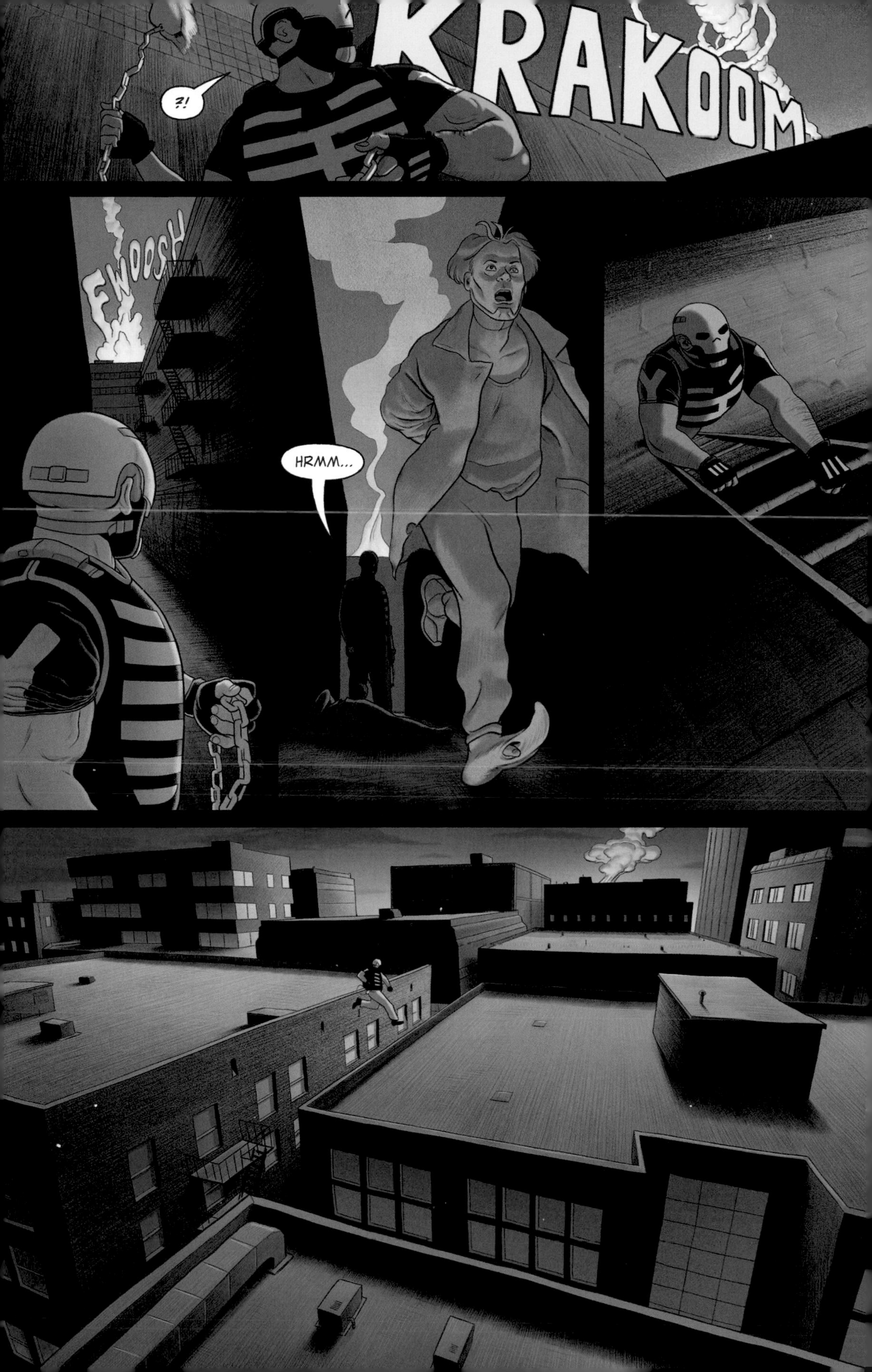

?!
KRAKOOM
FWOOSH
HRMM...

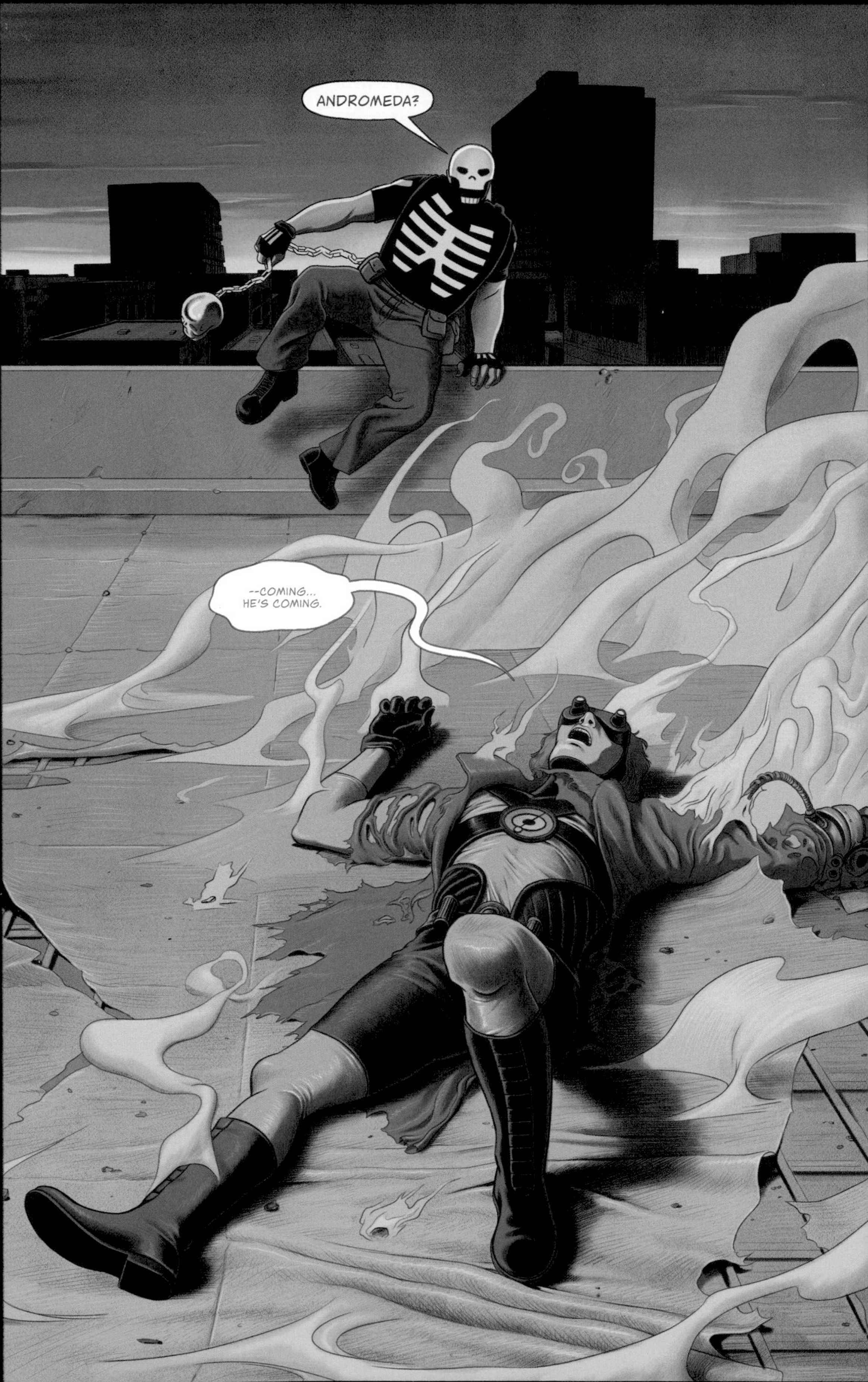
ANDROMEDA?
--COMING... HE'S COMING.

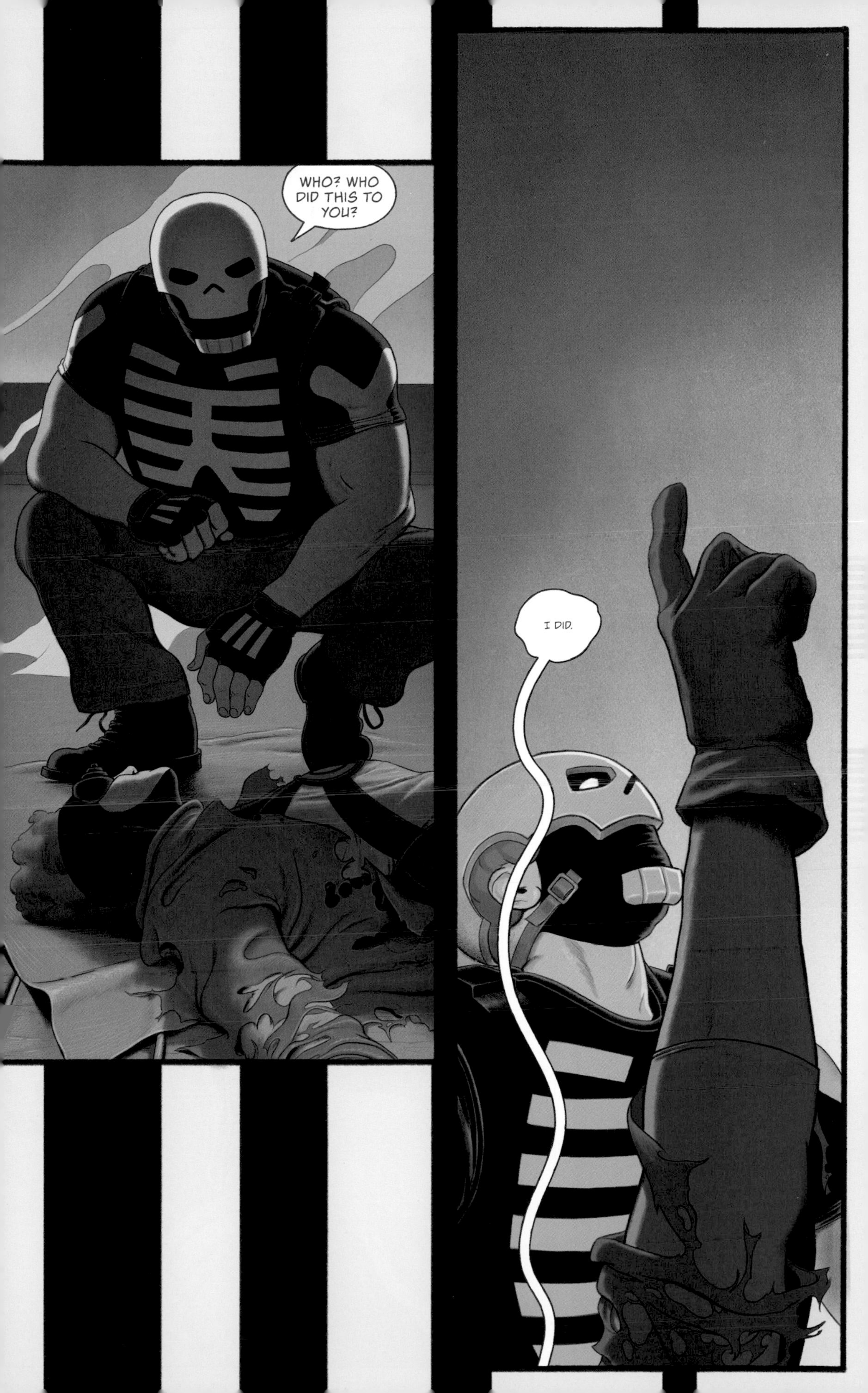
WHO? WHO DID THIS TO YOU?
I DID.

HMM, YOU REMIND ME OF SOMEONE. NOT AN EXACT COPY THOUGH. FASCINATING.

TSK, NO TIME FOR FURTHER STUDY, I'M AFRAID.

SHRAK

--UNGH!

NOW THEN, LAST CHANCE. TWO HEADS ARE BETTER THAN ONE AND ALL OF THAT?

DON'T DO THIS. WE ARE BETTER THAN THIS.

WE CERTAINLY ARE. AND THAT IS EXACTLY THE POINT.

AH-- AH--DID YOU REALLY THINK I WOULDN'T SEE A SHINY CHROME SKULL COMING?

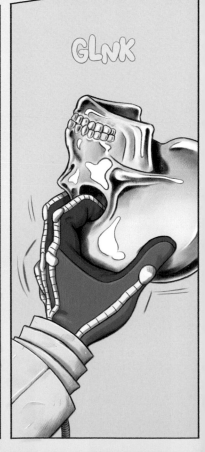

GLNK

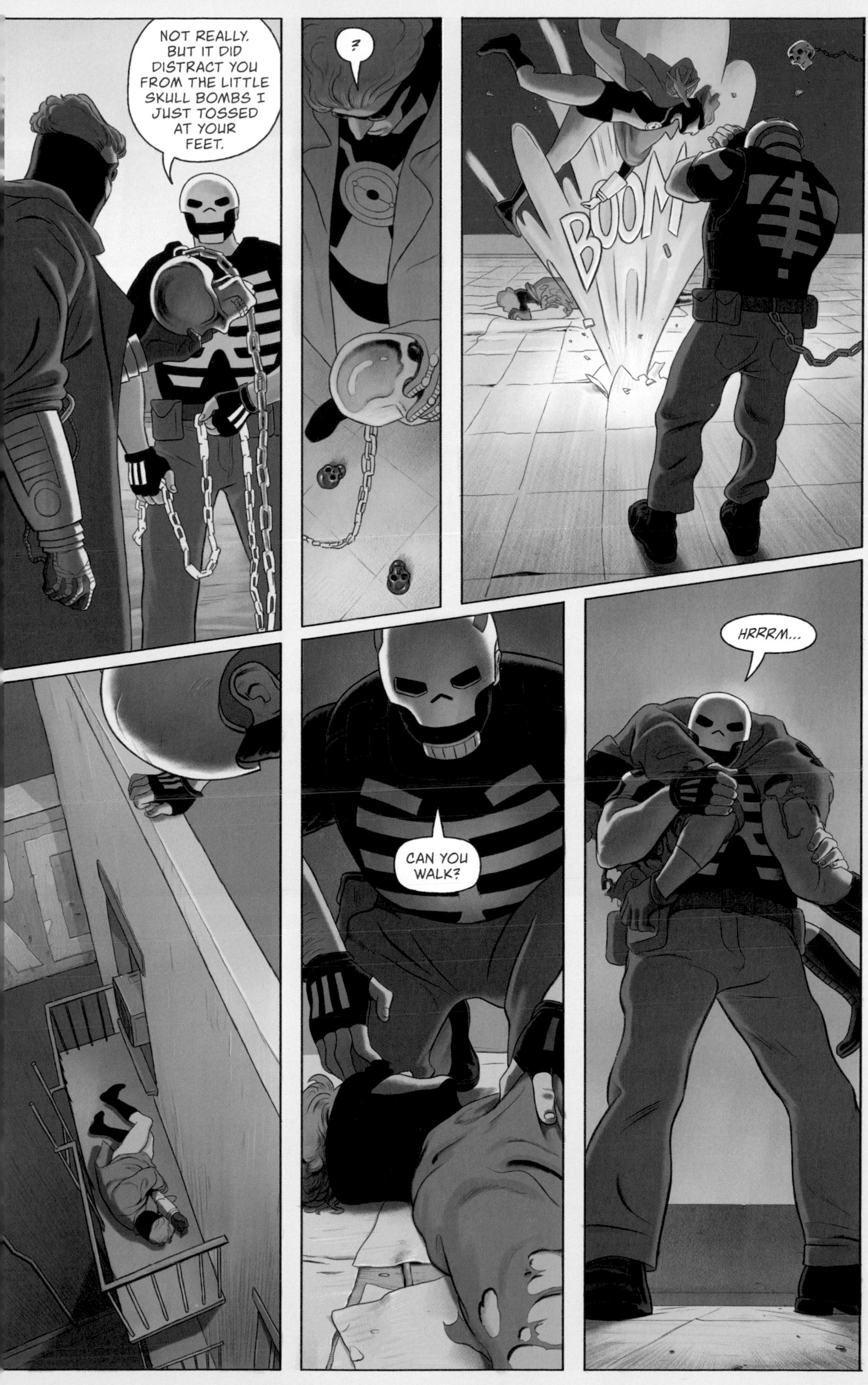
NOT REALLY. BUT IT DID DISTRACT YOU FROM THE LITTLE SKULL BOMBS I JUST TOSSED AT YOUR FEET.
?
BOOM
HRRRM...
CAN YOU WALK?

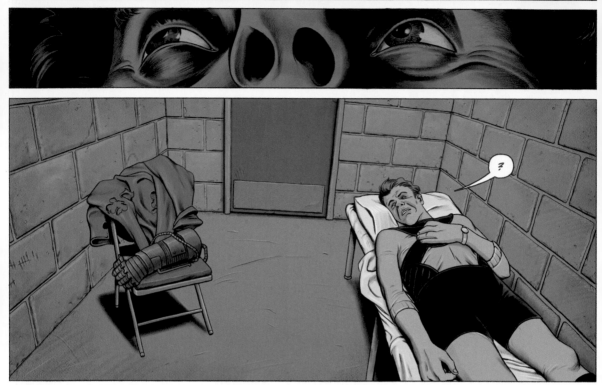

?

HELLO?

SKULLDIGGER?

OH, YOU'RE UP.

FEELING ANY BETTER?

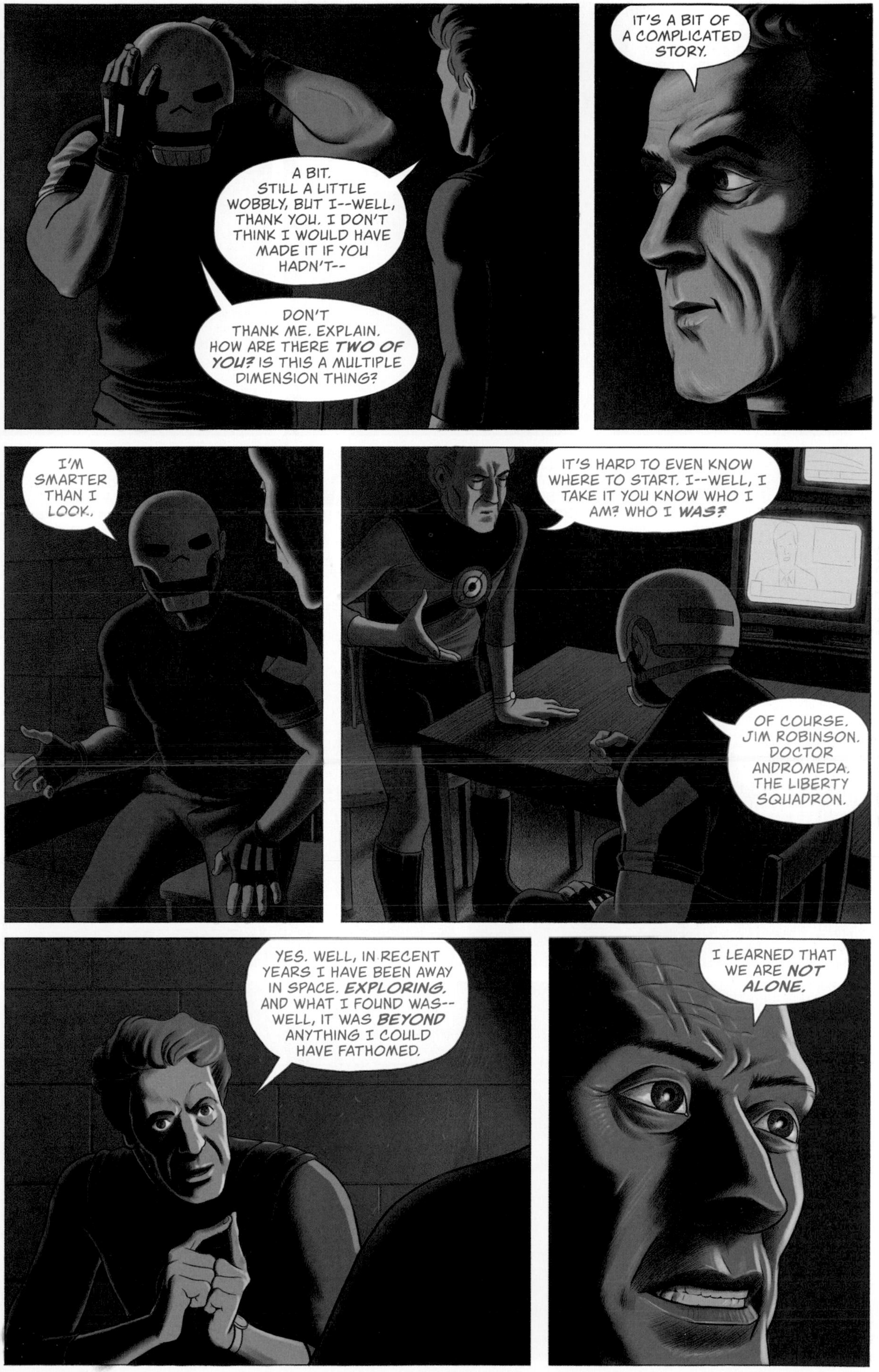
A BIT. STILL A LITTLE WOBBLY, BUT I--WELL, THANK YOU. I DON'T THINK I WOULD HAVE MADE IT IF YOU HADN'T--
DON'T THANK ME. EXPLAIN. HOW ARE THERE TWO OF YOU? IS THIS A MULTIPLE DIMENSION THING?
IT'S A BIT OF A COMPLICATED STORY.
I'M SMARTER THAN I LOOK.
IT'S HARD TO EVEN KNOW WHERE TO START. I--WELL, I TAKE IT YOU KNOW WHO I AM? WHO I WAS?
OF COURSE. JIM ROBINSON. DOCTOR ANDROMEDA. THE LIBERTY SQUADRON.
YES. WELL, IN RECENT YEARS I HAVE BEEN AWAY IN SPACE. EXPLORING. AND WHAT I FOUND WAS-- WELL, IT WAS BEYOND ANYTHING I COULD HAVE FATHOMED.
I LEARNED THAT WE ARE NOT ALONE.

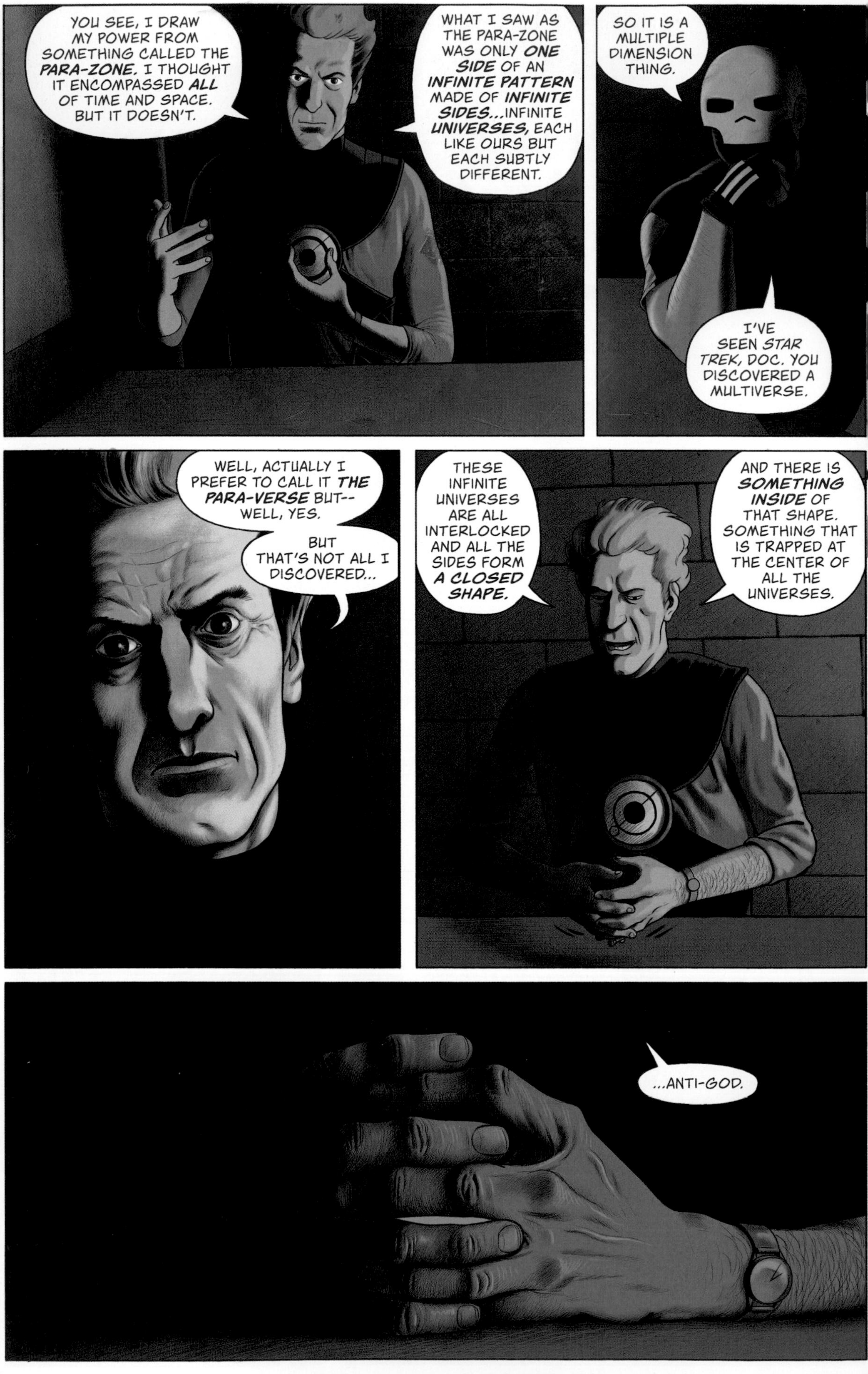
YOU SEE, I DRAW MY POWER FROM SOMETHING CALLED THE PARA-ZONE. I THOUGHT IT ENCOMPASSED ALL OF TIME AND SPACE. BUT IT DOESN'T.
WHAT I SAW AS THE PARA-ZONE WAS ONLY ONE SIDE OF AN INFINITE PATTERN MADE OF INFINITE SIDES... INFINITE UNIVERSES, EACH LIKE OURS BUT EACH SUBTLY DIFFERENT.
SO IT IS A MULTIPLE DIMENSION THING.
I'VE SEEN STAR TREK, DOC. YOU DISCOVERED A MULTIVERSE.
WELL, ACTUALLY I PREFER TO CALL IT THE PARA-VERSE BUT-- WELL, YES.
BUT THAT'S NOT ALL I DISCOVERED...
THESE INFINITE UNIVERSES ARE ALL INTERLOCKED AND ALL THE SIDES FORM A CLOSED SHAPE.
AND THERE IS SOMETHING INSIDE OF THAT SHAPE. SOMETHING THAT IS TRAPPED AT THE CENTER OF ALL THE UNIVERSES.
...ANTI-GOD.

ANTI-GOD IS DEAD.

WE ALL **THOUGHT** HE WAS. WE ALL **HOPED** HE WAS.

BUT I SAW HIM THERE--

"I SAW HIM **SLEEPING**."

I THINK WHEN BLACK HAMMER "DESTROYED" ANTI-GOD, HE REALLY JUST SENT HIM BACK TO WHERE HE CAME FROM.

AND NOW I THINK MY DOPPELGÄNGER MEANS TO **BRING HIM BACK**.

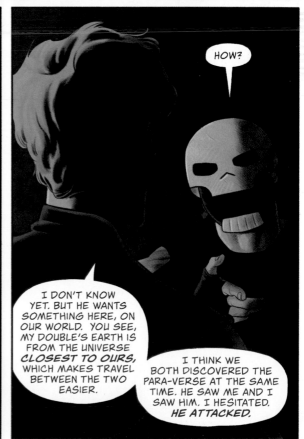

HOW?

I DON'T KNOW YET. BUT HE WANTS SOMETHING HERE, ON OUR WORLD. YOU SEE, MY DOUBLE'S EARTH IS FROM THE UNIVERSE **CLOSEST TO OURS**, WHICH MAKES TRAVEL BETWEEN THE TWO EASIER.

I THINK WE BOTH DISCOVERED THE PARA-VERSE AT THE SAME TIME. HE SAW ME AND I SAW HIM. I HESITATED. **HE ATTACKED.**

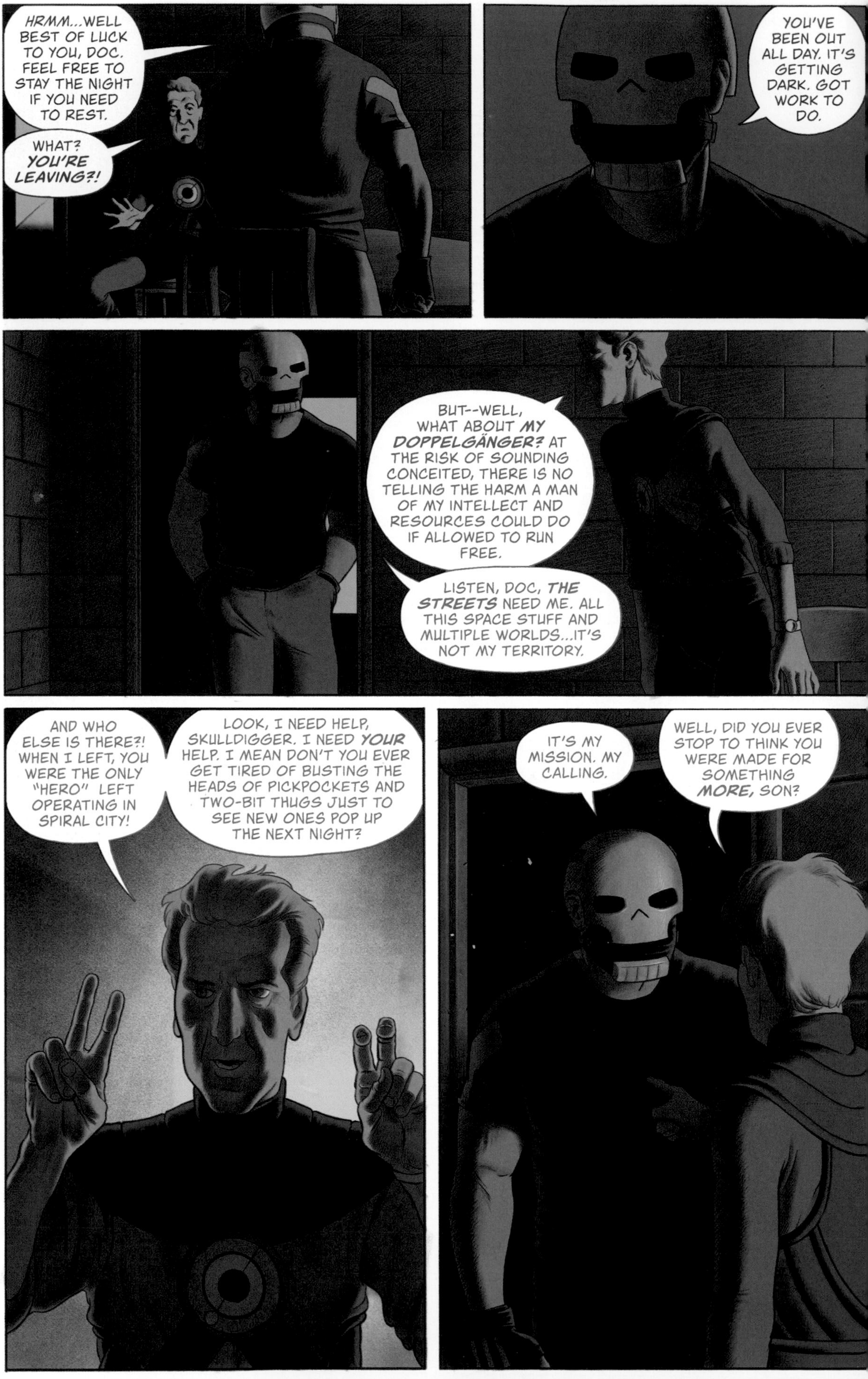
HRMM...WELL BEST OF LUCK TO YOU, DOC. FEEL FREE TO STAY THE NIGHT IF YOU NEED TO REST.
WHAT? YOU'RE LEAVING?!
YOU'VE BEEN OUT ALL DAY. IT'S GETTING DARK. GOT WORK TO DO.
BUT--WELL, WHAT ABOUT MY DOPPELGÄNGER? AT THE RISK OF SOUNDING CONCEITED, THERE IS NO TELLING THE HARM A MAN OF MY INTELLECT AND RESOURCES COULD DO IF ALLOWED TO RUN FREE.
LISTEN, DOC, THE STREETS NEED ME. ALL THIS SPACE STUFF AND MULTIPLE WORLDS...IT'S NOT MY TERRITORY.
AND WHO ELSE IS THERE?! WHEN I LEFT, YOU WERE THE ONLY "HERO" LEFT OPERATING IN SPIRAL CITY!
LOOK, I NEED HELP, SKULLDIGGER. I NEED YOUR HELP. I MEAN DON'T YOU EVER GET TIRED OF BUSTING THE HEADS OF PICKPOCKETS AND TWO-BIT THUGS JUST TO SEE NEW ONES POP UP THE NEXT NIGHT?
IT'S MY MISSION. MY CALLING.
WELL, DID YOU EVER STOP TO THINK YOU WERE MADE FOR SOMETHING MORE, SON?

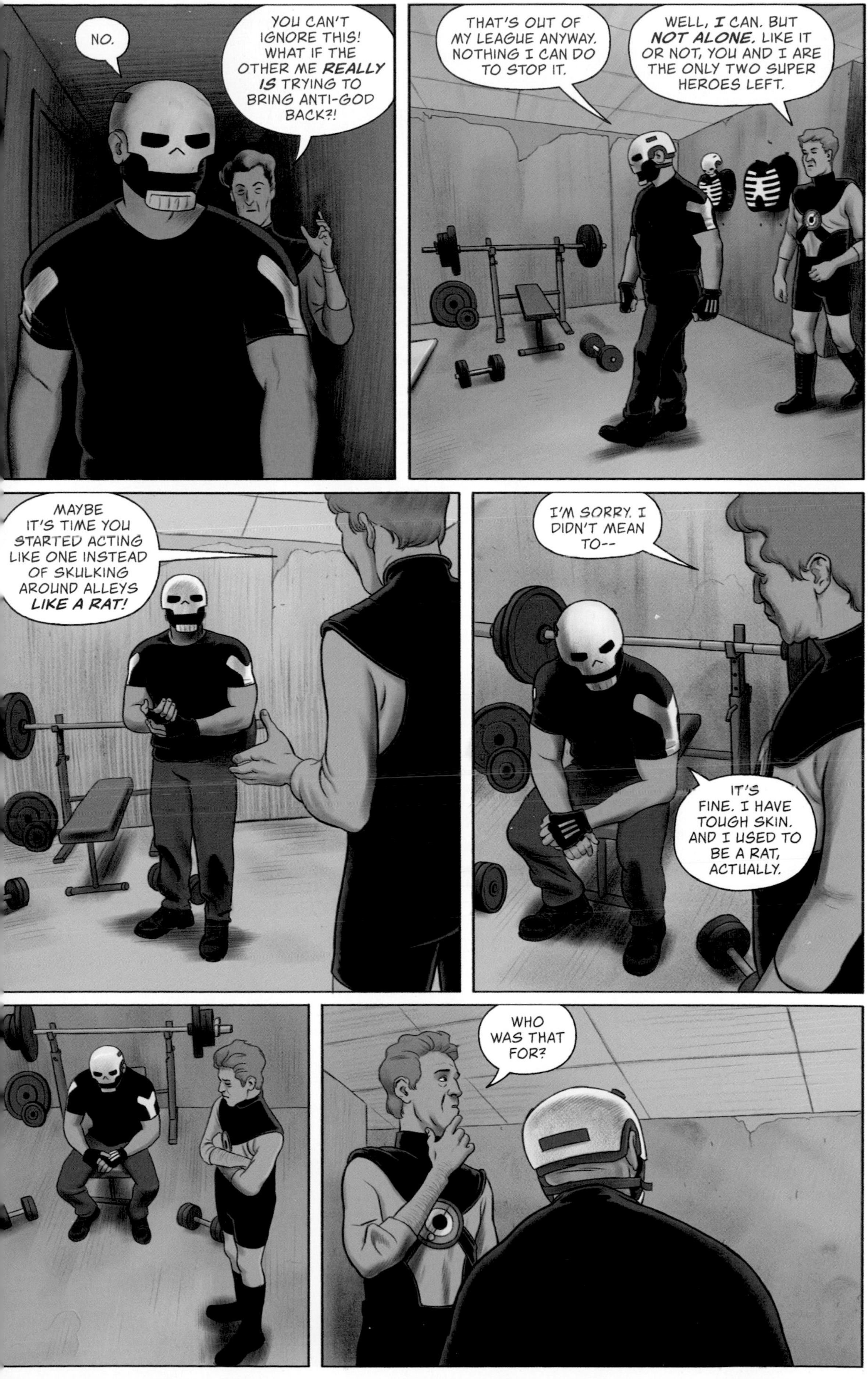
NO.
YOU CAN'T IGNORE THIS! WHAT IF THE OTHER ME REALLY IS TRYING TO BRING ANTI-GOD BACK?!
THAT'S OUT OF MY LEAGUE ANYWAY. NOTHING I CAN DO TO STOP IT.
WELL, I CAN. BUT NOT ALONE. LIKE IT OR NOT, YOU AND I ARE THE ONLY TWO SUPER HEROES LEFT.
MAYBE IT'S TIME YOU STARTED ACTING LIKE ONE INSTEAD OF SKULKING AROUND ALLEYS LIKE A RAT!
I'M SORRY. I DIDN'T MEAN TO--
IT'S FINE. I HAVE TOUGH SKIN. AND I USED TO BE A RAT, ACTUALLY.
WHO WAS THAT FOR?

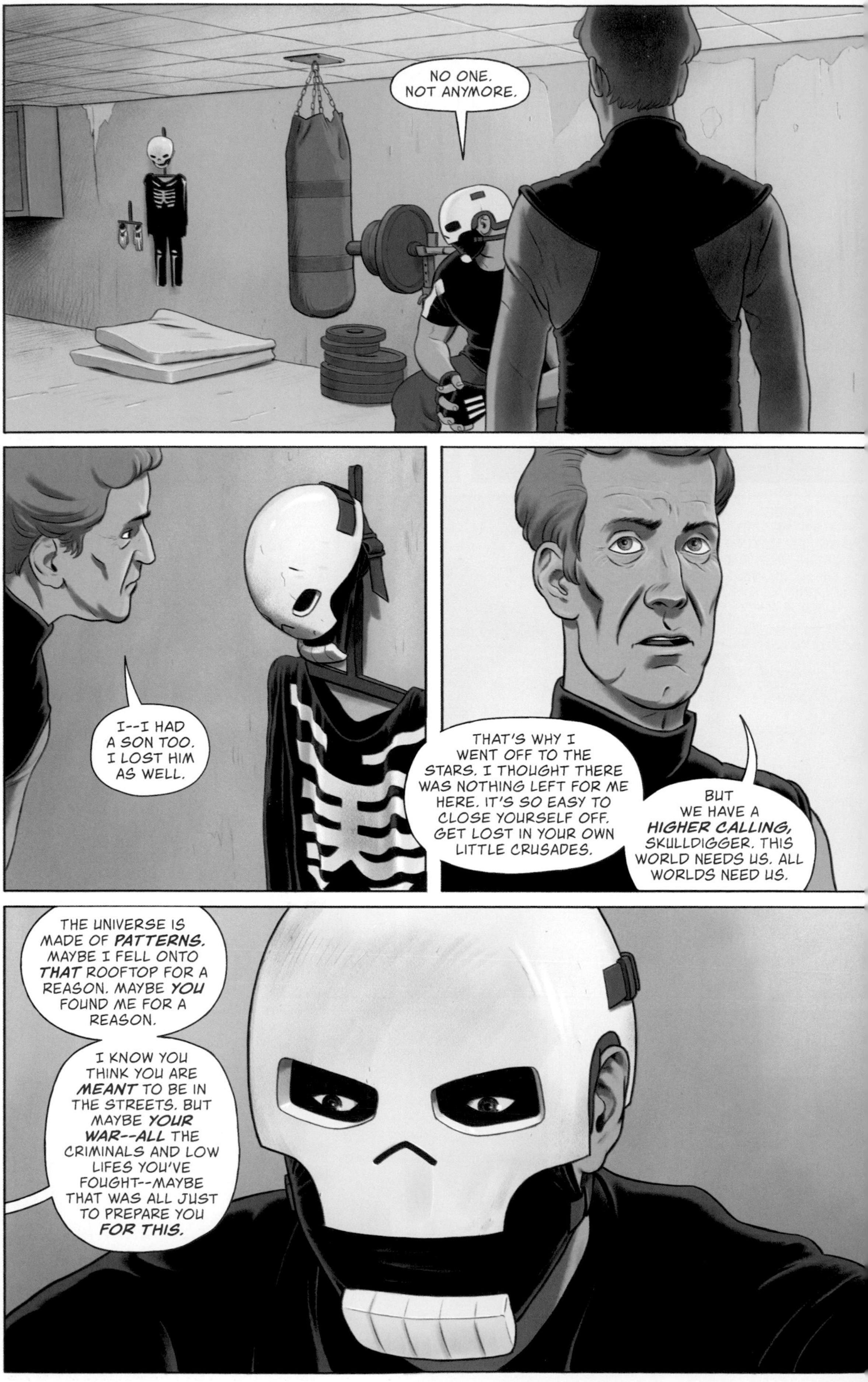
NO ONE. NOT ANYMORE.
I--I HAD A SON TOO. I LOST HIM AS WELL.
THAT'S WHY I WENT OFF TO THE STARS. I THOUGHT THERE WAS NOTHING LEFT FOR ME HERE. IT'S SO EASY TO CLOSE YOURSELF OFF. GET LOST IN YOUR OWN LITTLE CRUSADES.
BUT WE HAVE A HIGHER CALLING, SKULLDIGGER. THIS WORLD NEEDS US. ALL WORLDS NEED US.
THE UNIVERSE IS MADE OF PATTERNS. MAYBE I FELL ONTO THAT ROOFTOP FOR A REASON. MAYBE YOU FOUND ME FOR A REASON.
I KNOW YOU THINK YOU ARE MEANT TO BE IN THE STREETS. BUT MAYBE YOUR WAR--ALL THE CRIMINALS AND LOW LIFES YOU'VE FOUGHT--MAYBE THAT WAS ALL JUST TO PREPARE YOU FOR THIS.

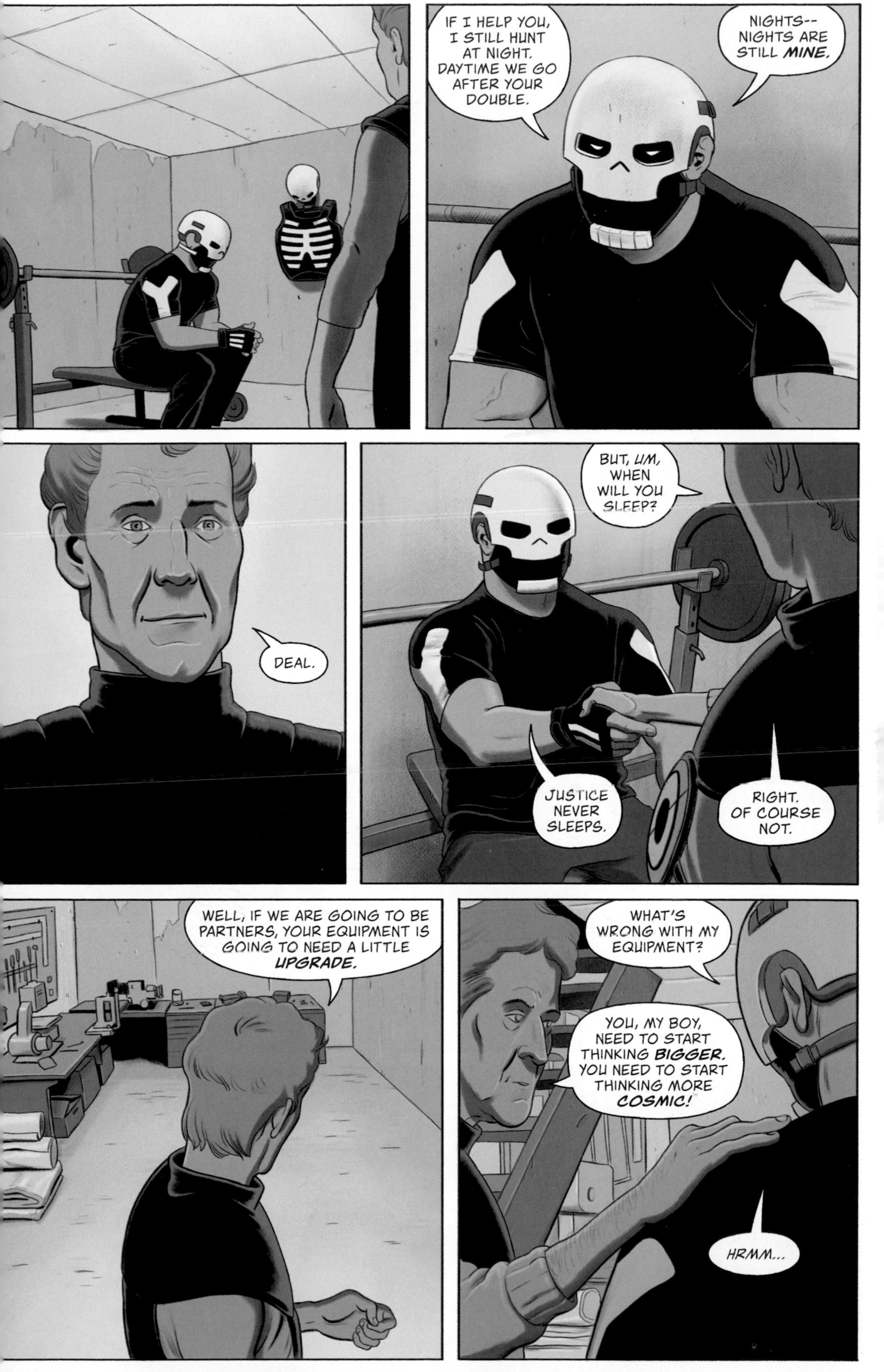
IF I HELP YOU, I STILL HUNT AT NIGHT. DAYTIME WE GO AFTER YOUR DOUBLE.
NIGHTS-- NIGHTS ARE STILL *MINE.*
DEAL.
BUT, *UM,* WHEN WILL YOU SLEEP?
JUSTICE NEVER SLEEPS.
RIGHT. OF COURSE NOT.
WELL, IF WE ARE GOING TO BE PARTNERS, YOUR EQUIPMENT IS GOING TO NEED A LITTLE ***UPGRADE.***
WHAT'S WRONG WITH MY EQUIPMENT?
YOU, MY BOY, NEED TO START THINKING ***BIGGER.*** YOU NEED TO START THINKING MORE ***COSMIC!***
HRMM...

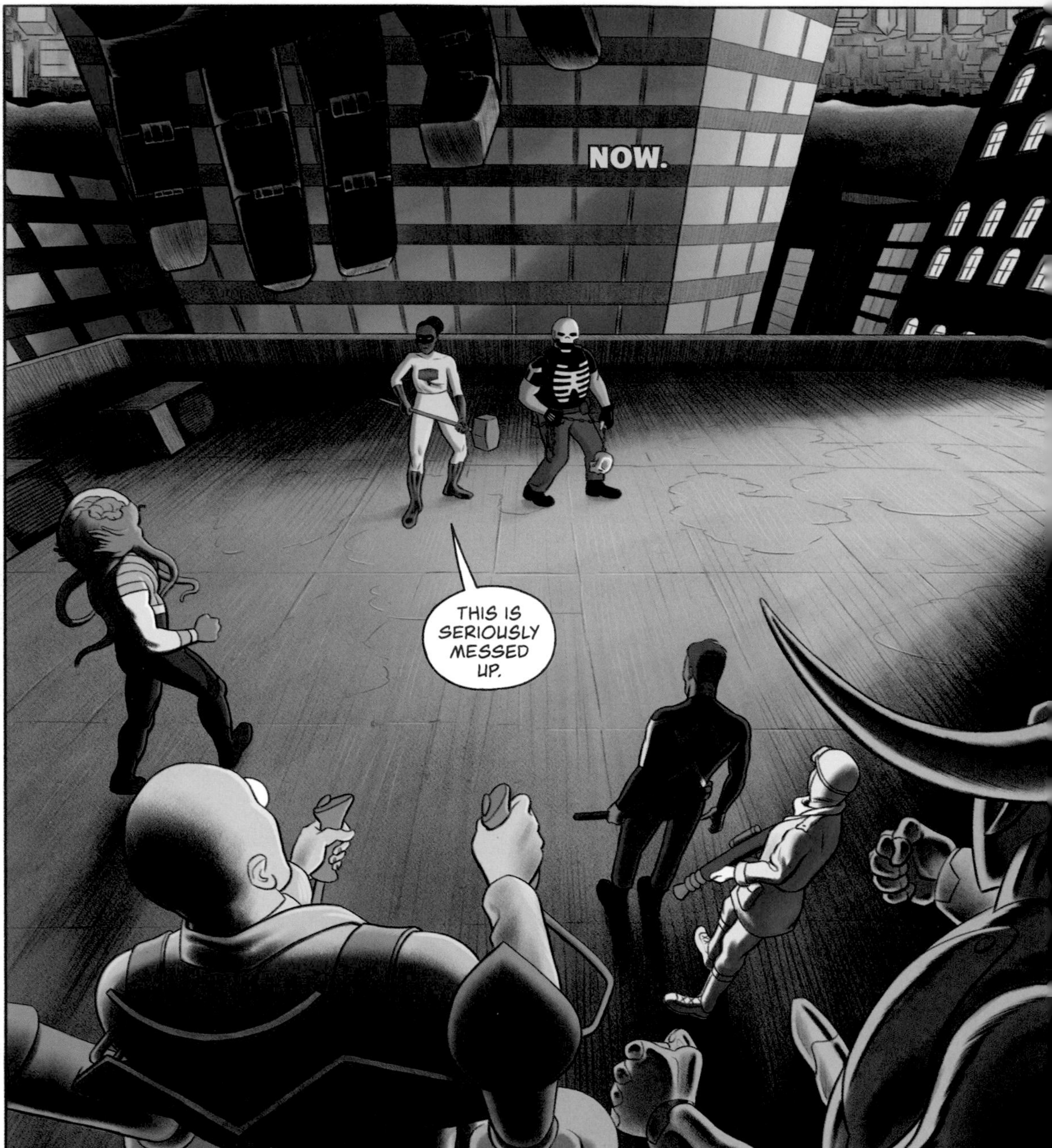
NOW.
THIS IS SERIOUSLY MESSED UP.

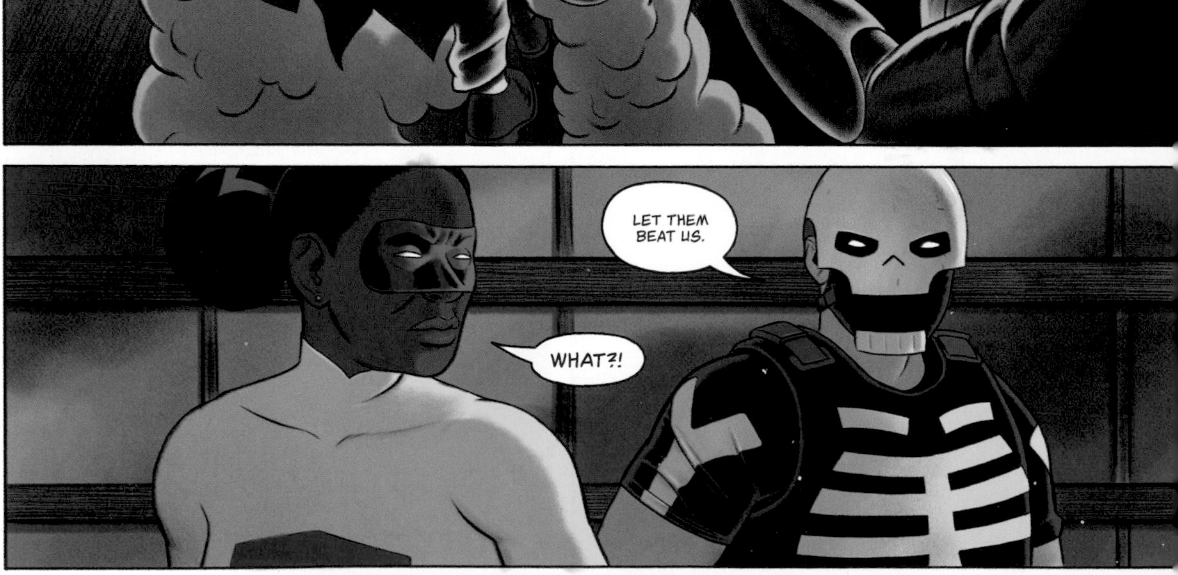
LET THEM BEAT US.
WHAT?!

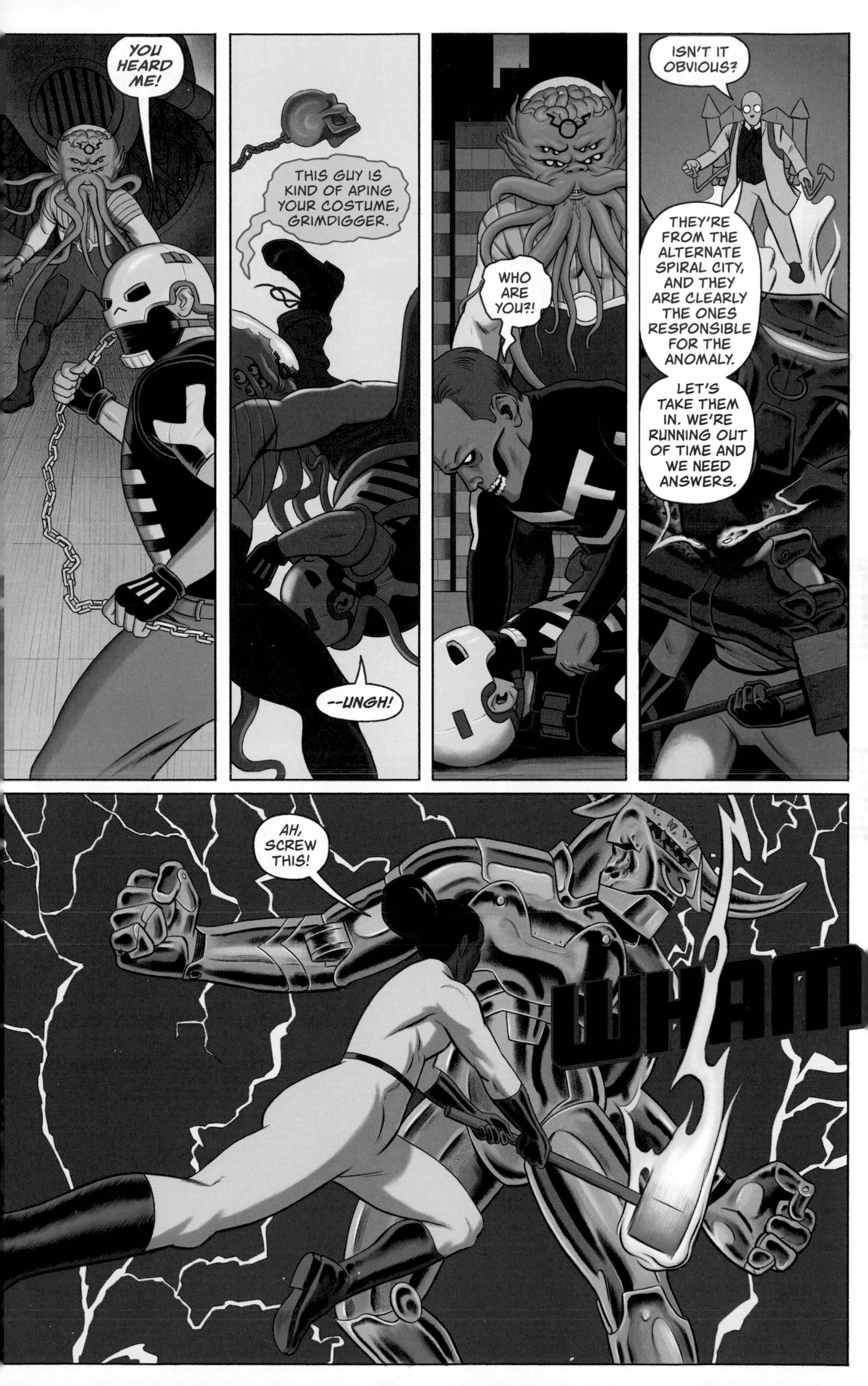
YOU HEARD ME!
THIS GUY IS KIND OF APING YOUR COSTUME, GRIMDIGGER.
--UNGH!
WHO ARE YOU?!
ISN'T IT OBVIOUS?
THEY'RE FROM THE ALTERNATE SPIRAL CITY, AND THEY ARE CLEARLY THE ONES RESPONSIBLE FOR THE ANOMALY.
LET'S TAKE THEM IN. WE'RE RUNNING OUT OF TIME AND WE NEED ANSWERS.
AH, SCREW THIS!
WHAM

KRRRAKKK

I GOT HER BOSS-- ARRRGH!

HANDS OFF, ASSHOLE.

FASCINATING. SHE *IS* A DUPLICATE OF OUR BLACK HAMMER. EVEN HER POWER LEVELS.

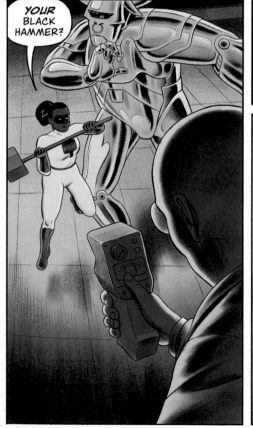

YOUR BLACK HAMMER?

INDEED. LUCKILY I'VE ALREADY SPENT A LIFETIME LEARNING HOW TO DEAL WITH YOU.

HEY!

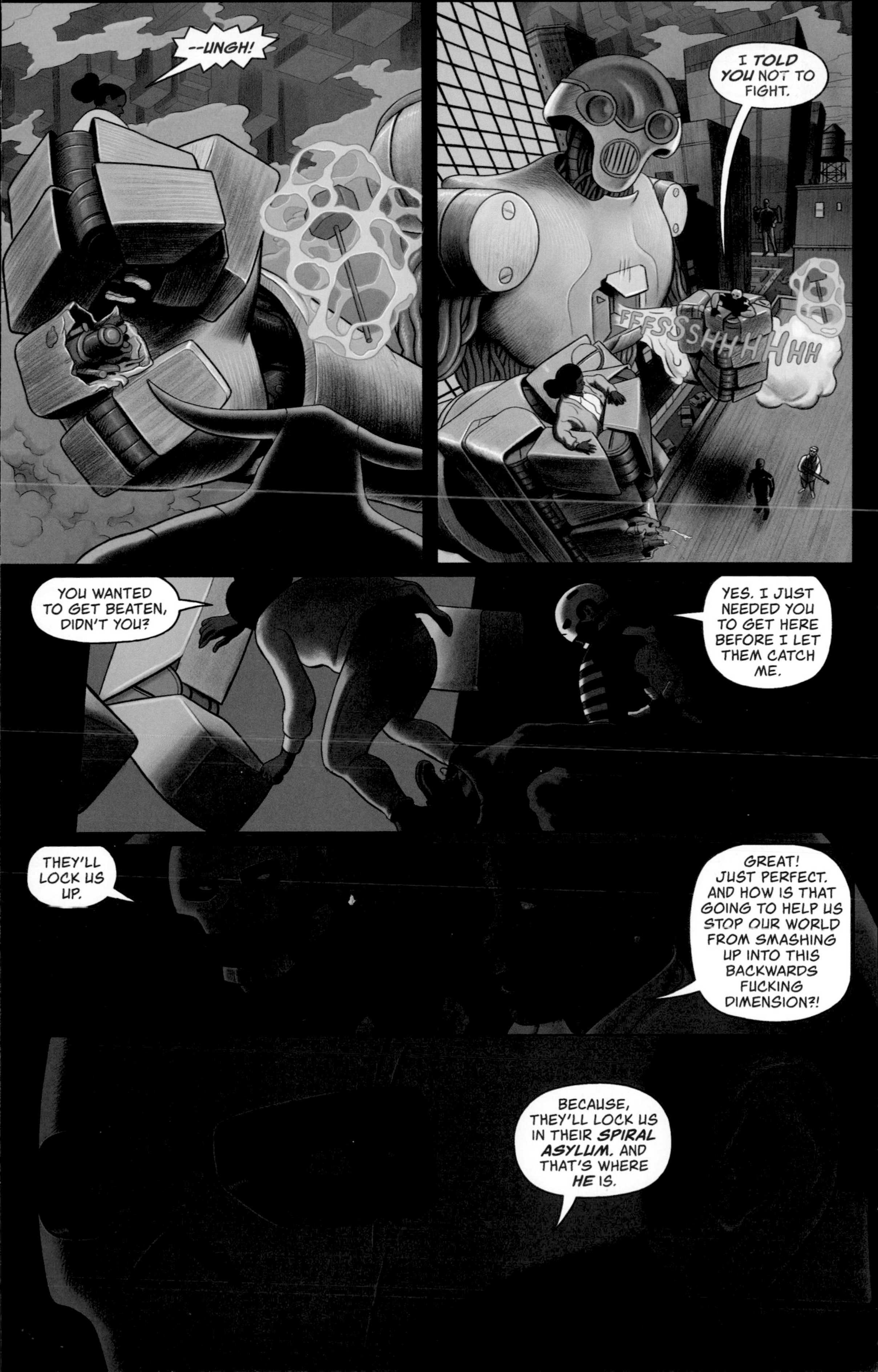
--UNGH!
I TOLD YOU NOT TO FIGHT.
FFFSSSHHHHHhh
YOU WANTED TO GET BEATEN, DIDN'T YOU?
YES. I JUST NEEDED YOU TO GET HERE BEFORE I LET THEM CATCH ME.
THEY'LL LOCK US UP.
GREAT! JUST PERFECT. AND HOW IS THAT GOING TO HELP US STOP OUR WORLD FROM SMASHING UP INTO THIS BACKWARDS FUCKING DIMENSION?!
BECAUSE, THEY'LL LOCK US IN THEIR SPIRAL ASYLUM. AND THAT'S WHERE HE IS.

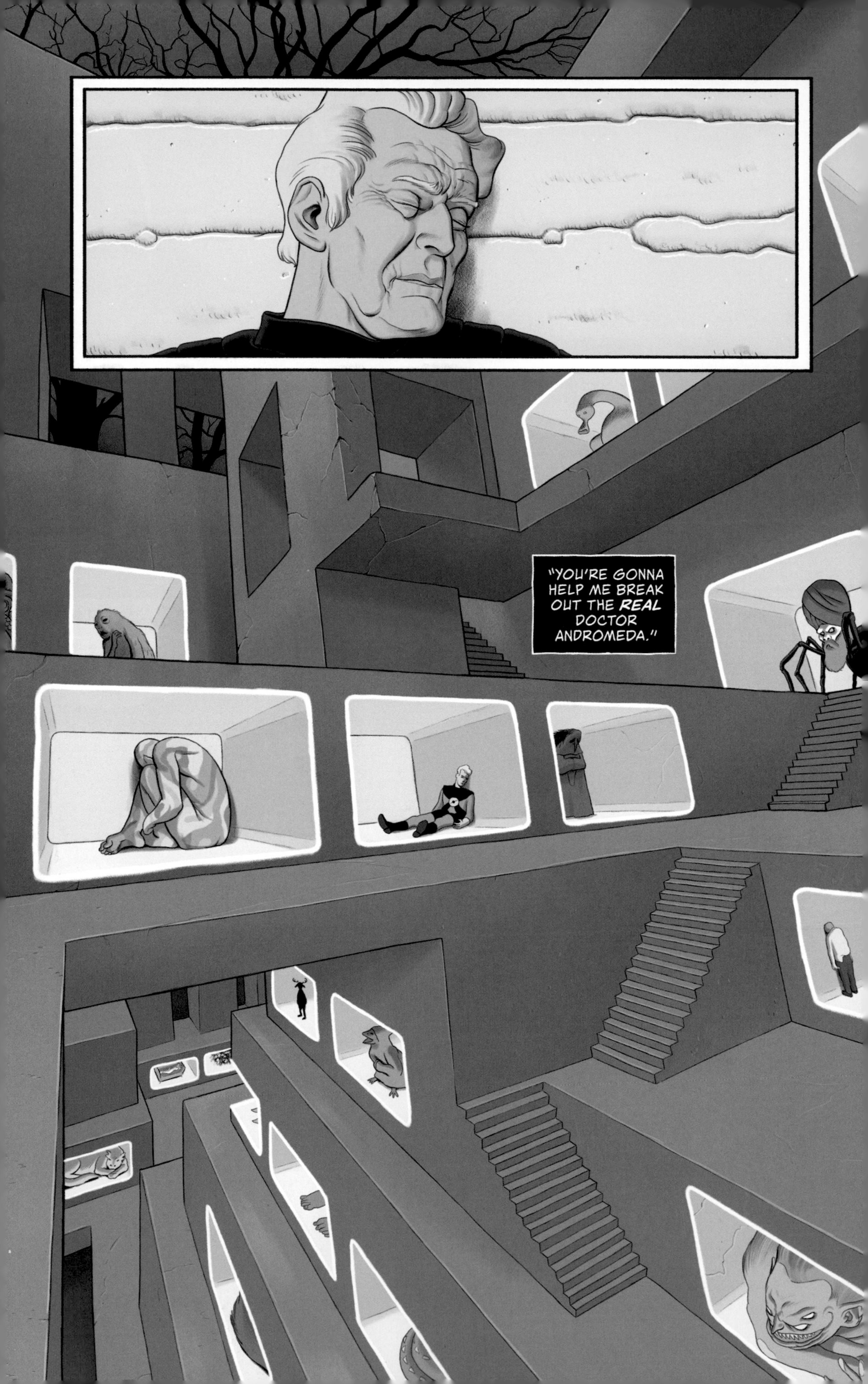
"YOU'RE GONNA HELP ME BREAK OUT THE ***REAL*** DOCTOR ANDROMEDA."

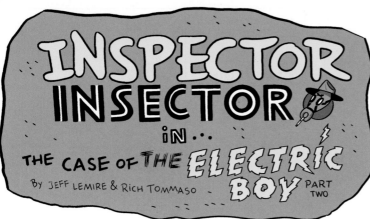

INSPECTOR INSECTOR IN...
THE CASE OF THE ELECTRIC BOY PART TWO
BY JEFF LEMIRE & RICH TOMMASO

Panel 1

--WHERE WE GOING?!

TO FIND A FRIEND. AND YES, FOR THE TENTH TIME, WE'RE **ALMOST THERE**, KID.

Panel 2

I JUST TOLD YOU I THINK THAT I'M DEAD! COLONEL WEIRD **SHOT** ME AND MY DAD AND MY SISTER WITH A RAY GUN! WHY WON'T YOU TAKE ME SERIOUSLY?!

Panel 3

OH, I'M TAKING YOU SERIOUSLY, KID. BUT YOU AIN'T DEAD. YOU'RE JUST **UNIMAGINED**.

Panel 4

WHAT'S THAT SUPPOSED TO MEAN?!

MEANS YOU WERE AND THEN YOU WEREN'T ANYMORE. NOT THE SAME THING AS BEING DEAD. TRUST ME.

Panel 5

TAKE A SEAT, SQUIRT. WANT A CUPPA JOE? A CIGARETTE?

I'M **NINE**.

Panel 6

HEY! WAKE UP! WE GOT COMPANY!

Panel 7

WHO ARE YOU TALKING TO?

MY PARTNERS...

Panel 8

QUACK! QUACK!

AH, QUIT YOUR SQUAWKING. WE GOT A NEW CASE.

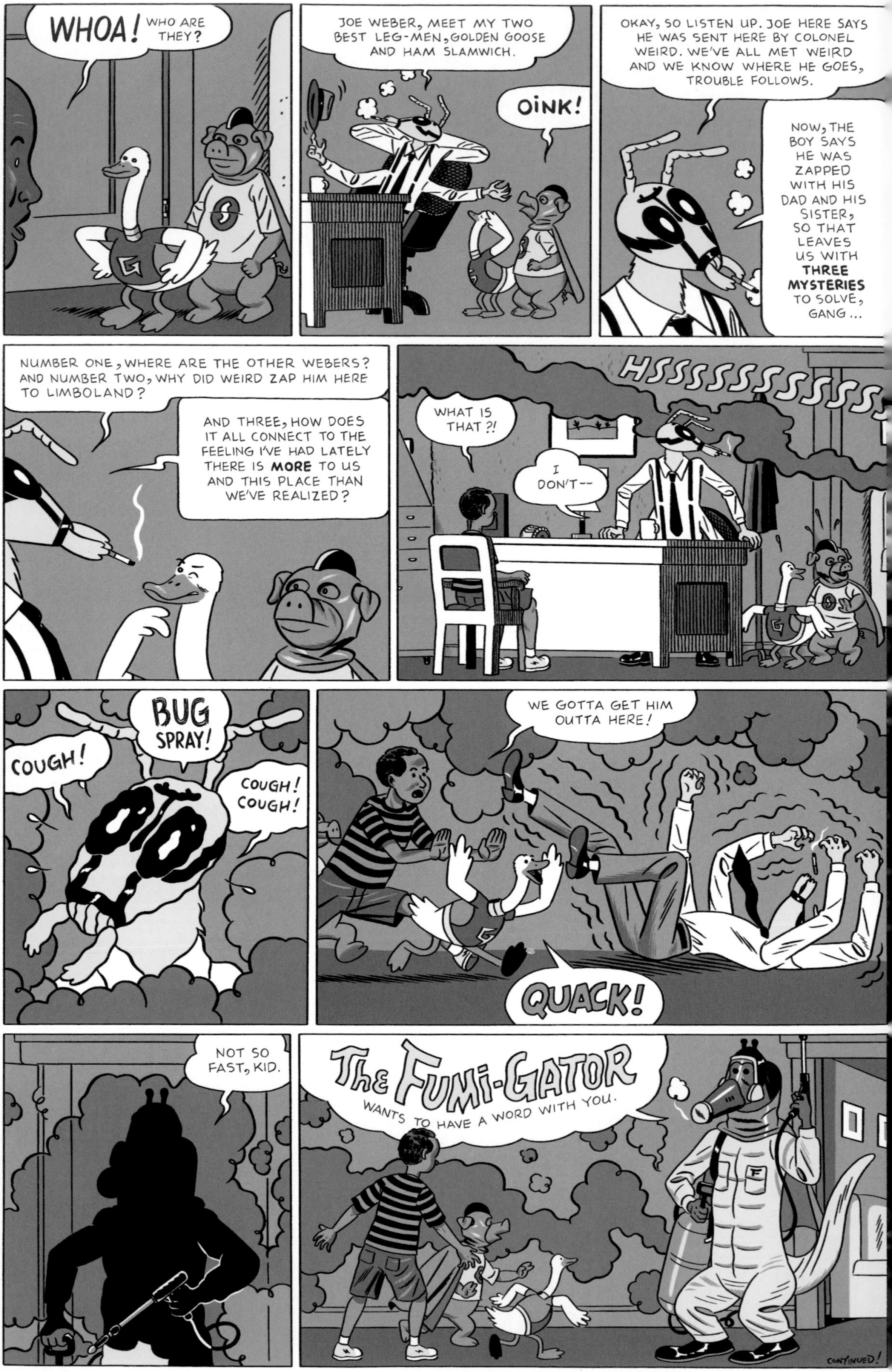
WHOA! WHO ARE THEY?
JOE WEBER, MEET MY TWO BEST LEG-MEN, GOLDEN GOOSE AND HAM SLAMWICH.
OINK!
OKAY, SO LISTEN UP. JOE HERE SAYS HE WAS SENT HERE BY COLONEL WEIRD. WE'VE ALL MET WEIRD AND WE KNOW WHERE HE GOES, TROUBLE FOLLOWS.
NOW, THE BOY SAYS HE WAS ZAPPED WITH HIS DAD AND HIS SISTER, SO THAT LEAVES US WITH THREE MYSTERIES TO SOLVE, GANG...
NUMBER ONE, WHERE ARE THE OTHER WEBERS? AND NUMBER TWO, WHY DID WEIRD ZAP HIM HERE TO LIMBOLAND?
AND THREE, HOW DOES IT ALL CONNECT TO THE FEELING I'VE HAD LATELY THERE IS MORE TO US AND THIS PLACE THAN WE'VE REALIZED?
HSSSSSSSSSSS
WHAT IS THAT?!
I DON'T--
COUGH!
BUG SPRAY!
COUGH! COUGH!
WE GOTTA GET HIM OUTTA HERE!
QUACK!
NOT SO FAST, KID.
The FUMI-GATOR WANTS TO HAVE A WORD WITH YOU.
CONTINUED!

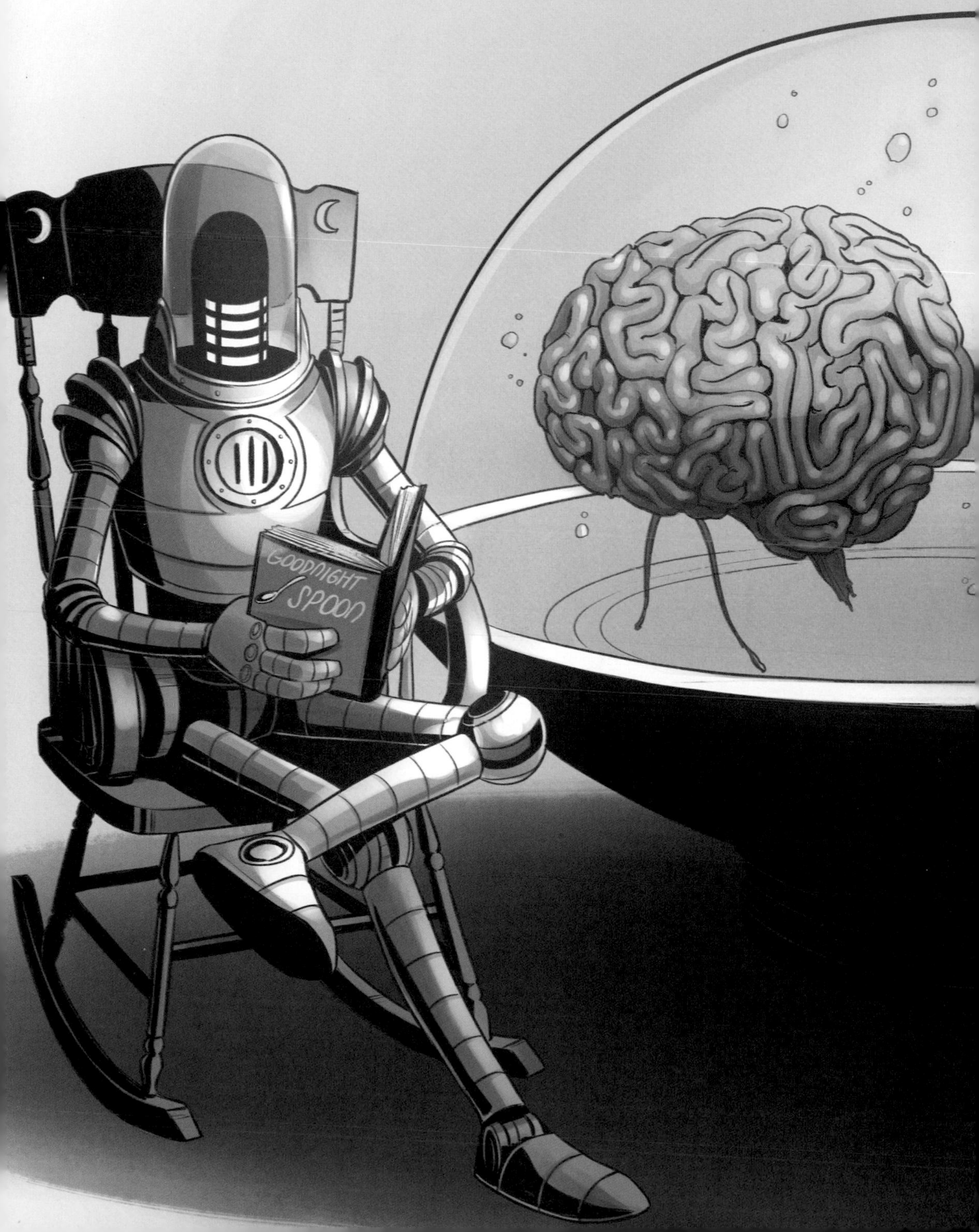
GOODNIGHT
SPOON

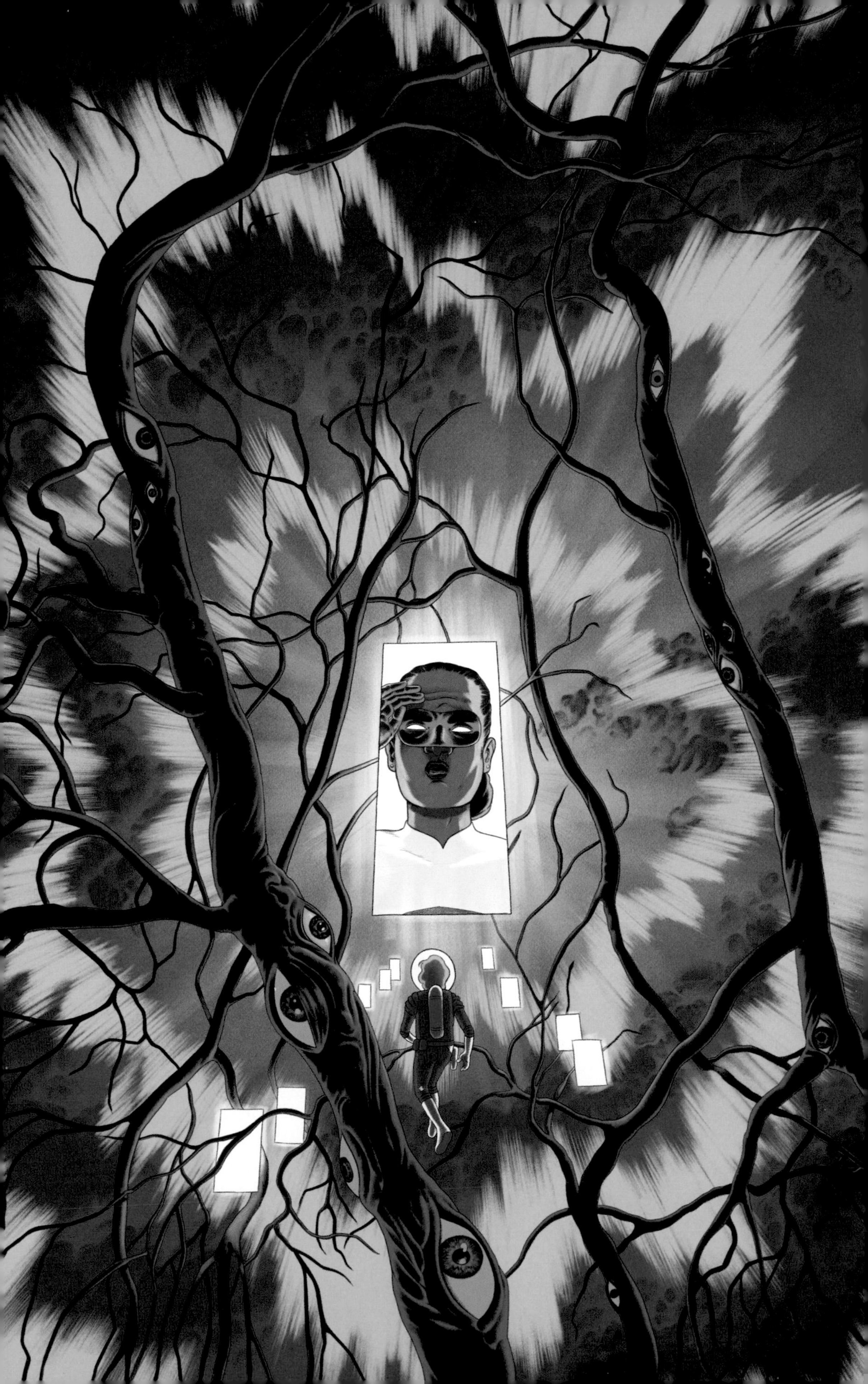

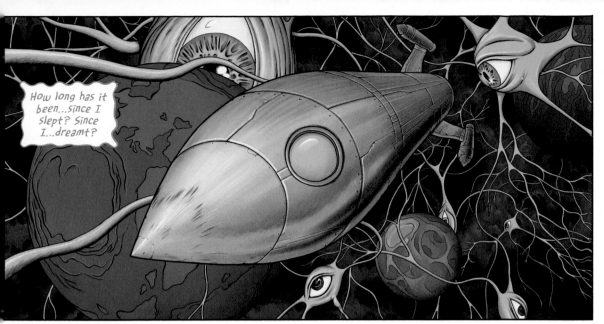

How long has it been...since I slept? Since I...dreamt?

I cannot remember when I last...slept. Should I? **Can I** even if I wanted to?

Perhaps I should...shave?

Do I...shave today? I don't--why don't I know?

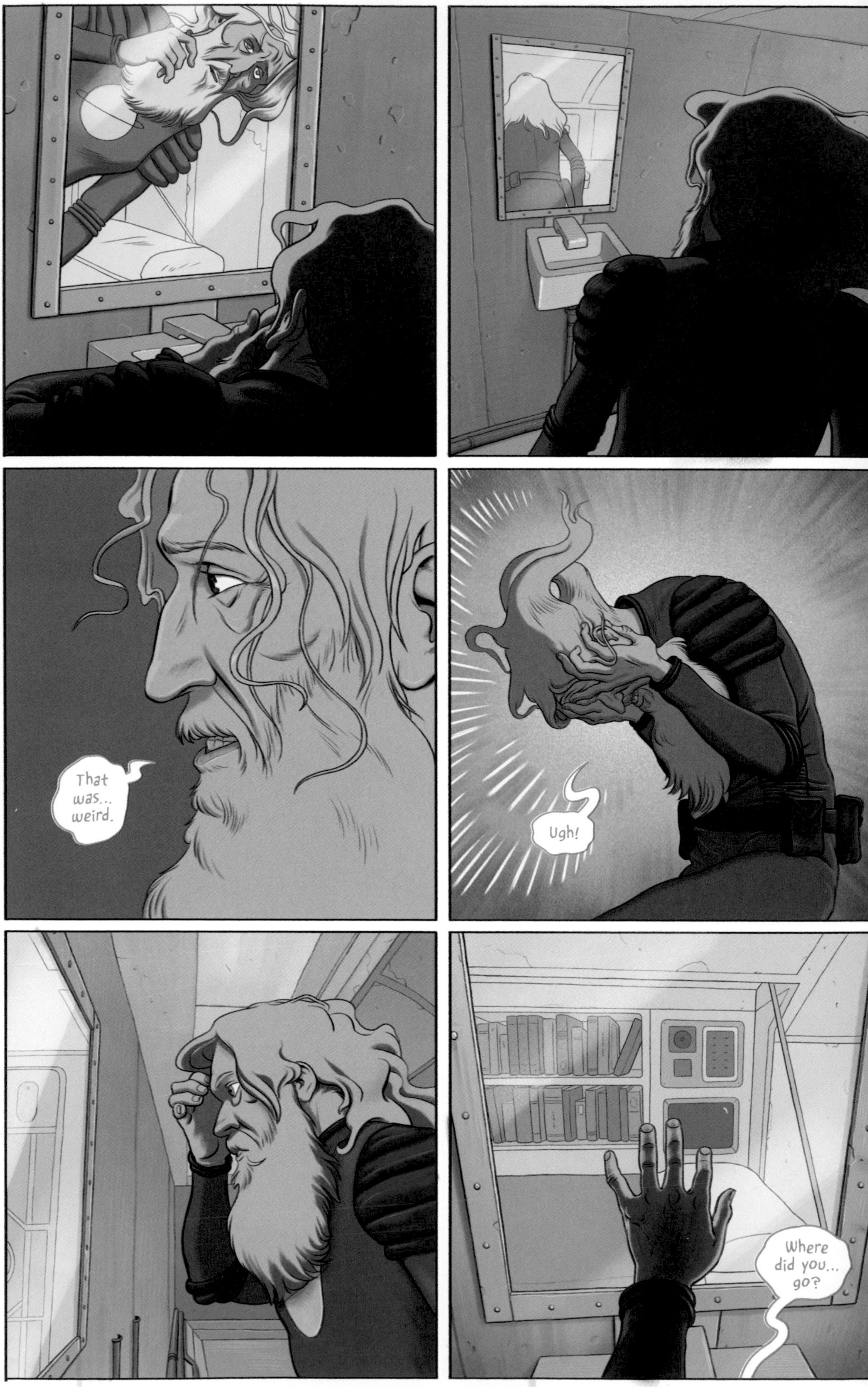
That was... weird.
Ugh!
Where did you... go?

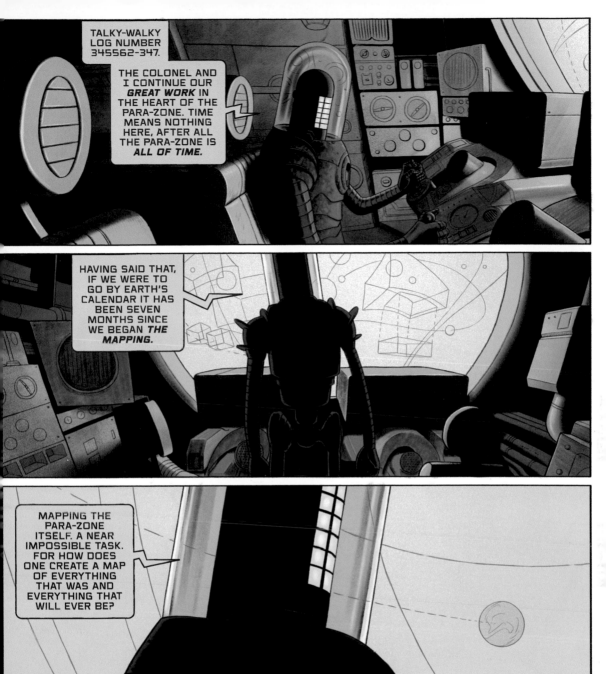

TALKY-WALKY LOG NUMBER 345562-347.

THE COLONEL AND I CONTINUE OUR *GREAT WORK* IN THE HEART OF THE PARA-ZONE. TIME MEANS NOTHING HERE, AFTER ALL THE PARA-ZONE IS *ALL OF TIME.*

HAVING SAID THAT, IF WE WERE TO GO BY EARTH'S CALENDAR IT HAS BEEN SEVEN MONTHS SINCE WE BEGAN *THE MAPPING.*

MAPPING THE PARA-ZONE ITSELF. A NEAR IMPOSSIBLE TASK. FOR HOW DOES ONE CREATE A MAP OF EVERYTHING THAT WAS AND EVERYTHING THAT WILL EVER BE?

WELL, I AM NOT JUST ANYONE. NOR IS RANDALL. I HAVE CREATED THE UNIVERSE'S MOST POWERFUL COMPUTER. I CALL IT "ARCHIVE."

HE IS--WELL, HE IS BEAUTIFUL. LIKE MY OWN CHILD. AND WITH ARCHIVE I AM ACTUALLY SUCCEEDING IN CREATING A FRAMEWORK TO *CATALOGUE THE INFINITE.*

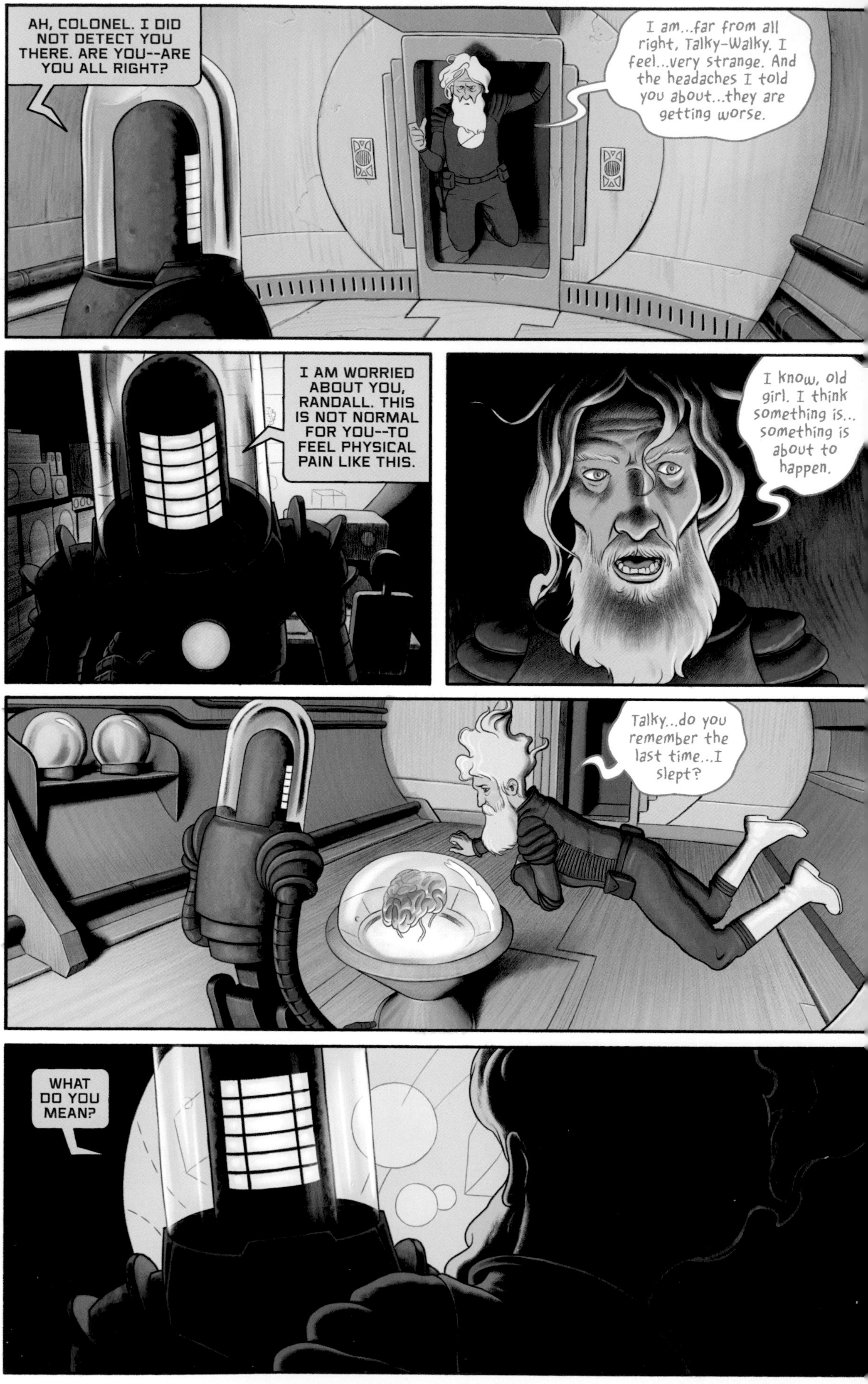
AH, COLONEL. I DID NOT DETECT YOU THERE. ARE YOU--ARE YOU ALL RIGHT?
I am...far from all right, Talky-Walky. I feel...very strange. And the headaches I told you about...they are getting worse.
I AM WORRIED ABOUT YOU, RANDALL. THIS IS NOT NORMAL FOR YOU--TO FEEL PHYSICAL PAIN LIKE THIS.
I know, old girl. I think something is... something is about to happen.
Talky...do you remember the last time...I slept?
WHAT DO YOU MEAN?

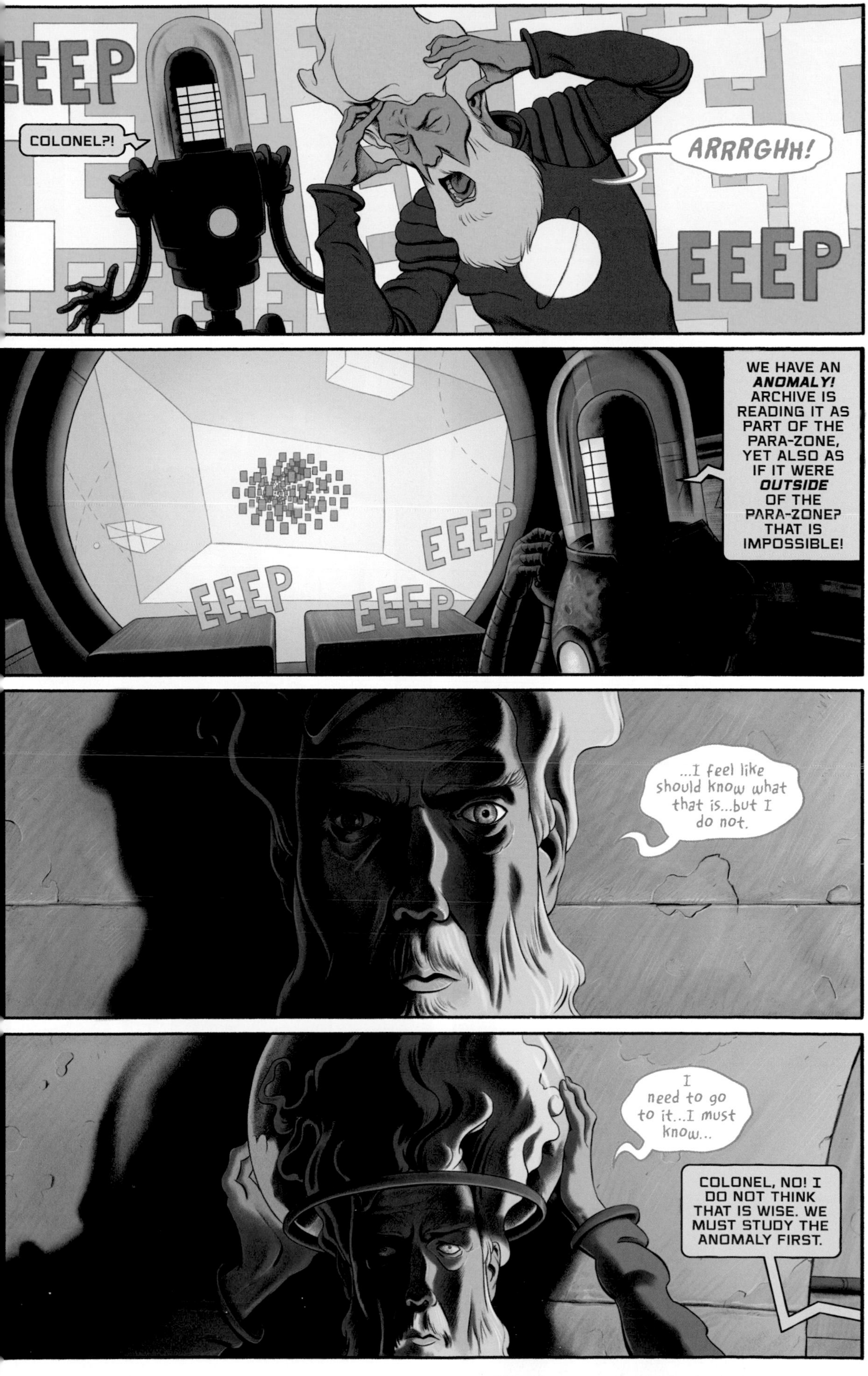
EEEP
COLONEL?!
ARRRGHH!
EEEP
WE HAVE AN ANOMALY! ARCHIVE IS READING IT AS PART OF THE PARA-ZONE, YET ALSO AS IF IT WERE OUTSIDE OF THE PARA-ZONE? THAT IS IMPOSSIBLE!
EEEP
EEEP
EEEP
...I feel like should know what that is...but I do not.
I need to go to it...I must know...
COLONEL, NO! I DO NOT THINK THAT IS WISE. WE MUST STUDY THE ANOMALY FIRST.

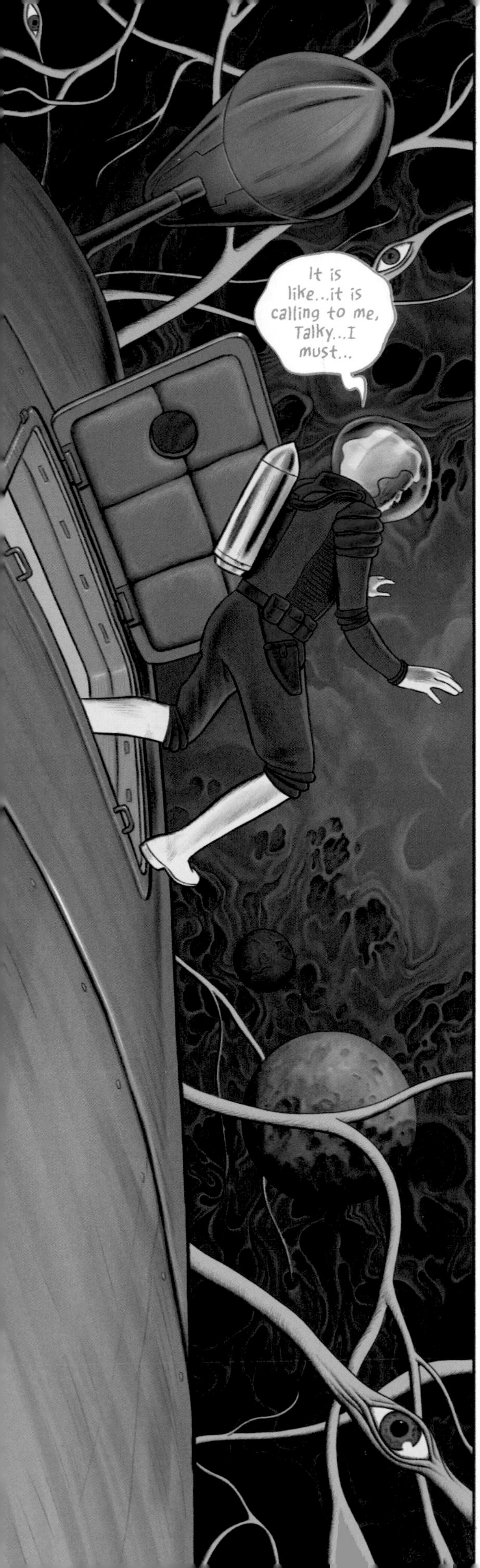
It is like...it is calling to me, Talky...I must...

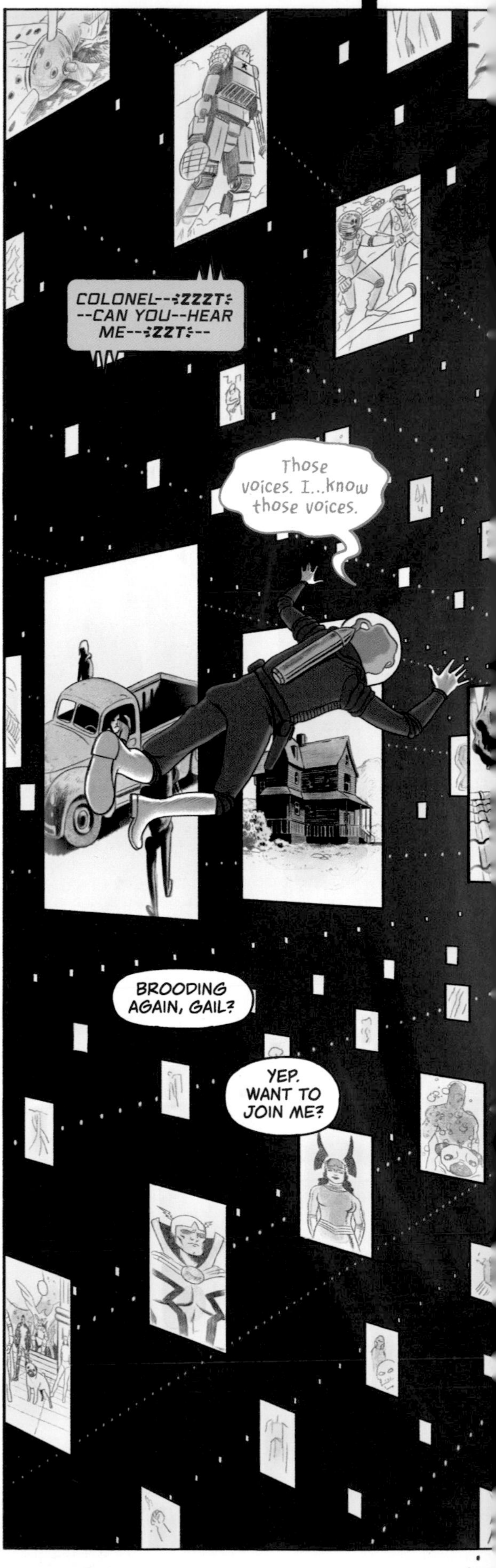
COLONEL--ZZZT--CAN YOU--HEAR ME--ZZT--
Those voices. I...know those voices.
BROODING AGAIN, GAIL?
YEP. WANT TO JOIN ME?

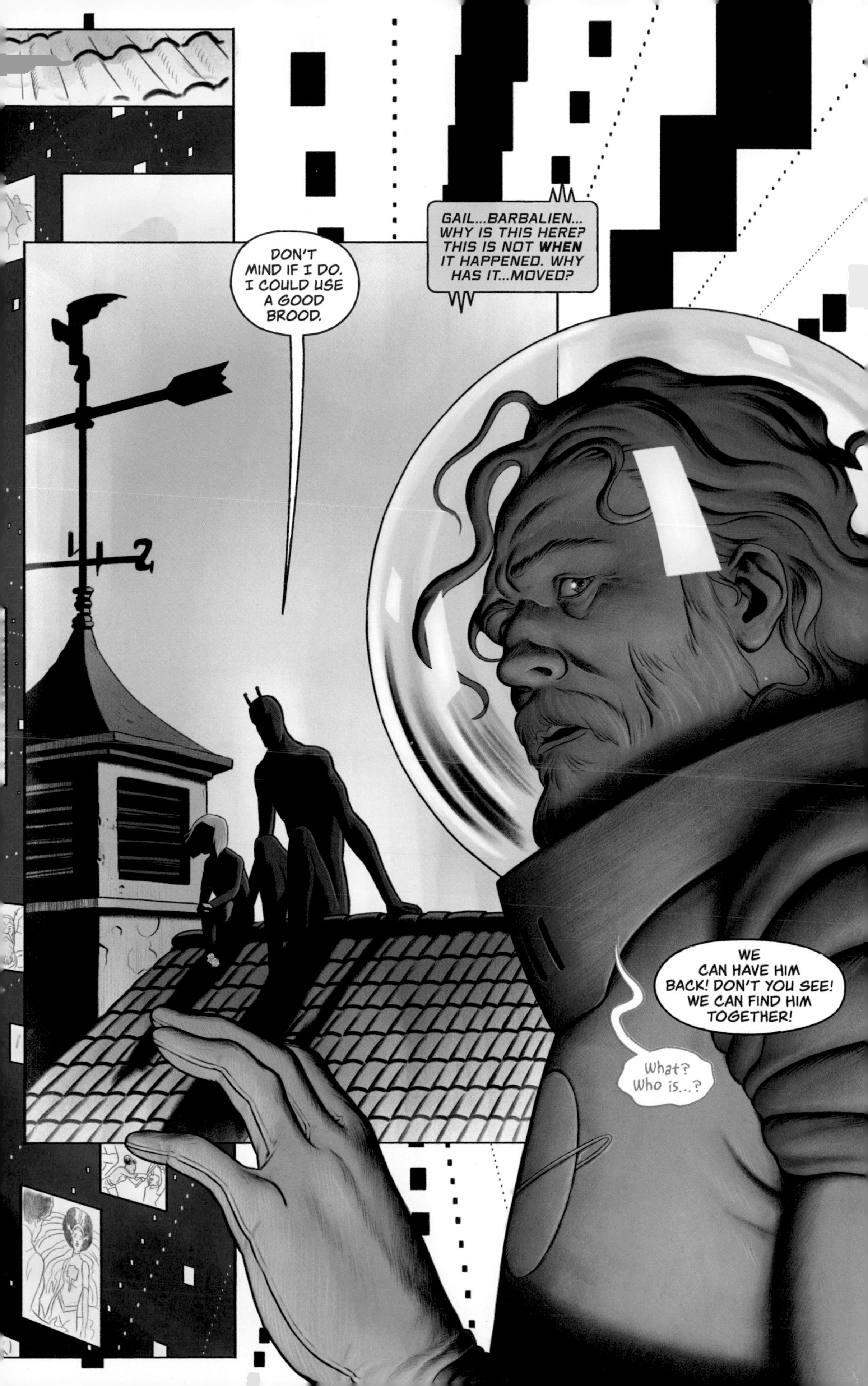
DON'T MIND IF I DO. I COULD USE A GOOD BROOD.
GAIL...BARBALIEN... WHY IS THIS HERE? THIS IS NOT WHEN IT HAPPENED. WHY HAS IT...MOVED?
WE CAN HAVE HIM BACK! DON'T YOU SEE! WE CAN FIND HIM TOGETHER!
What? Who is...?

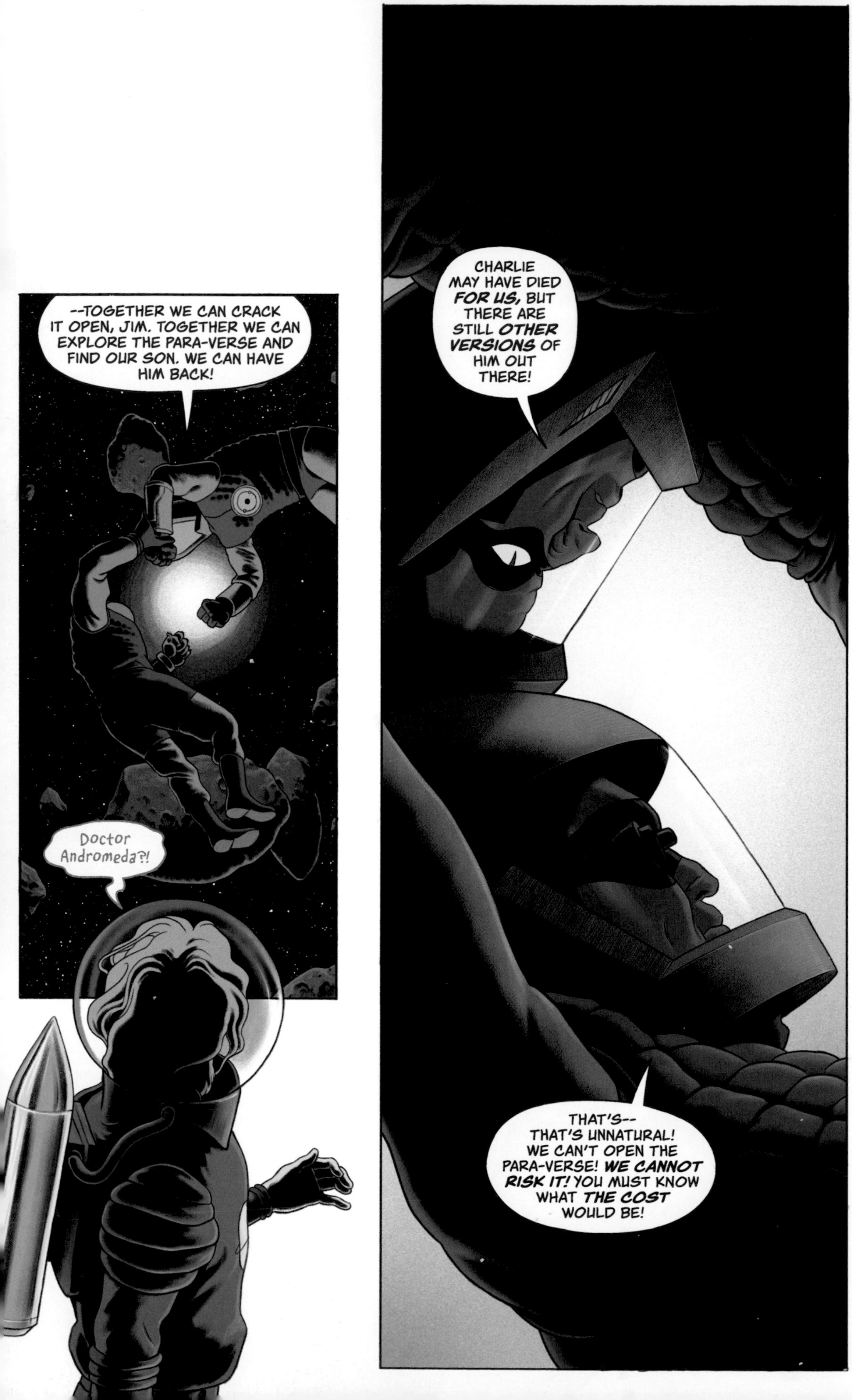
--TOGETHER WE CAN CRACK IT OPEN, JIM. TOGETHER WE CAN EXPLORE THE PARA-VERSE AND FIND OUR SON. WE CAN HAVE HIM BACK!
Doctor Andromeda?!
CHARLIE MAY HAVE DIED FOR US, BUT THERE ARE STILL OTHER VERSIONS OF HIM OUT THERE!
THAT'S-- THAT'S UNNATURAL! WE CAN'T OPEN THE PARA-VERSE! WE CANNOT RISK IT! YOU MUST KNOW WHAT THE COST WOULD BE!

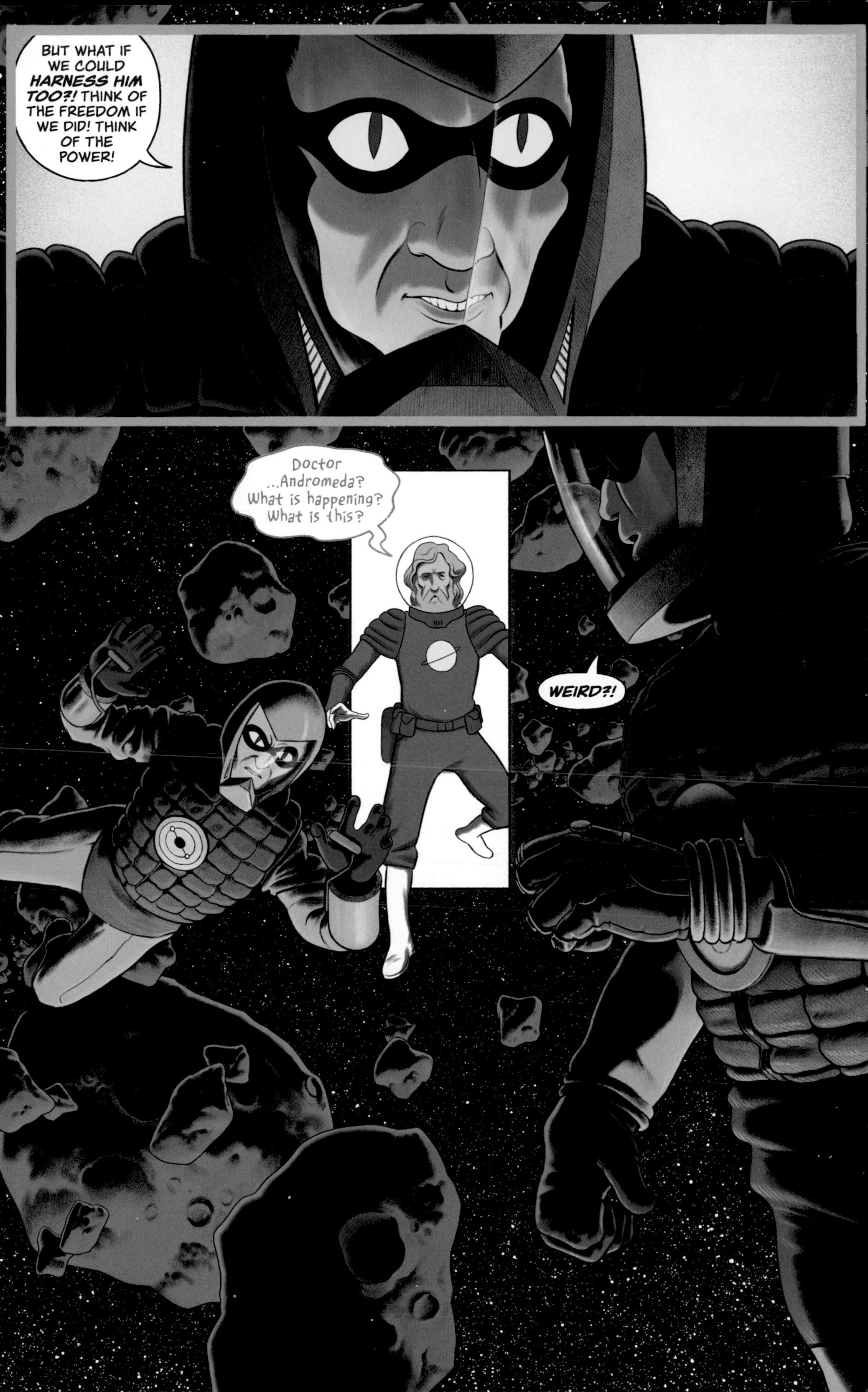
BUT WHAT IF WE COULD **HARNESS HIM TOO?!** THINK OF THE FREEDOM IF WE DID! THINK OF THE POWER!
Doctor ...Andromeda? What is happening? What is this?
WEIRD?!

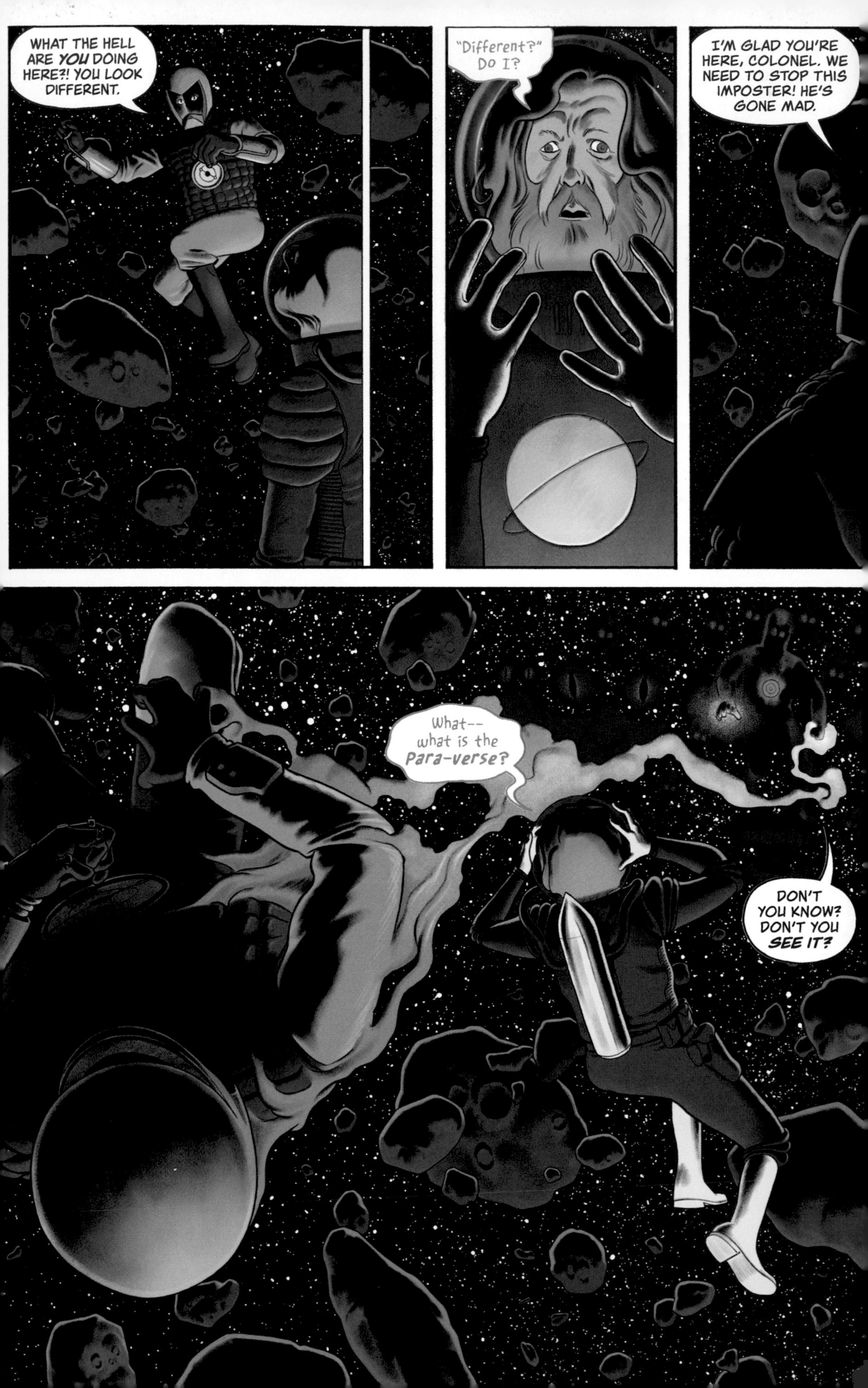
WHAT THE HELL ARE YOU DOING HERE?! YOU LOOK DIFFERENT.
"Different?" Do I?
I'M GLAD YOU'RE HERE, COLONEL. WE NEED TO STOP THIS IMPOSTER! HE'S GONE MAD.
What-- what is the Para-verse?
DON'T YOU KNOW? DON'T YOU SEE IT?

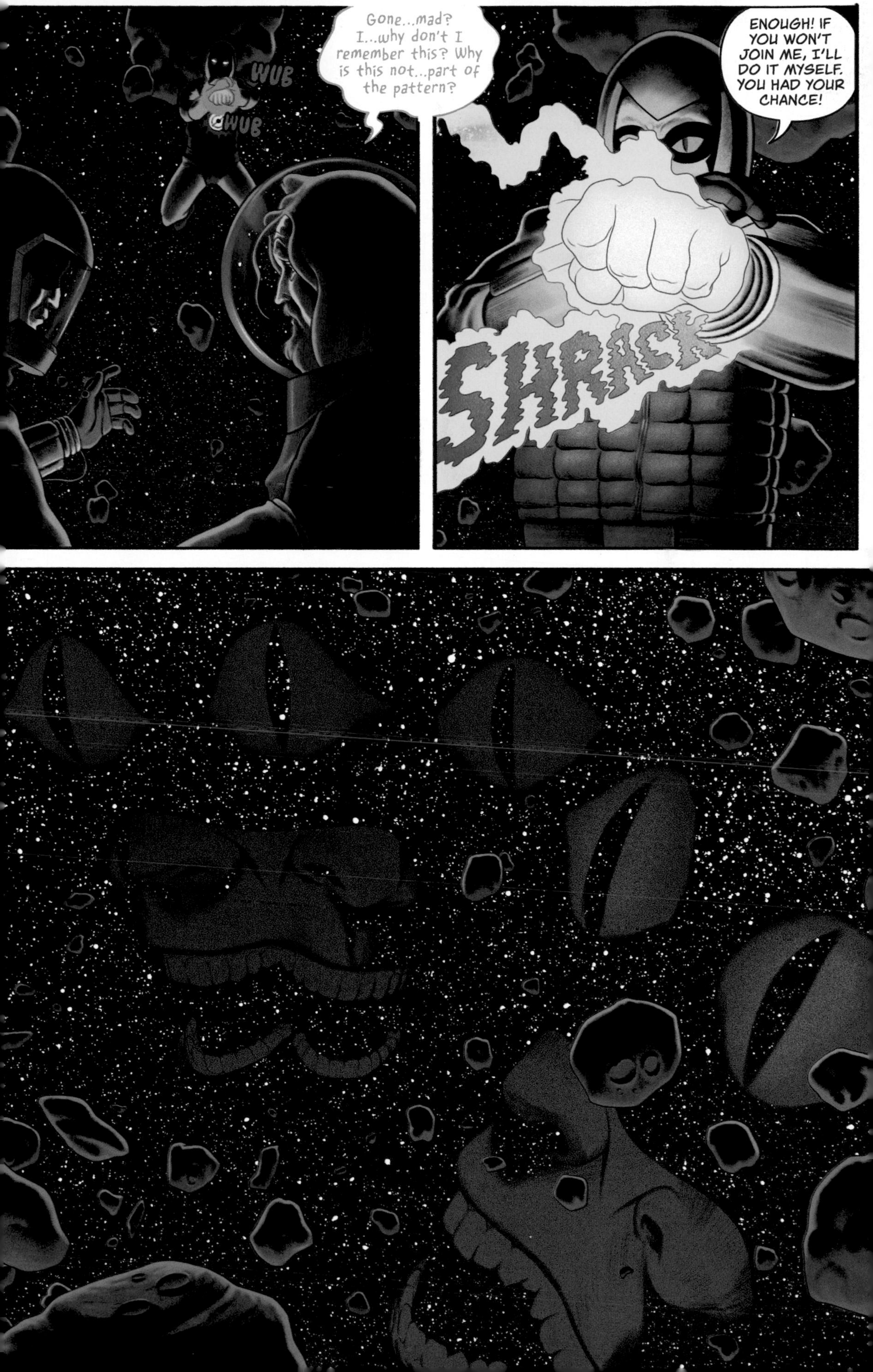
WUB
WUB
Gone...mad? I...why don't I remember this? Why is this not...part of the pattern?
ENOUGH! IF YOU WON'T JOIN ME, I'LL DO IT MYSELF. YOU HAD YOUR CHANCE!
SHRACK

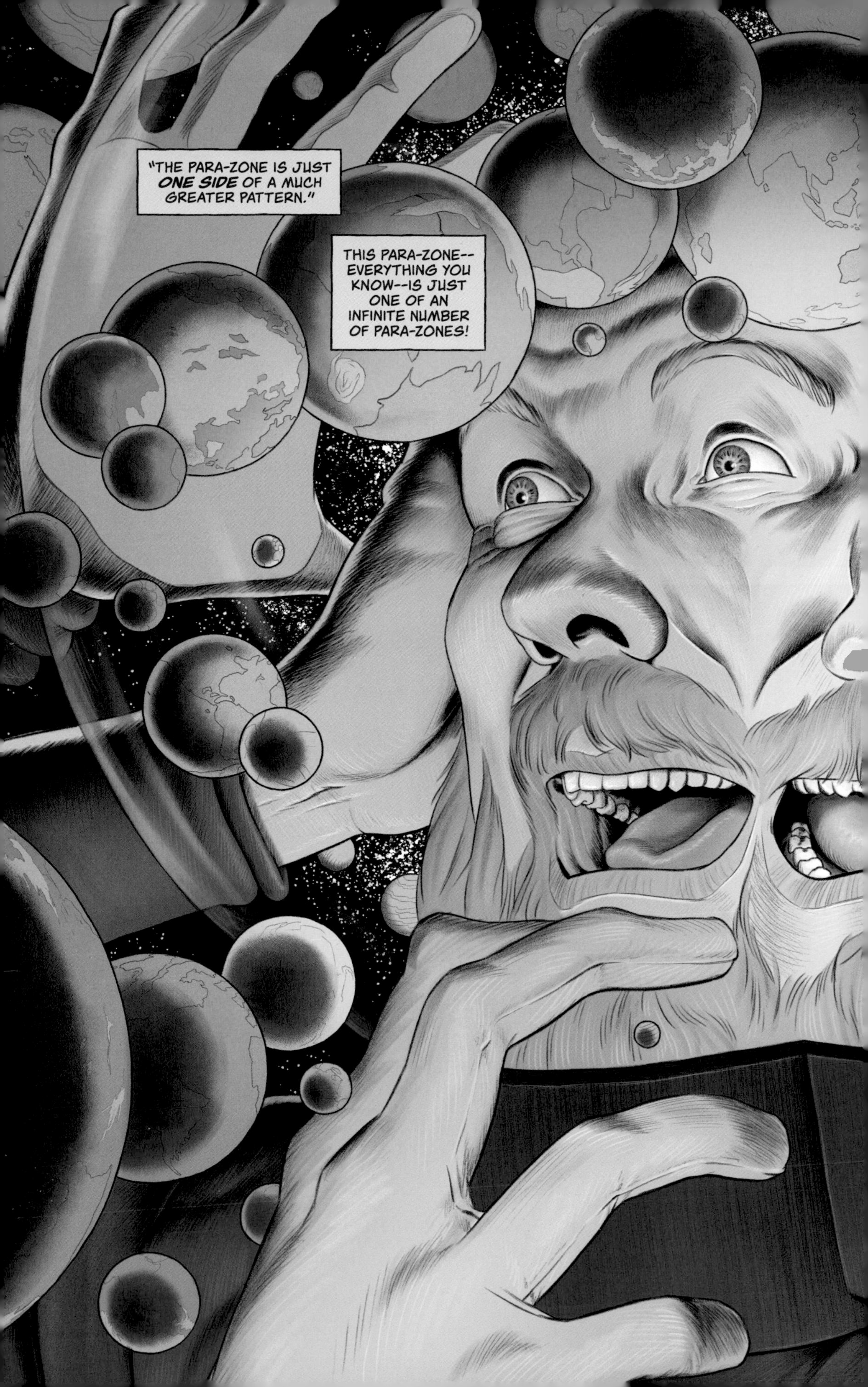
"THE PARA-ZONE IS JUST *ONE SIDE* OF A MUCH GREATER PATTERN."
THIS PARA-ZONE--EVERYTHING YOU KNOW--IS JUST ONE OF AN INFINITE NUMBER OF PARA-ZONES!

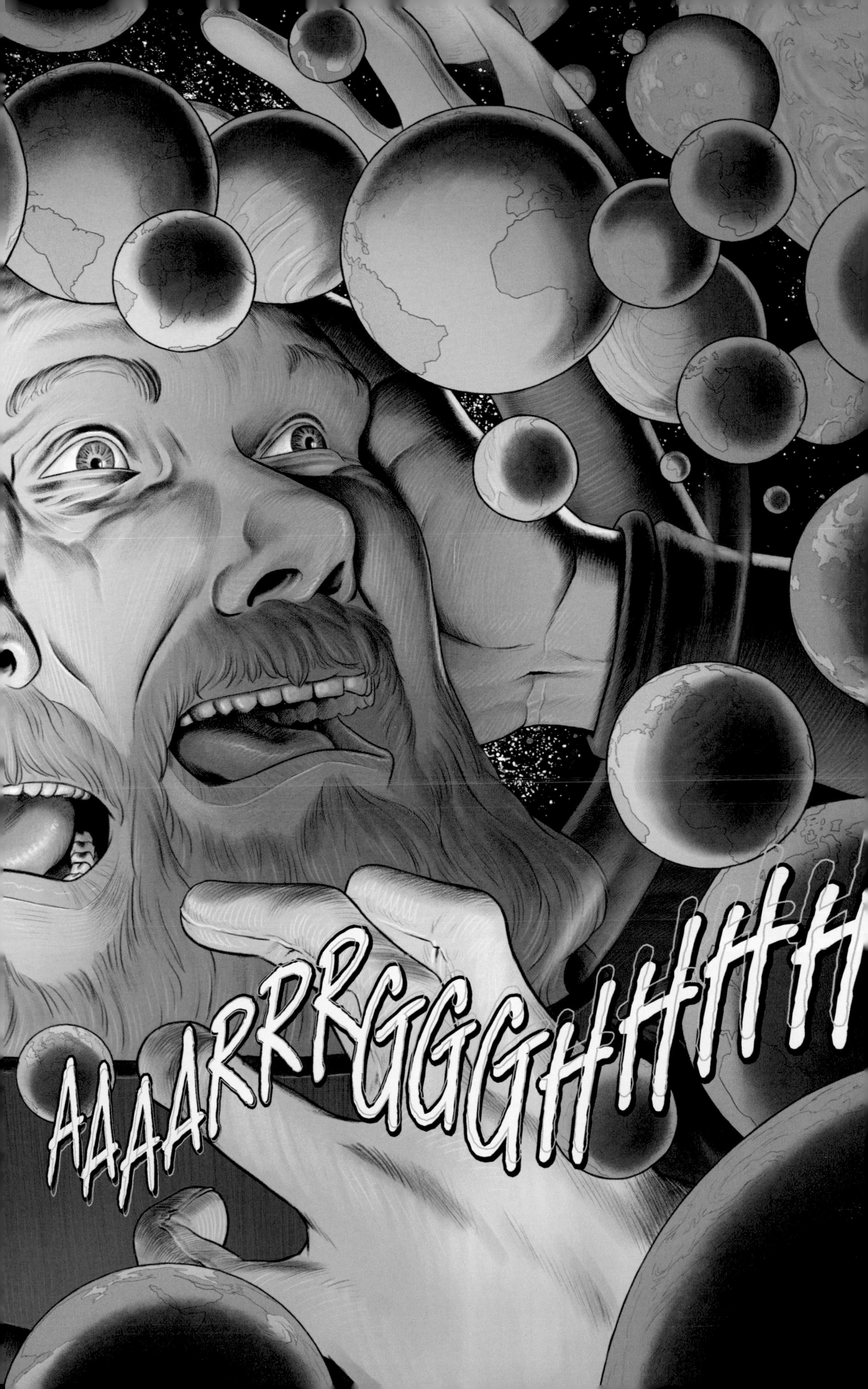
AAAARRRGGGHHHHH

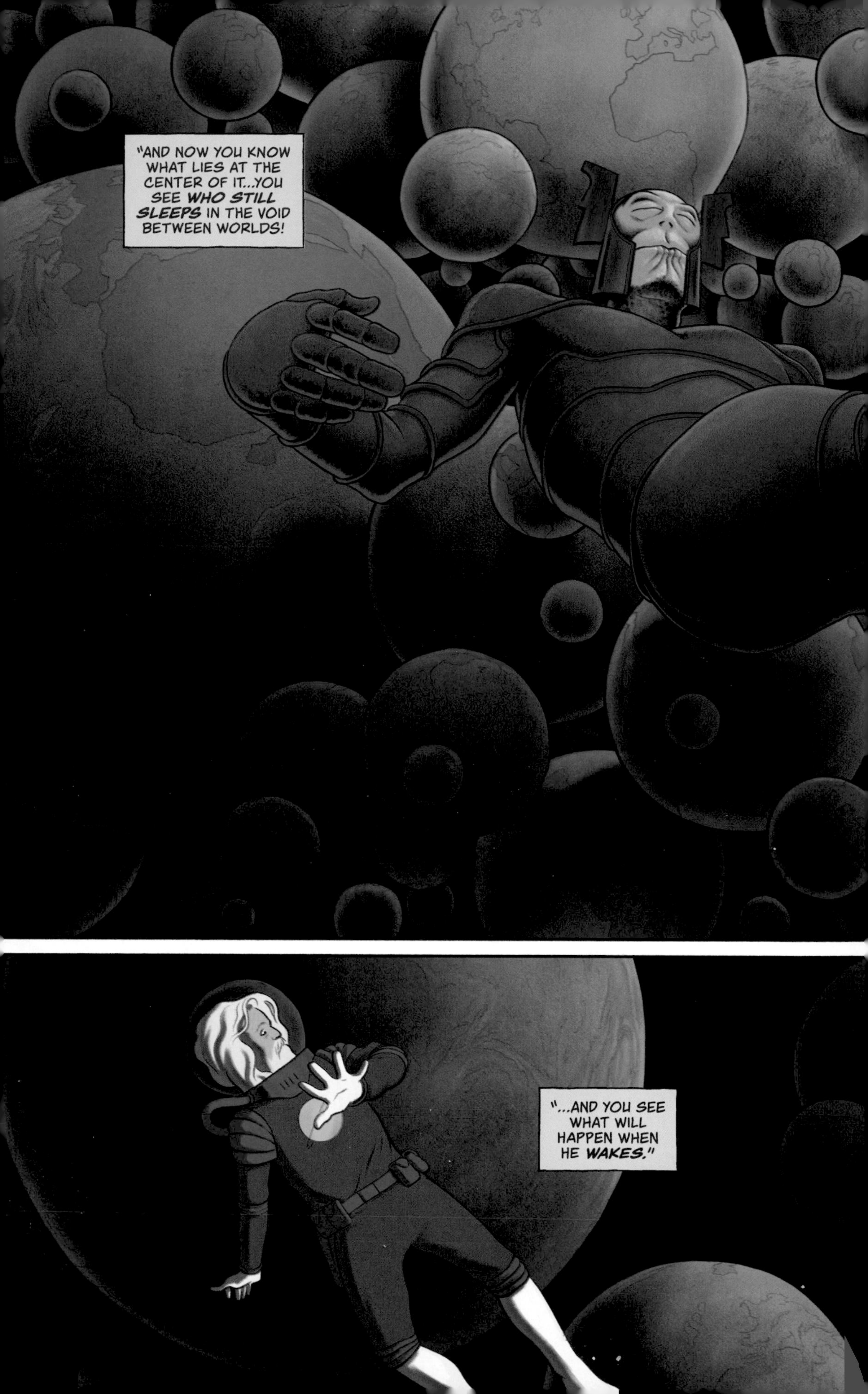
"AND NOW YOU KNOW WHAT LIES AT THE CENTER OF IT...YOU SEE WHO STILL SLEEPS IN THE VOID BETWEEN WORLDS!
"...AND YOU SEE WHAT WILL HAPPEN WHEN HE WAKES."

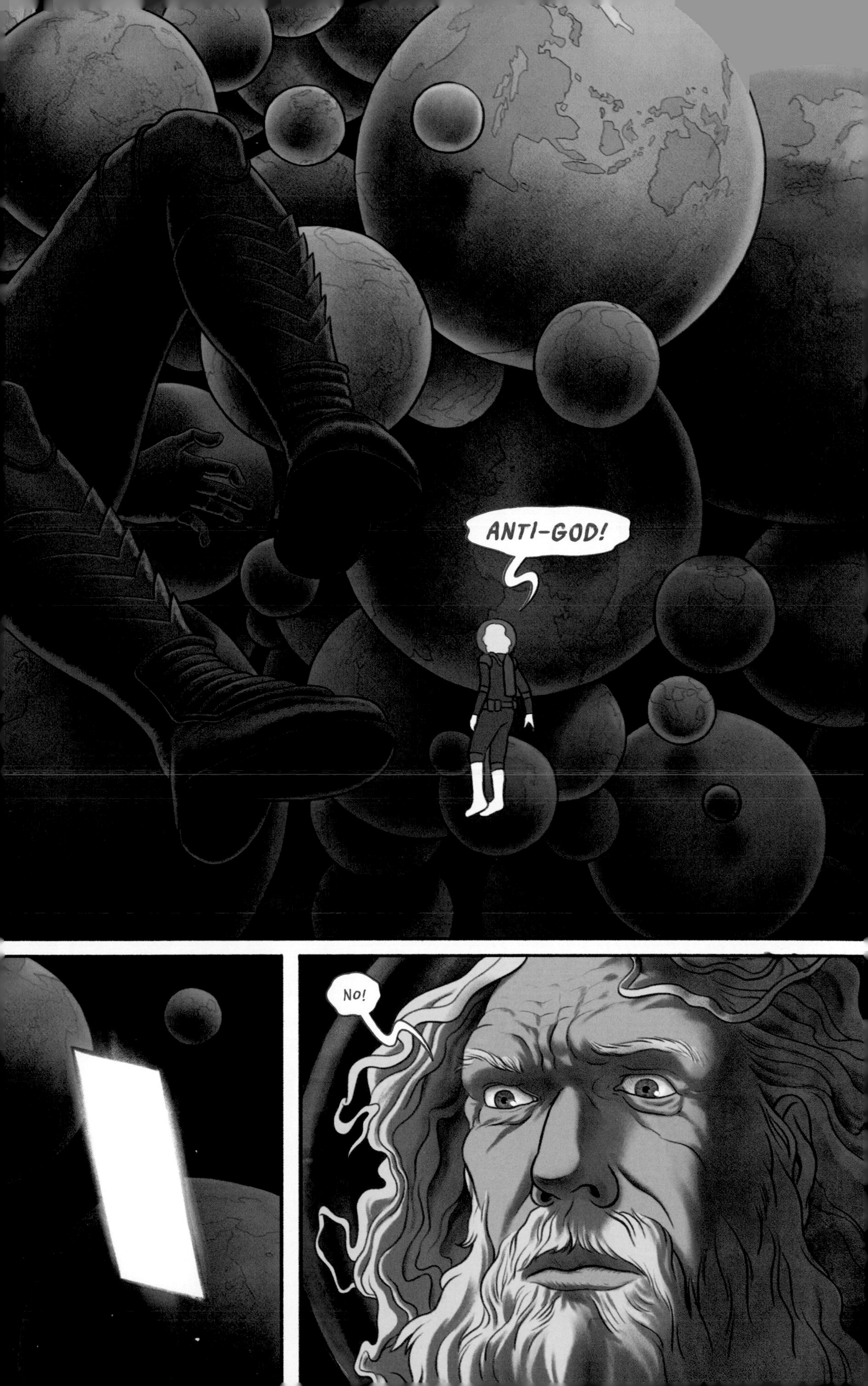
ANTI-GOD!
No!

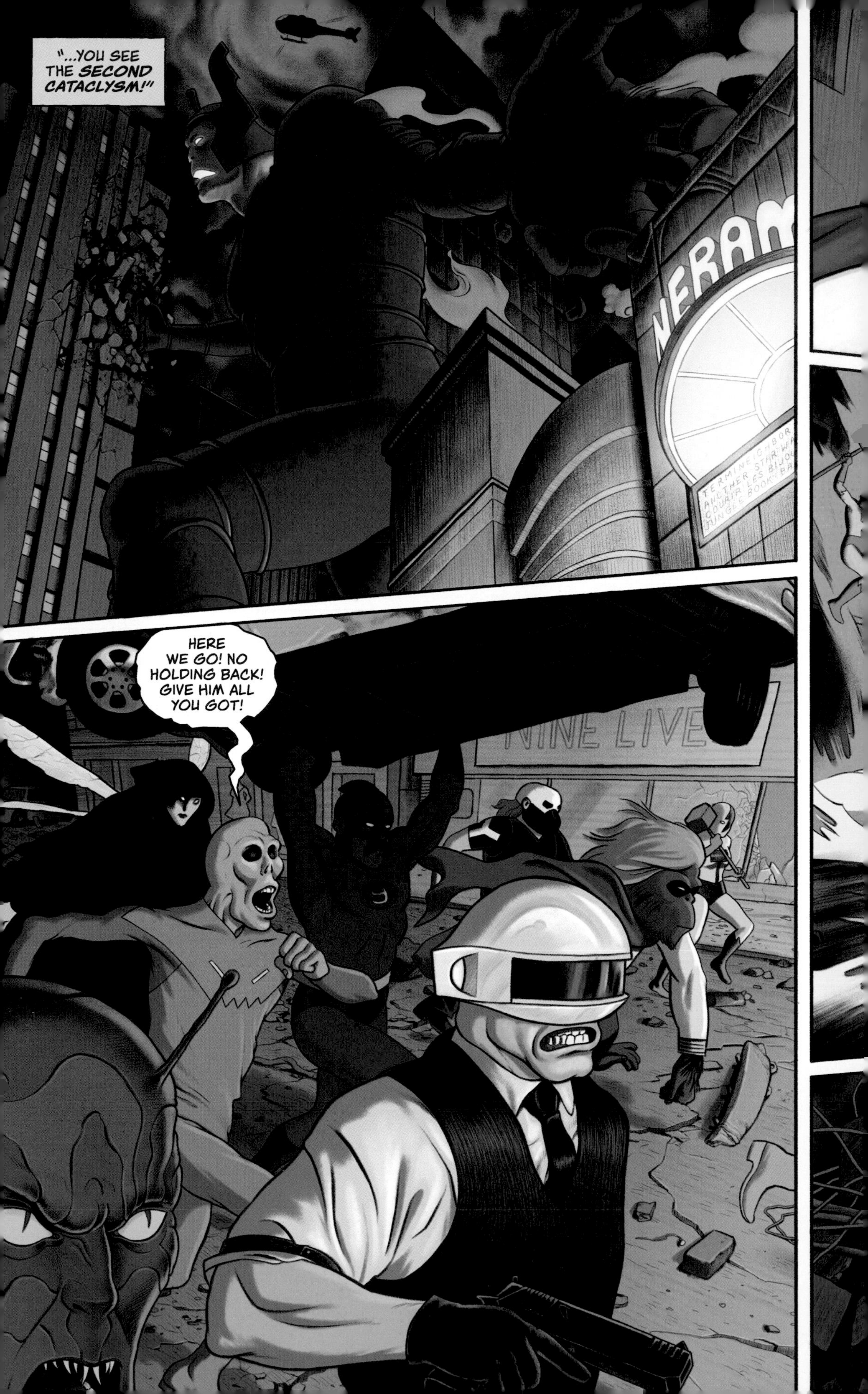
"...YOU SEE THE *SECOND CATACLYSM!*"
HERE WE GO! NO HOLDING BACK! GIVE HIM ALL YOU GOT!

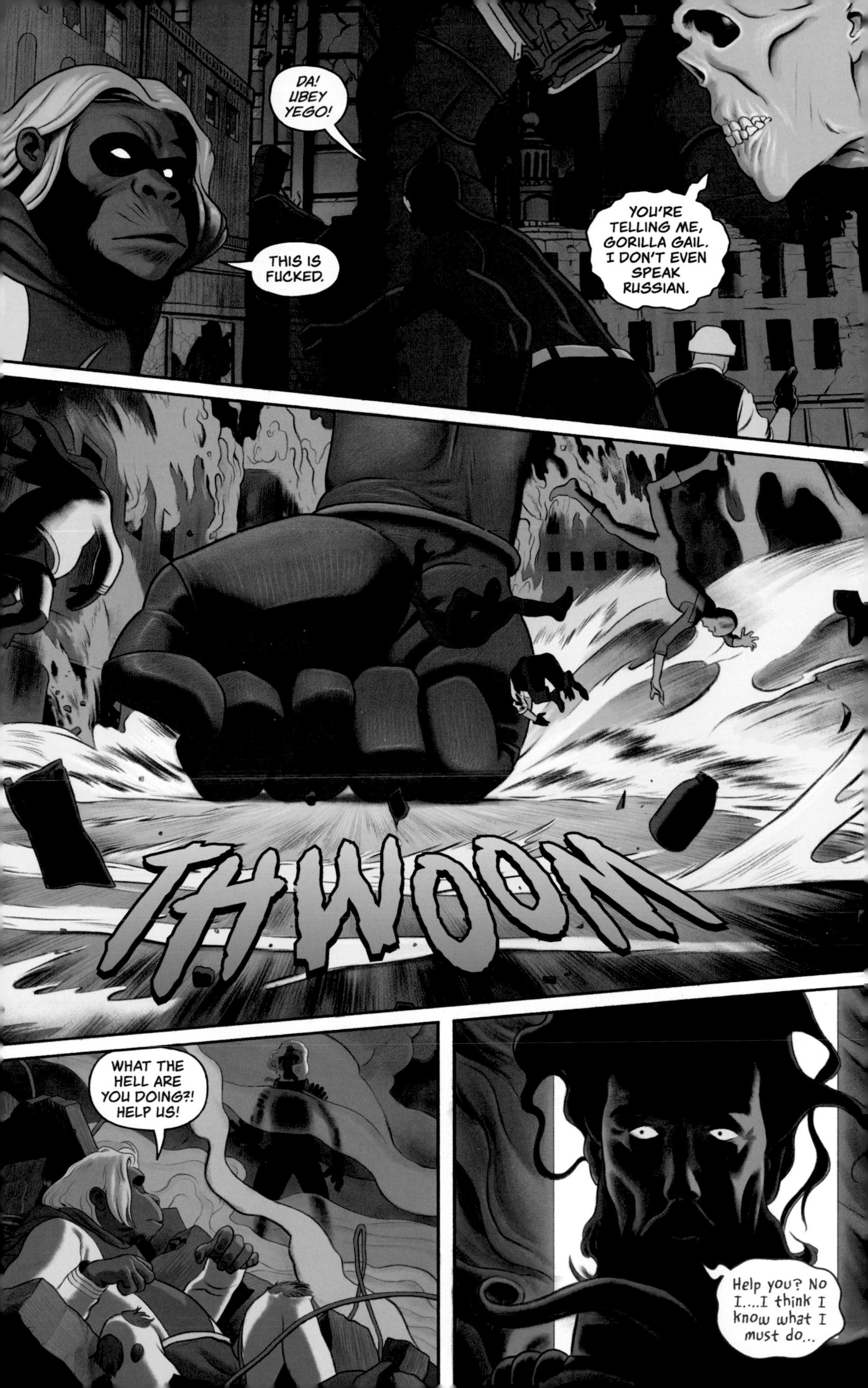
DA! UBEY YEGO!
THIS IS FUCKED.
YOU'RE TELLING ME, GORILLA GAIL. I DON'T EVEN SPEAK RUSSIAN.
THWOOM
WHAT THE HELL ARE YOU DOING?! HELP US!
Help you? No I....I think I know what I must do...

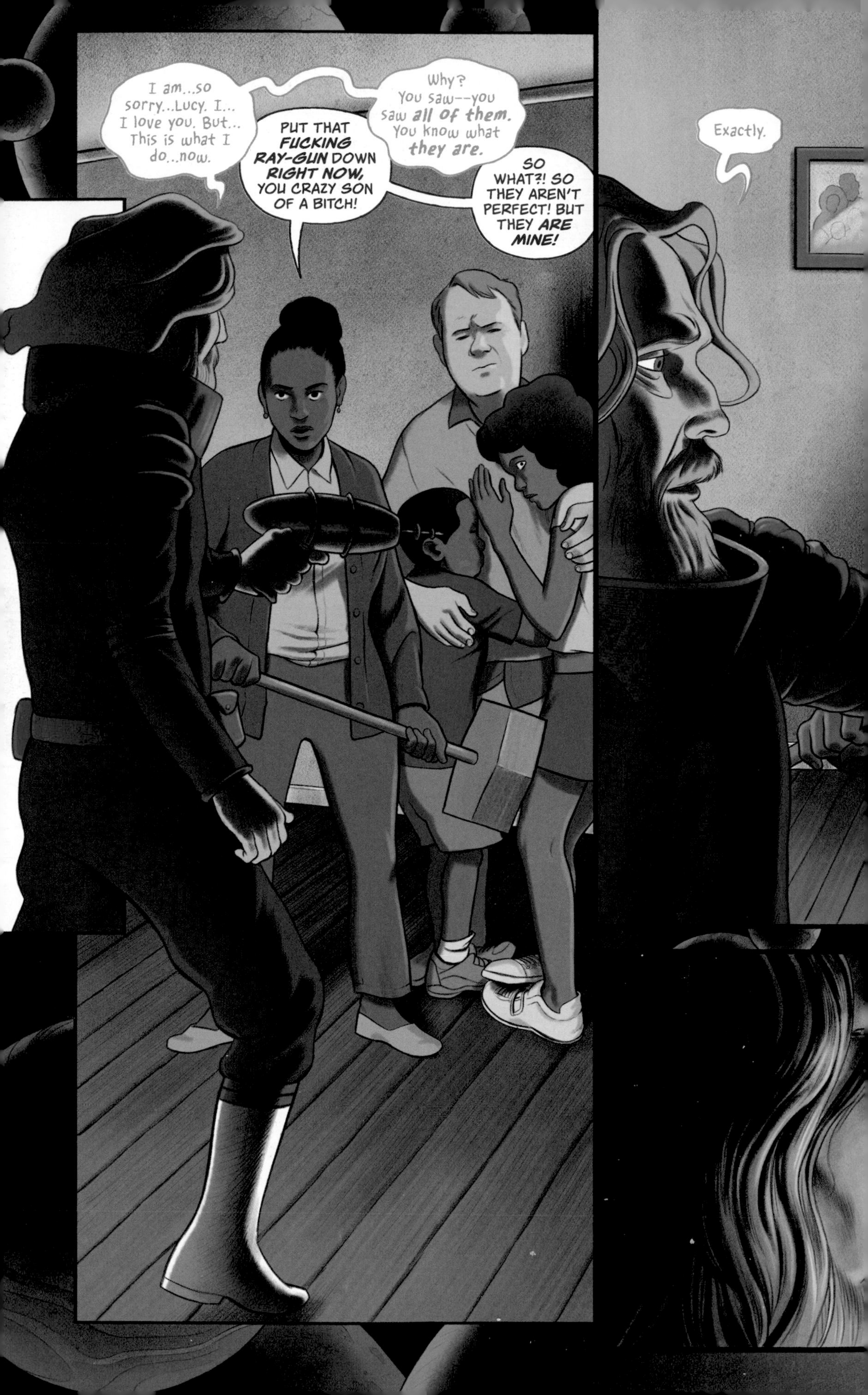
I am...so sorry...Lucy. I... I love you. But... This is what I do...now.
PUT THAT FUCKING RAY-GUN DOWN RIGHT NOW, YOU CRAZY SON OF A BITCH!
Why? You saw--you saw all of them. You know what they are.
SO WHAT?! SO THEY AREN'T PERFECT! BUT THEY ARE MINE!
Exactly.

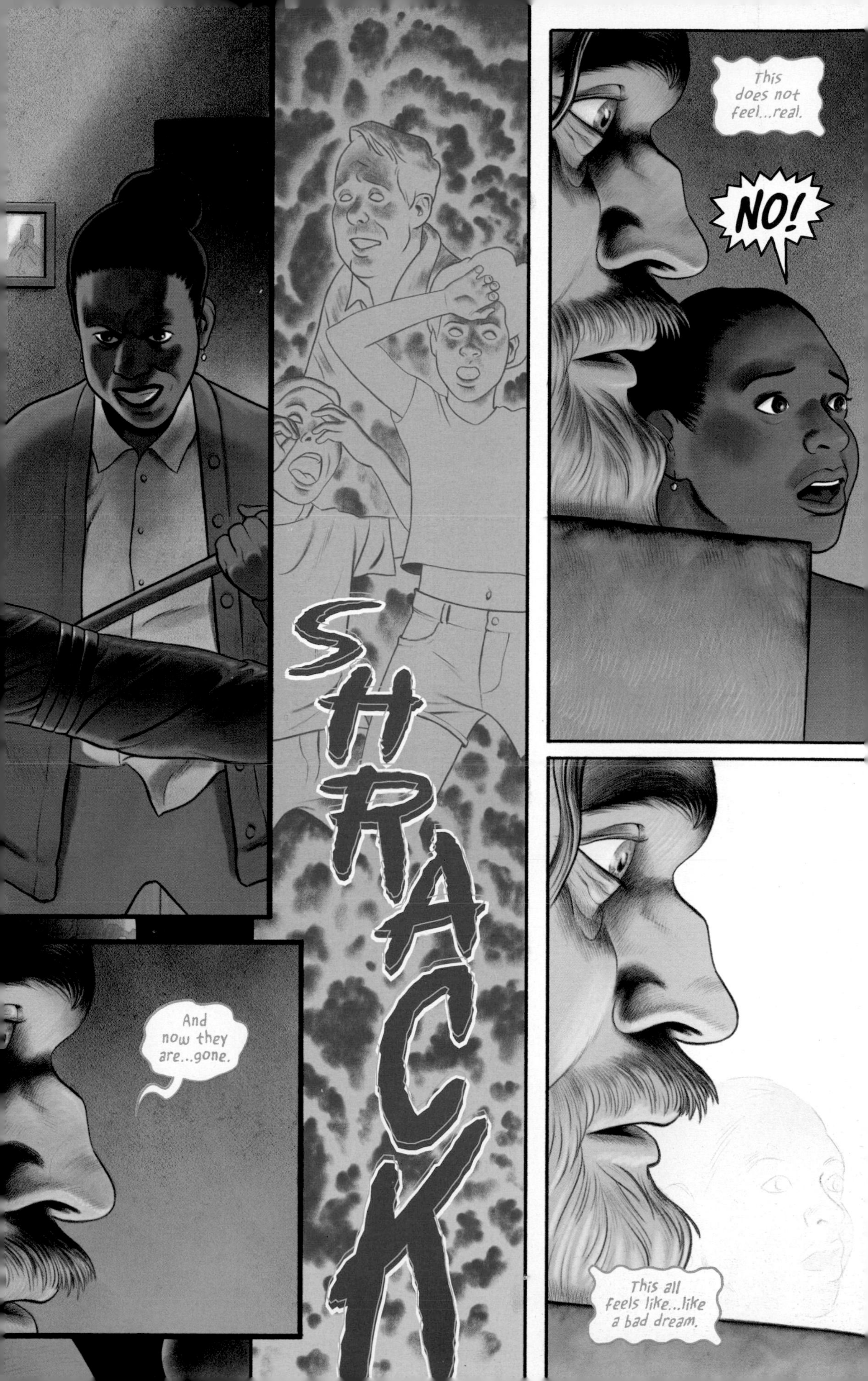
SHRACK
And now they are...gone.
This does not feel...real.
NO!
This all feels like...like a bad dream.

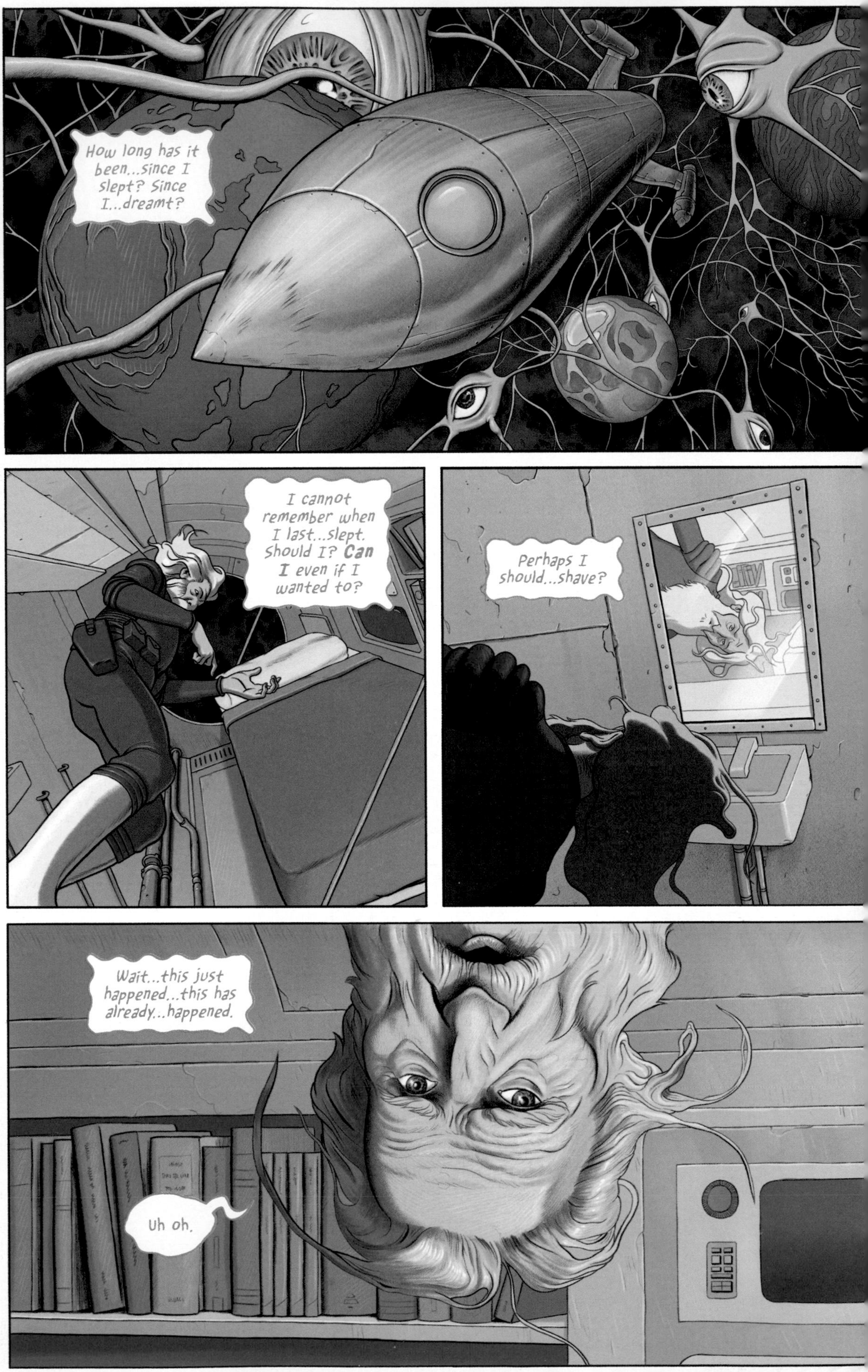
How long has it been...since I slept? Since I...dreamt?
I cannot remember when I last...slept. Should I? **Can I** even if I wanted to?
Perhaps I should...shave?
Wait...this just happened...this has already...happened.
Uh oh.

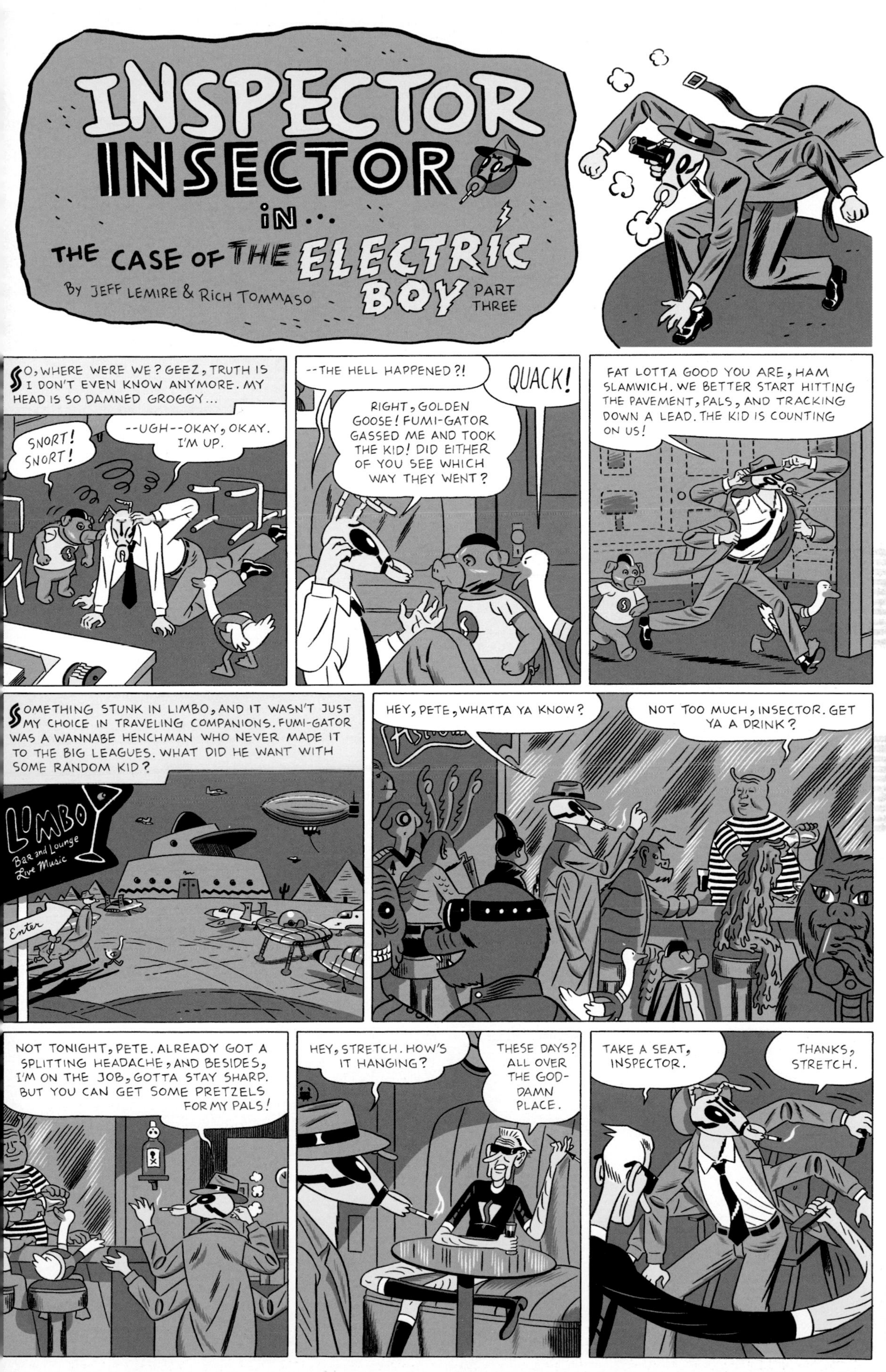
INSPECTOR INSECTOR
IN...
THE CASE OF THE ELECTRIC BOY
BY JEFF LEMIRE & RICH TOMMASO
PART THREE
SO, WHERE WERE WE? GEEZ, TRUTH IS I DON'T EVEN KNOW ANYMORE. MY HEAD IS SO DAMNED GROGGY...
SNORT! SNORT!
--UGH--OKAY, OKAY. I'M UP.
--THE HELL HAPPENED?!
QUACK!
RIGHT, GOLDEN GOOSE! FUMI-GATOR GASSED ME AND TOOK THE KID! DID EITHER OF YOU SEE WHICH WAY THEY WENT?
FAT LOTTA GOOD YOU ARE, HAM SLAMWICH. WE BETTER START HITTING THE PAVEMENT, PALS, AND TRACKING DOWN A LEAD. THE KID IS COUNTING ON US!
SOMETHING STUNK IN LIMBO, AND IT WASN'T JUST MY CHOICE IN TRAVELING COMPANIONS. FUMI-GATOR WAS A WANNABE HENCHMAN WHO NEVER MADE IT TO THE BIG LEAGUES. WHAT DID HE WANT WITH SOME RANDOM KID?
LIMBO
Bar and Lounge
Live Music
Enter
HEY, PETE, WHATTA YA KNOW?
NOT TOO MUCH, INSECTOR. GET YA A DRINK?
NOT TONIGHT, PETE. ALREADY GOT A SPLITTING HEADACHE, AND BESIDES, I'M ON THE JOB, GOTTA STAY SHARP. BUT YOU CAN GET SOME PRETZELS FOR MY PALS!
HEY, STRETCH. HOW'S IT HANGING?
THESE DAYS? ALL OVER THE GOD-DAMN PLACE.
TAKE A SEAT, INSPECTOR.
THANKS, STRETCH.

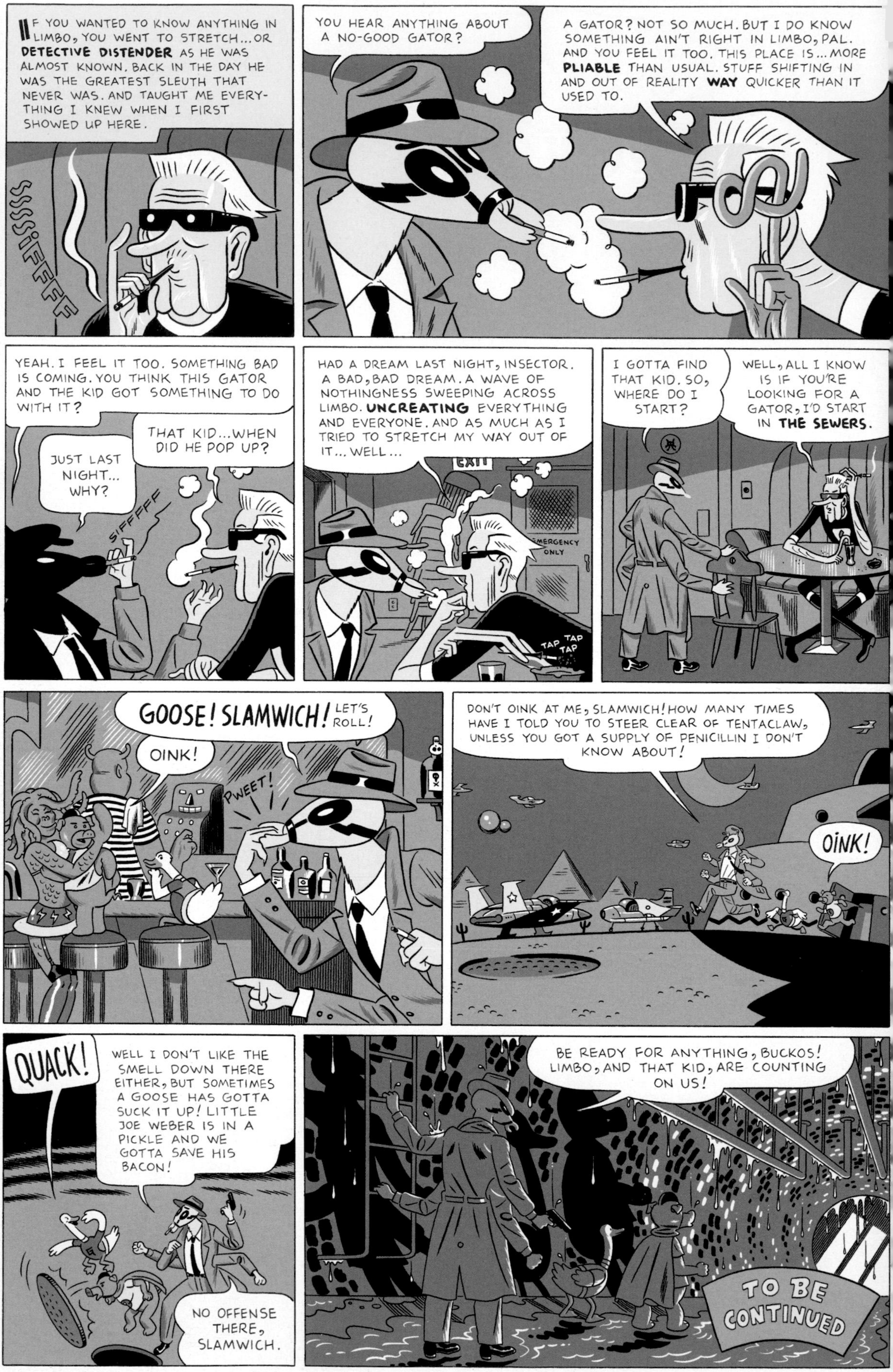
IF YOU WANTED TO KNOW ANYTHING IN LIMBO, YOU WENT TO STRETCH... OR DETECTIVE DISTENDER AS HE WAS ALMOST KNOWN. BACK IN THE DAY HE WAS THE GREATEST SLEUTH THAT NEVER WAS. AND TAUGHT ME EVERYTHING I KNEW WHEN I FIRST SHOWED UP HERE.
YOU HEAR ANYTHING ABOUT A NO-GOOD GATOR?
A GATOR? NOT SO MUCH. BUT I DO KNOW SOMETHING AIN'T RIGHT IN LIMBO, PAL. AND YOU FEEL IT TOO. THIS PLACE IS... MORE PLIABLE THAN USUAL. STUFF SHIFTING IN AND OUT OF REALITY WAY QUICKER THAN IT USED TO.
YEAH. I FEEL IT TOO. SOMETHING BAD IS COMING. YOU THINK THIS GATOR AND THE KID GOT SOMETHING TO DO WITH IT?
THAT KID... WHEN DID HE POP UP?
JUST LAST NIGHT... WHY?
HAD A DREAM LAST NIGHT, INSECTOR. A BAD, BAD DREAM. A WAVE OF NOTHINGNESS SWEEPING ACROSS LIMBO. UNCREATING EVERYTHING AND EVERYONE. AND AS MUCH AS I TRIED TO STRETCH MY WAY OUT OF IT... WELL...
EXIT
TAP TAP TAP
I GOTTA FIND THAT KID. SO, WHERE DO I START?
WELL, ALL I KNOW IS IF YOU'RE LOOKING FOR A GATOR, I'D START IN THE SEWERS.
GOOSE! SLAMWICH! LET'S ROLL!
OINK!
PWEET!
DON'T OINK AT ME, SLAMWICH! HOW MANY TIMES HAVE I TOLD YOU TO STEER CLEAR OF TENTACLAW, UNLESS YOU GOT A SUPPLY OF PENICILLIN I DON'T KNOW ABOUT!
OINK!
QUACK!
WELL I DON'T LIKE THE SMELL DOWN THERE EITHER, BUT SOMETIMES A GOOSE HAS GOTTA SUCK IT UP! LITTLE JOE WEBER IS IN A PICKLE AND WE GOTTA SAVE HIS BACON!
NO OFFENSE THERE, SLAMWICH.
BE READY FOR ANYTHING, BUCKOS! LIMBO, AND THAT KID, ARE COUNTING ON US!
TO BE CONTINUED

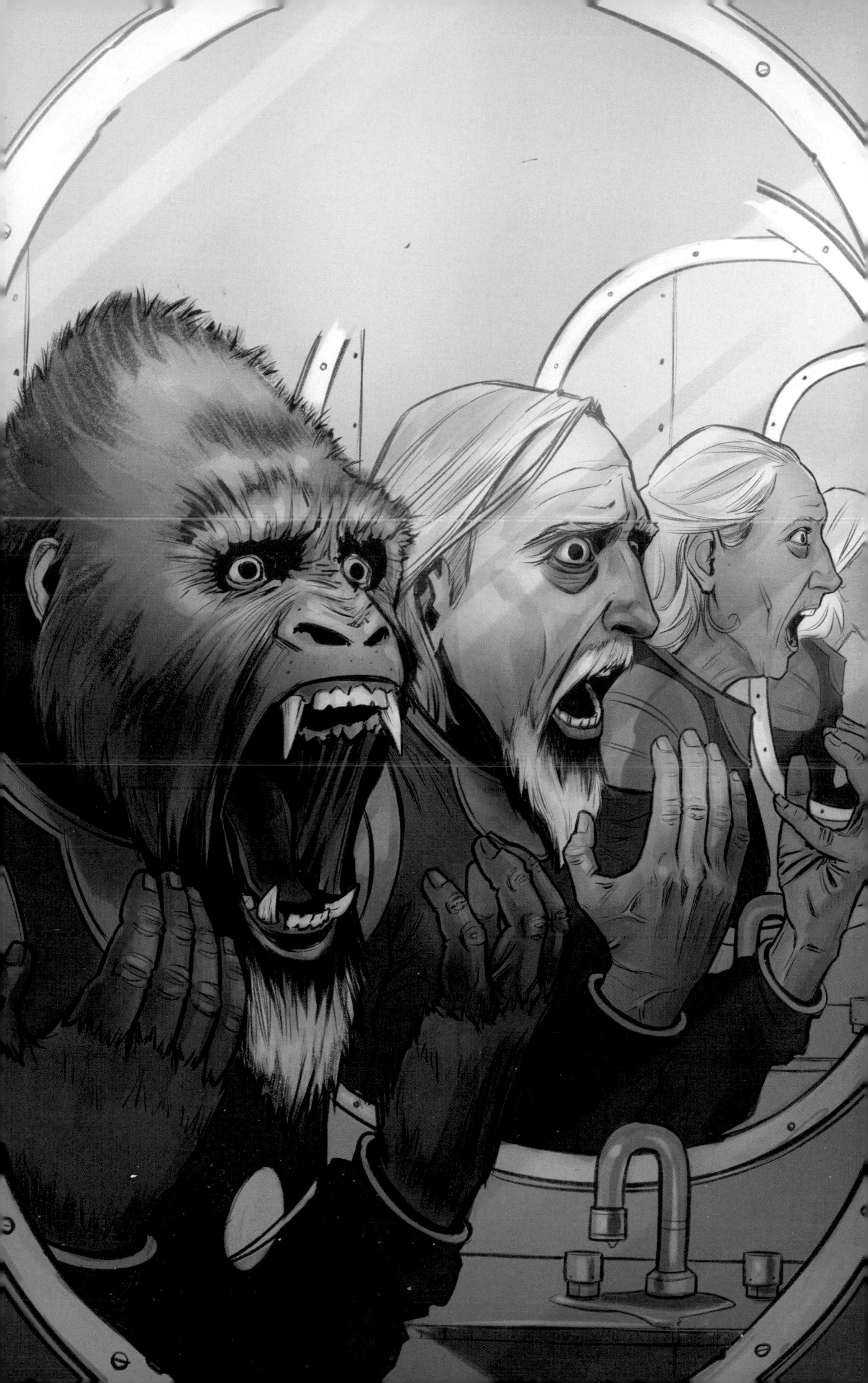

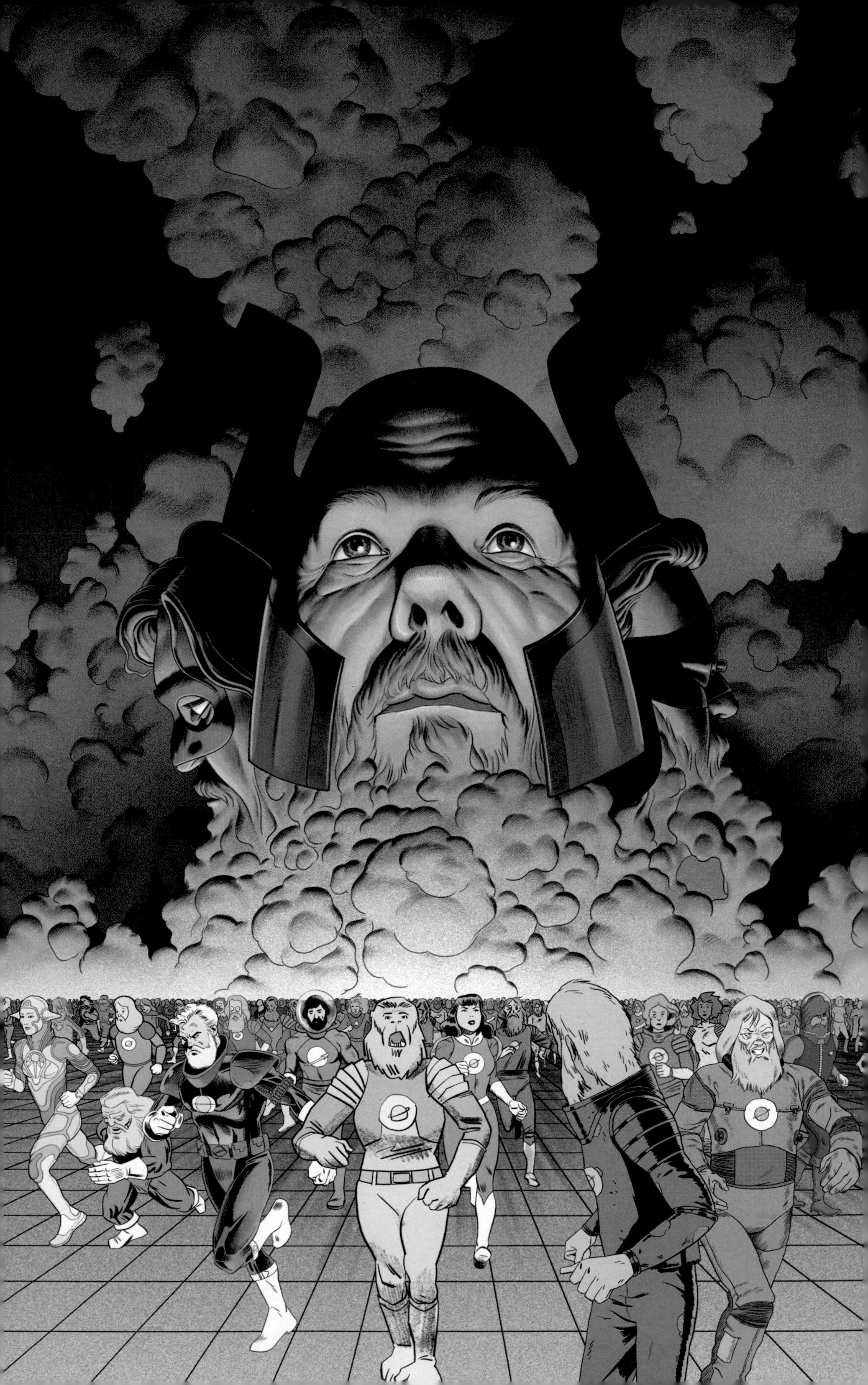

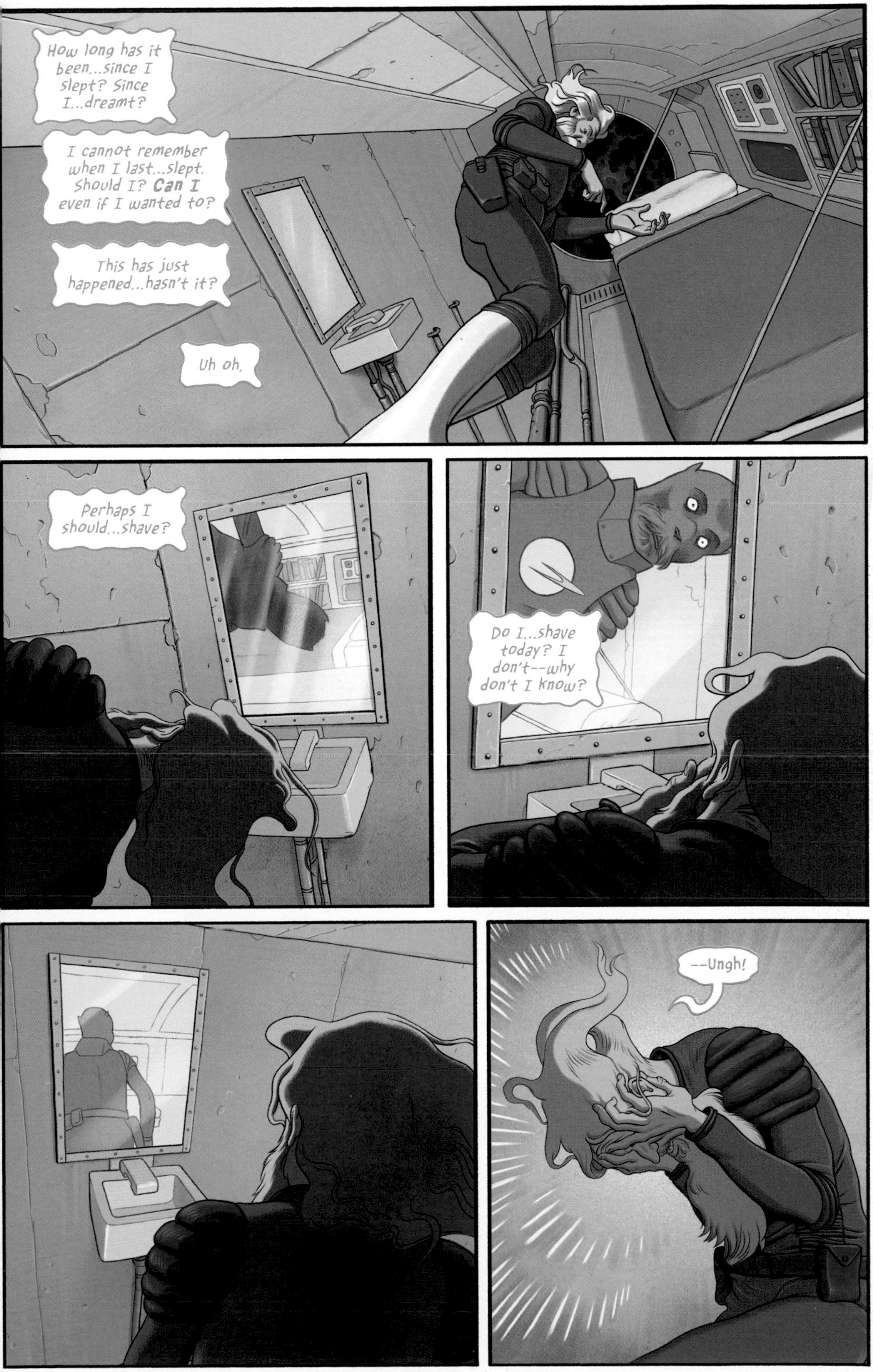
How long has it been...since I slept? Since I...dreamt?
I cannot remember when I last...slept. Should I? **Can I** even if I wanted to?
This has just happened...hasn't it?
Uh oh.
Perhaps I should...shave?
Do I...shave today? I don't--why don't I know?
--Ungh!

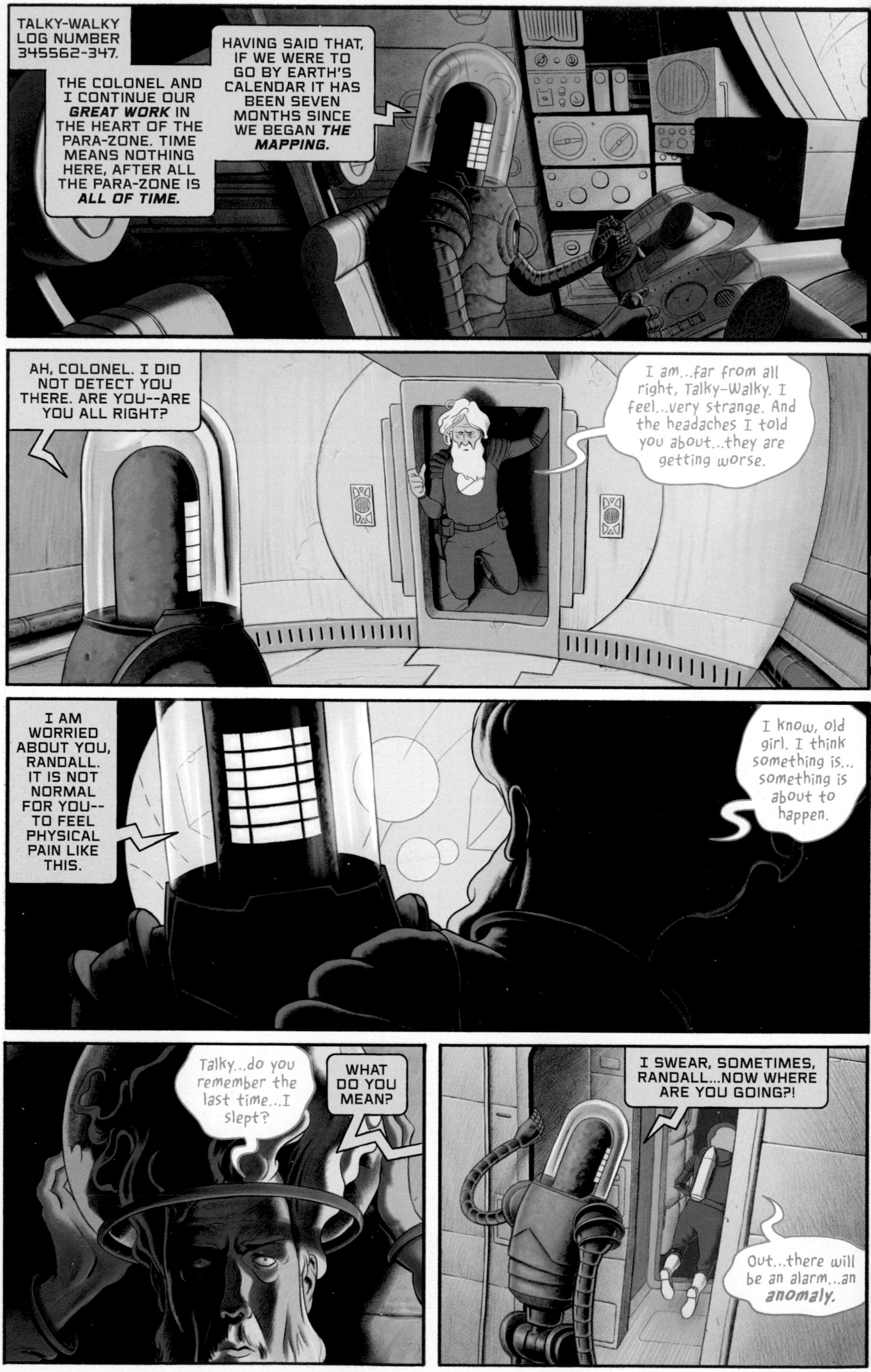
TALKY-WALKY LOG NUMBER 345562-347.
THE COLONEL AND I CONTINUE OUR GREAT WORK IN THE HEART OF THE PARA-ZONE. TIME MEANS NOTHING HERE, AFTER ALL THE PARA-ZONE IS ALL OF TIME.
HAVING SAID THAT, IF WE WERE TO GO BY EARTH'S CALENDAR IT HAS BEEN SEVEN MONTHS SINCE WE BEGAN THE MAPPING.
AH, COLONEL. I DID NOT DETECT YOU THERE. ARE YOU--ARE YOU ALL RIGHT?
I am...far from all right, Talky-Walky. I feel...very strange. And the headaches I told you about...they are getting worse.
I AM WORRIED ABOUT YOU, RANDALL. IT IS NOT NORMAL FOR YOU-- TO FEEL PHYSICAL PAIN LIKE THIS.
I know, old girl. I think something is... something is about to happen.
Talky...do you remember the last time...I slept?
WHAT DO YOU MEAN?
I SWEAR, SOMETIMES, RANDALL...NOW WHERE ARE YOU GOING?!
Out...there will be an alarm...an anomaly.

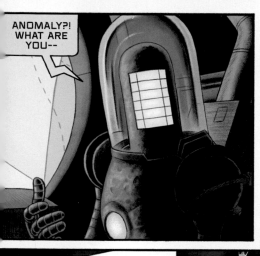

ANOMALY?! WHAT ARE YOU--

OH.

EEEP

EEEP

EEEP

WHAT IS IT, COLONEL?!

The Cataclysm... The *Second* Cataclysm...

SECOND CATACLYSM?! COLONEL...THERE WAS NO SECOND CATACLYSM. IT ONLY HAPPENED ONCE. ANTI-GOD WAS DESTROYED.

No, Talky. He is just... sleeping...

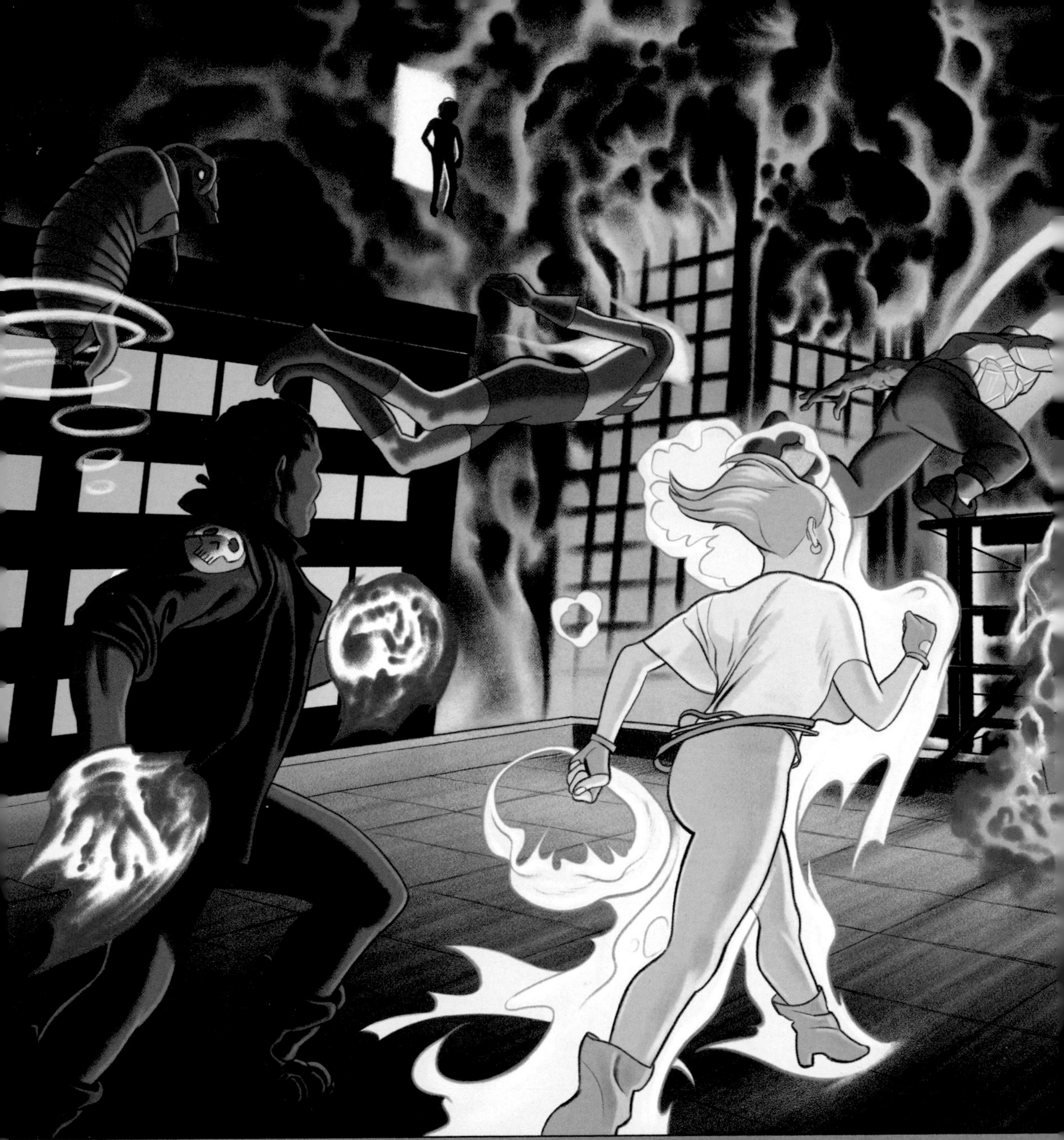

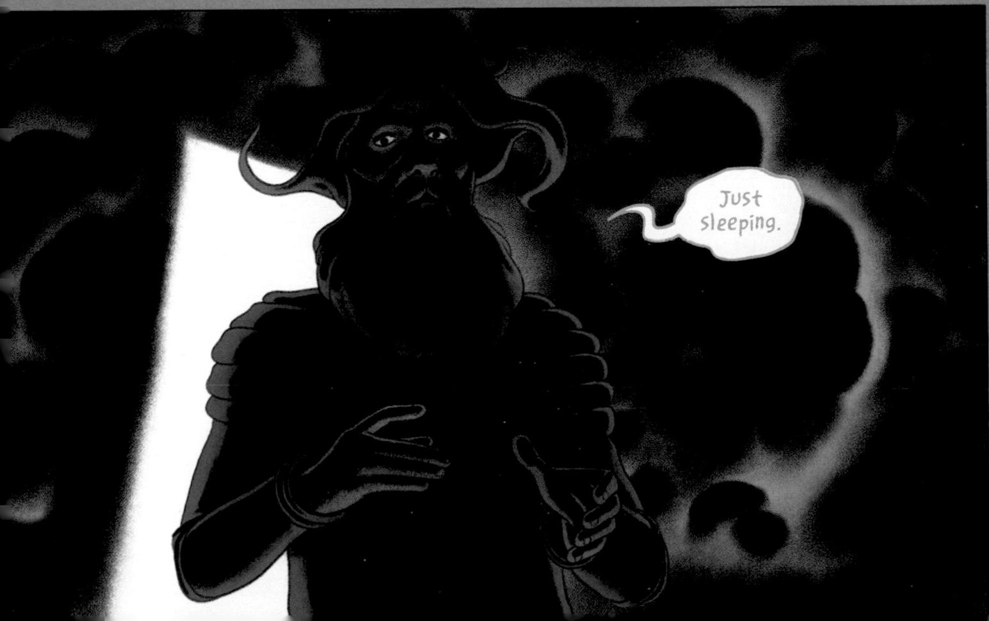
Just sleeping.

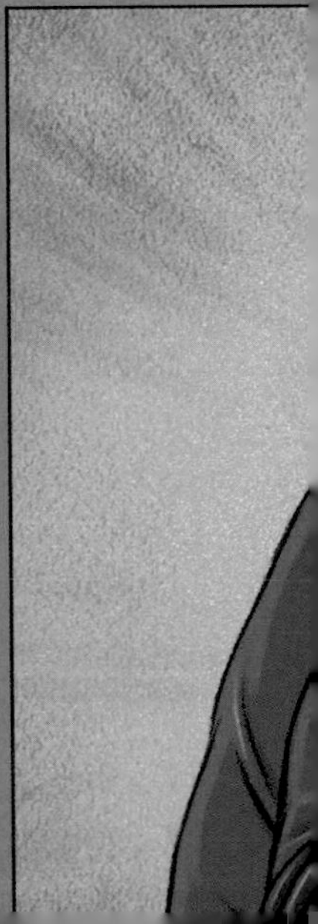

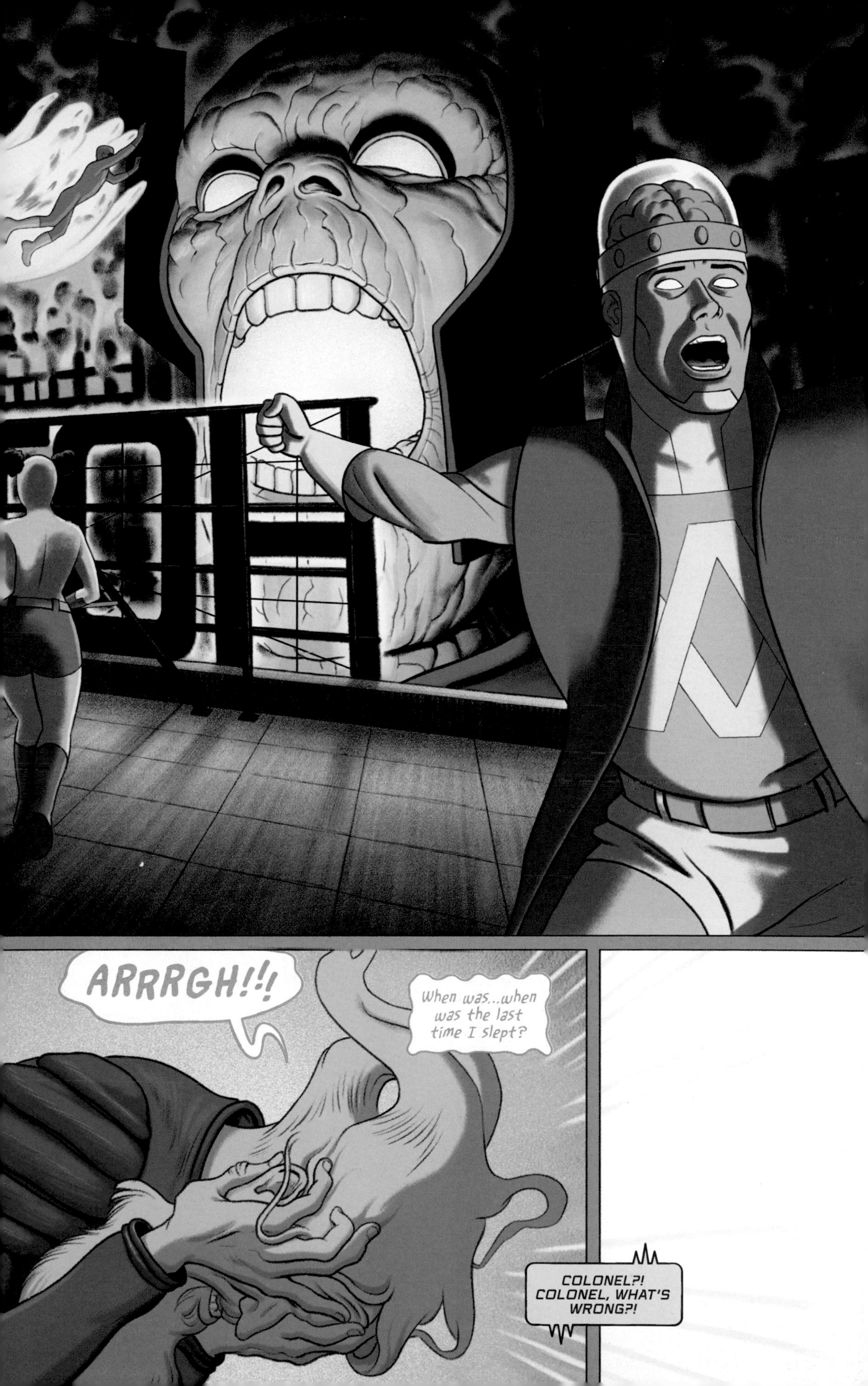
ARRRGH!!!
When was...when was the last time I slept?
COLONEL?! COLONEL, WHAT'S WRONG?!

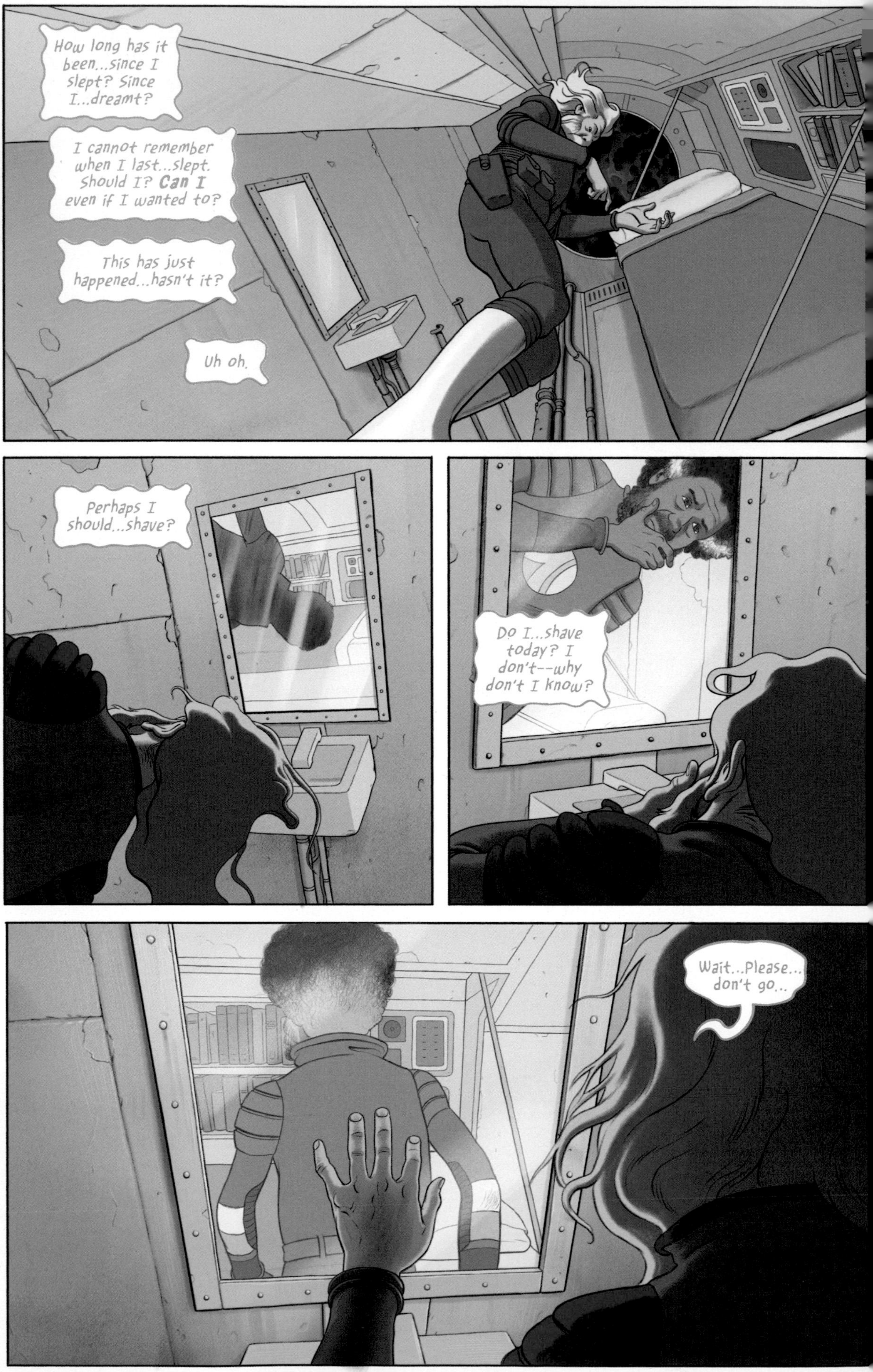
How long has it been...since I slept? Since I...dreamt?
I cannot remember when I last...slept. Should I? Can I even if I wanted to?
This has just happened...hasn't it?
Uh oh.
Perhaps I should...shave?
Do I...shave today? I don't--why don't I know?
Wait...Please... don't go...

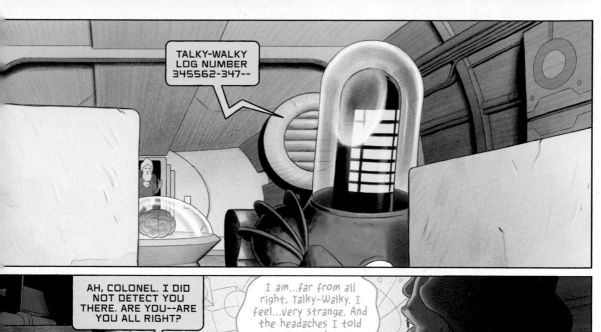

TALKY-WALKY LOG NUMBER 345562-347--

AH, COLONEL. I DID NOT DETECT YOU THERE. ARE YOU--ARE YOU ALL RIGHT?

I am...far from all right, Talky-Walky. I feel...very strange. And the headaches I told you about...they are getting worse.

But that's not...all. Something else is...happening to me. The... Anomaly...

ANOMOLY? WHAT ANOM--

EE
EEEP

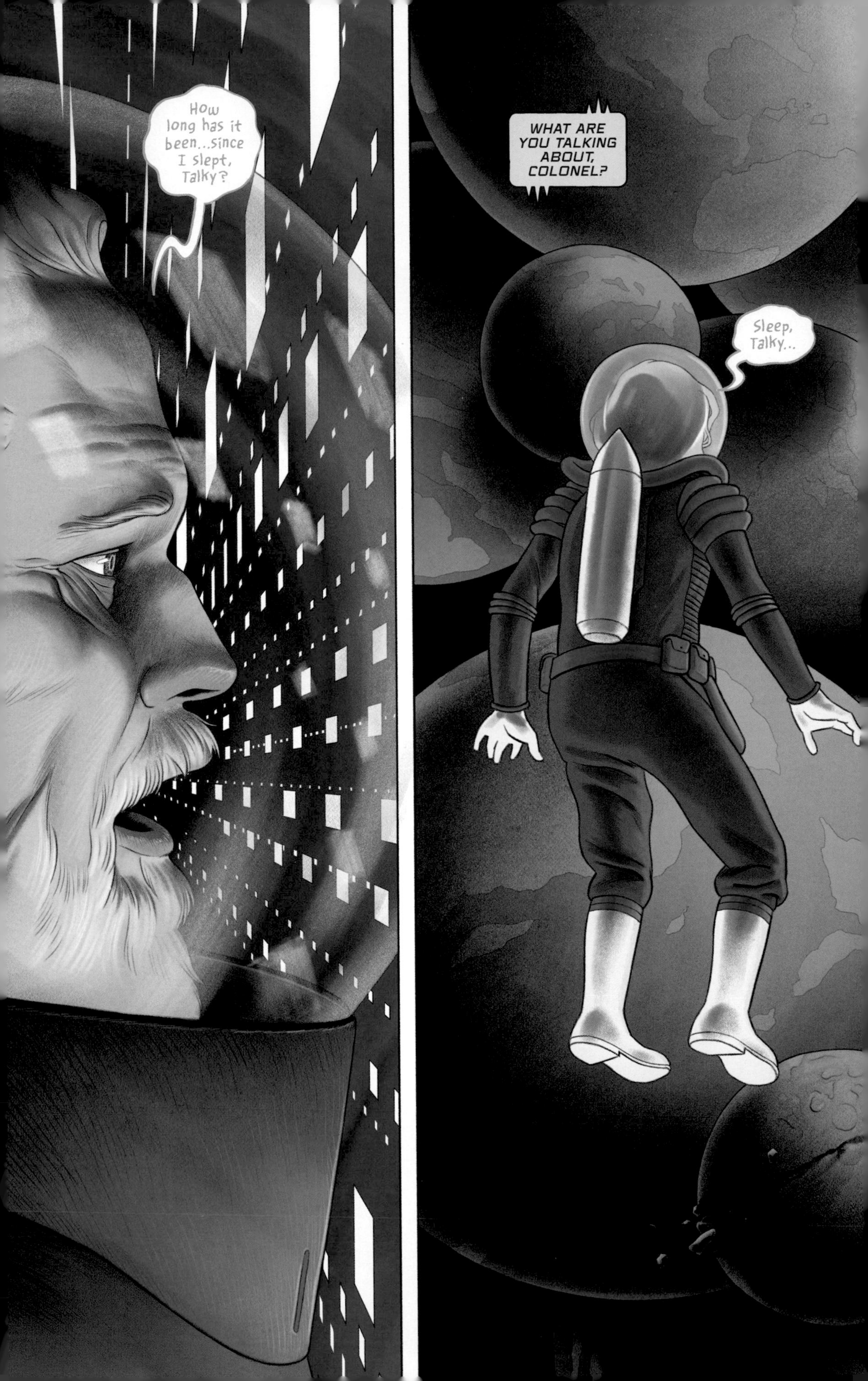
How long has it been...since I slept, Talky?
WHAT ARE YOU TALKING ABOUT, COLONEL?
Sleep, Talky...

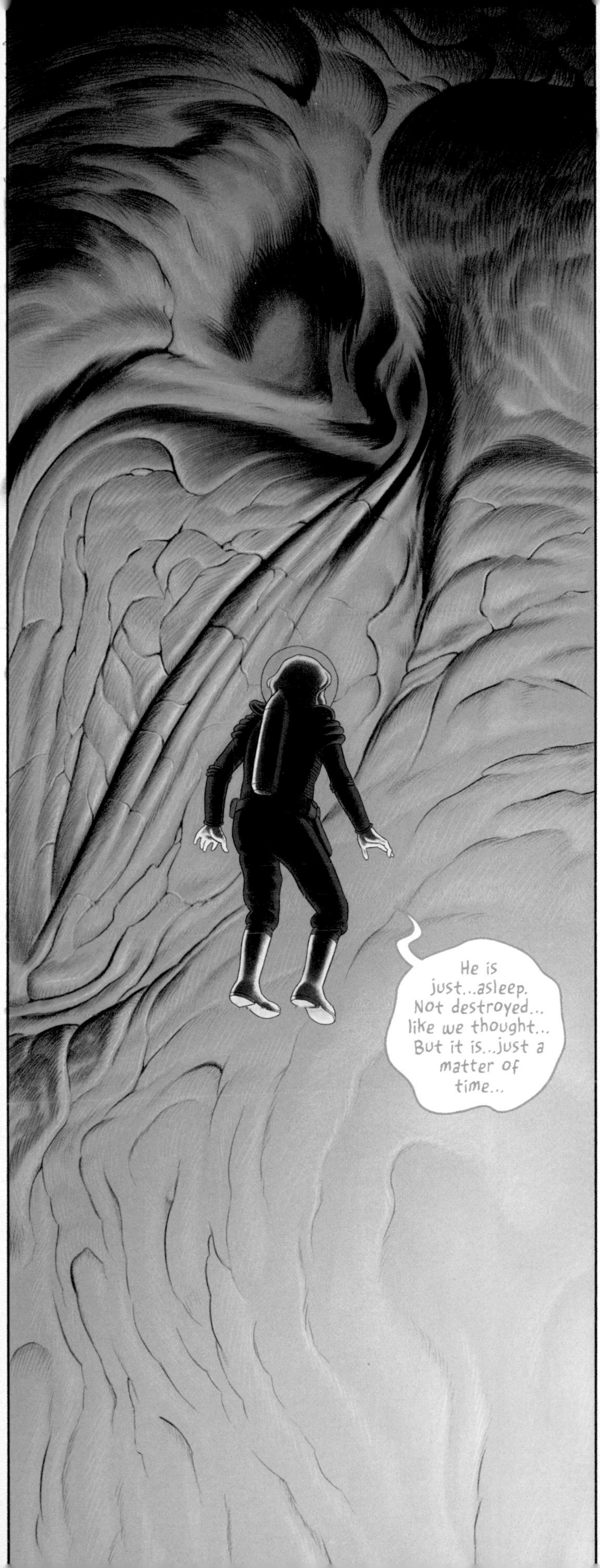
He is just...asleep. Not destroyed... like we thought... But it is...just a matter of time...

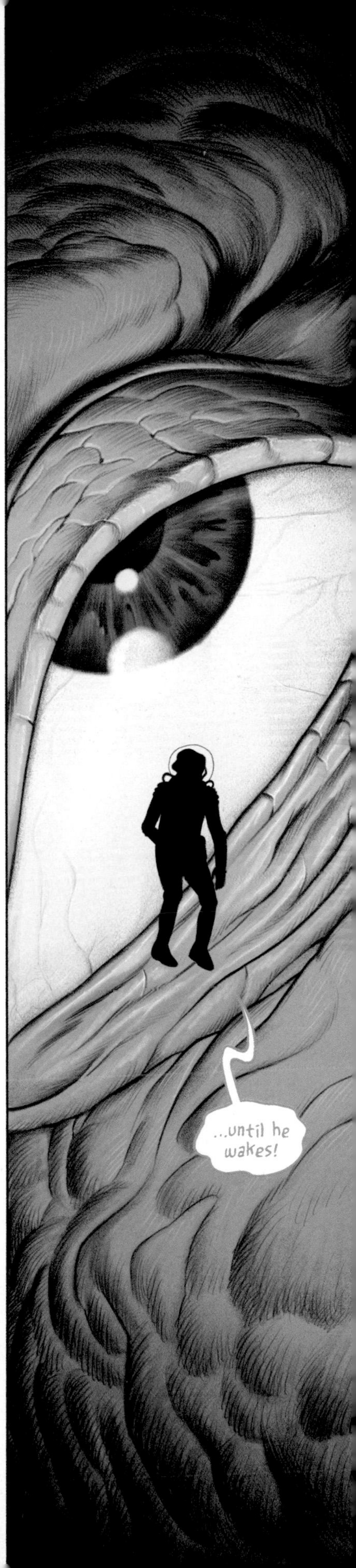
...until he wakes!

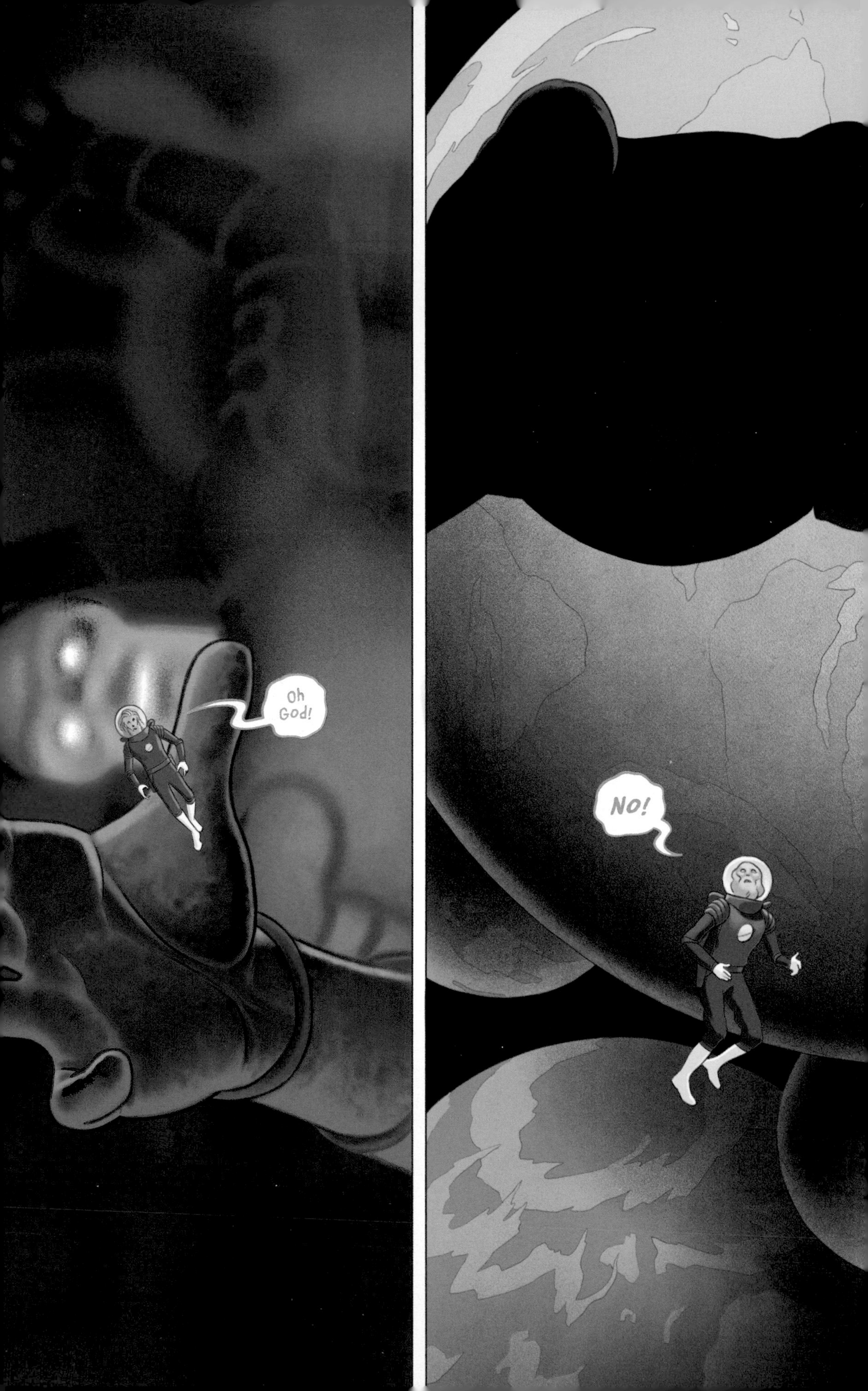
Oh God!
No!

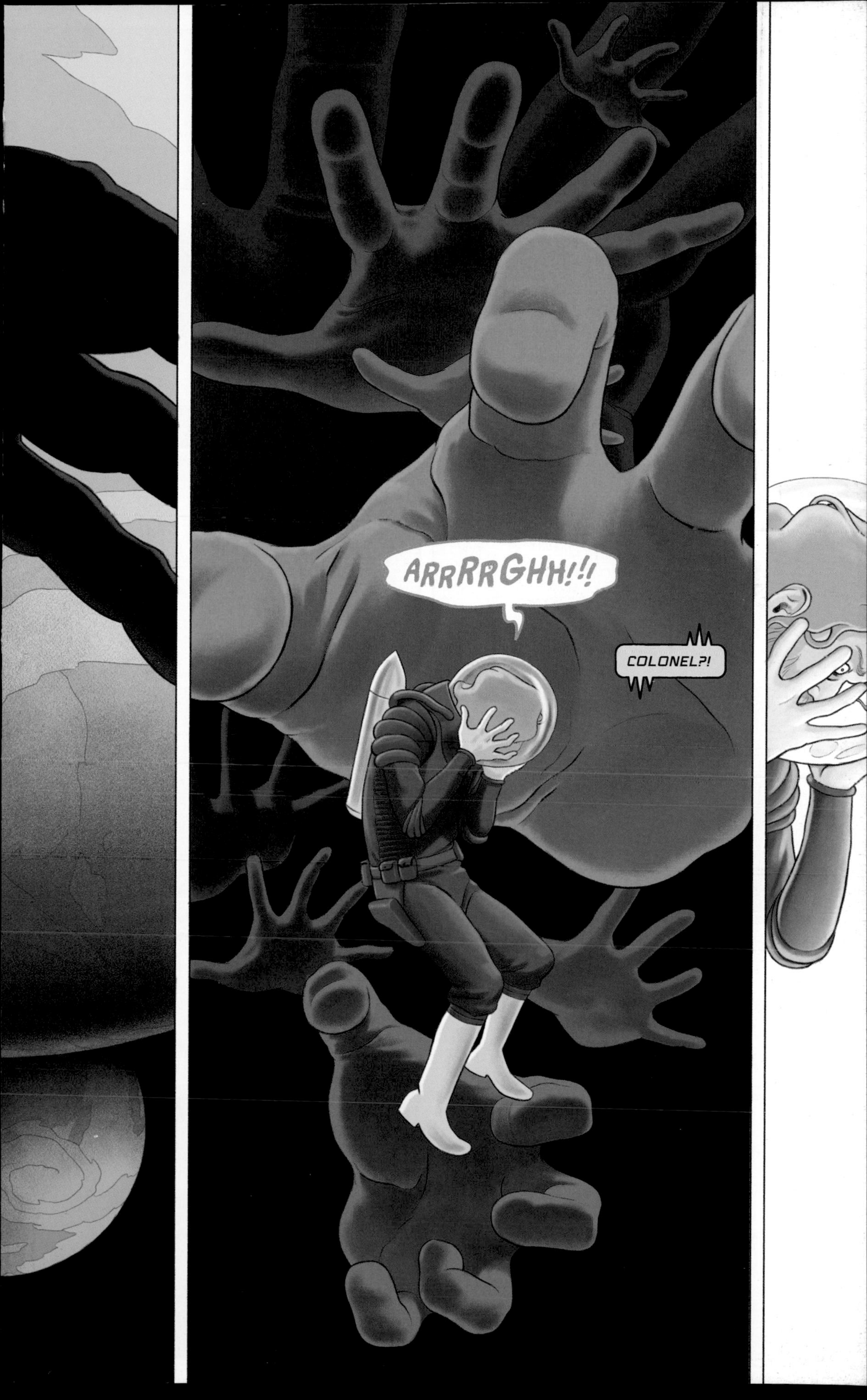
ARRRRGHH!!!
COLONEL?!

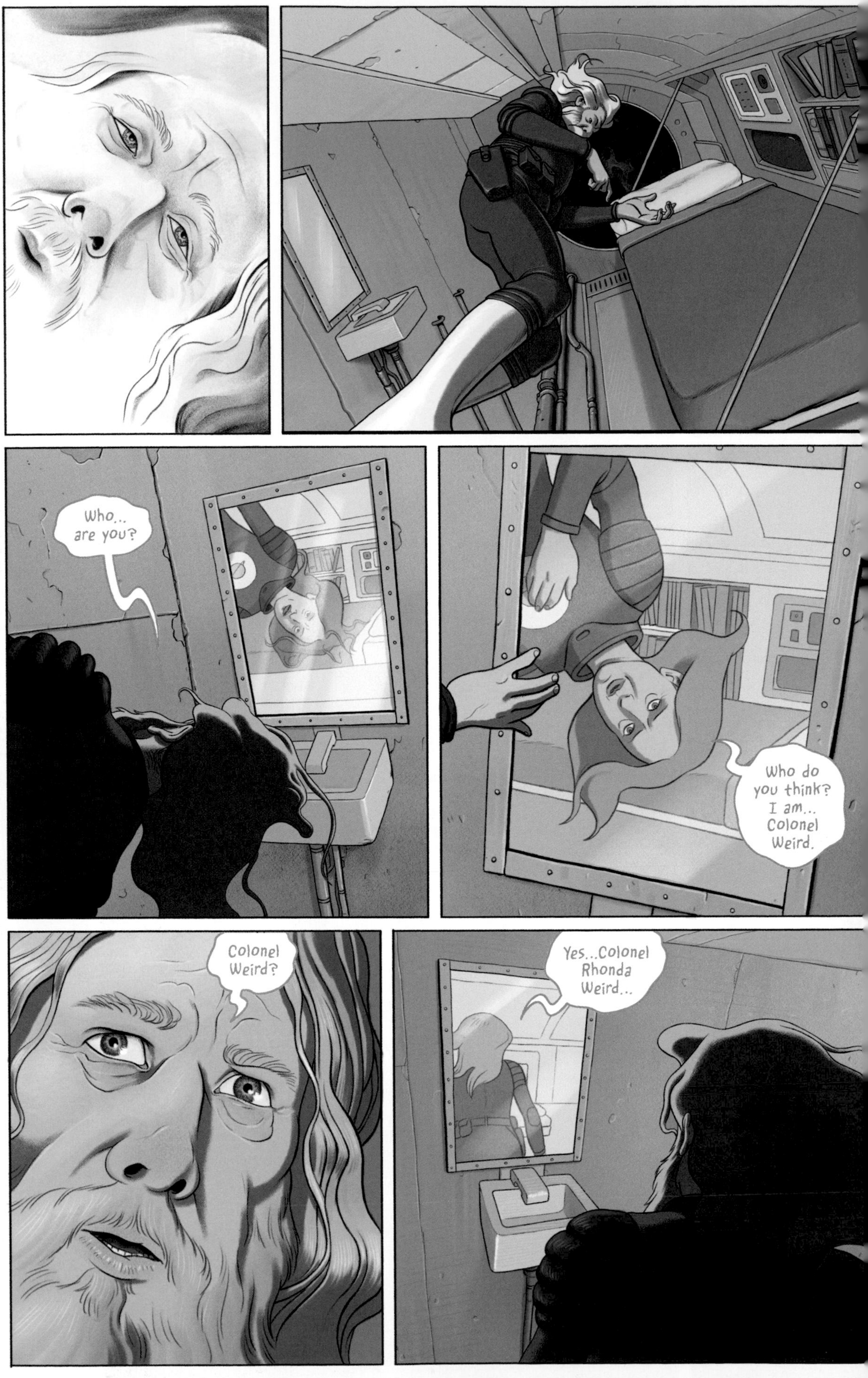
Who... are you?
Who do you think? I am... Colonel Weird.
Colonel Weird?
Yes...Colonel Rhonda Weird...

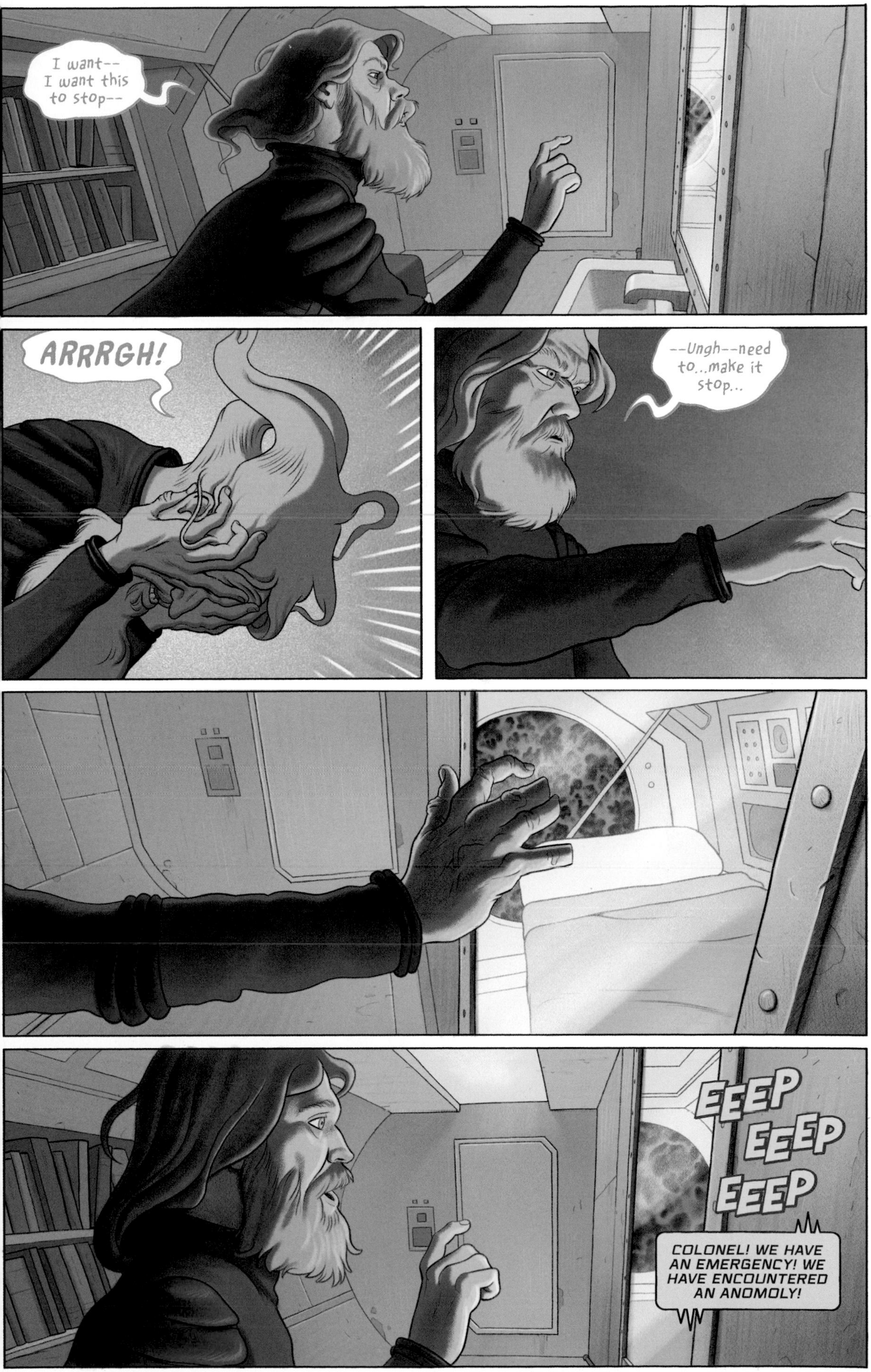
I want--
I want this to stop--
ARRRGH!
--Ungh--need to...make it stop...
EEEP EEEP EEEP
COLONEL! WE HAVE AN EMERGENCY! WE HAVE ENCOUNTERED AN ANOMOLY!

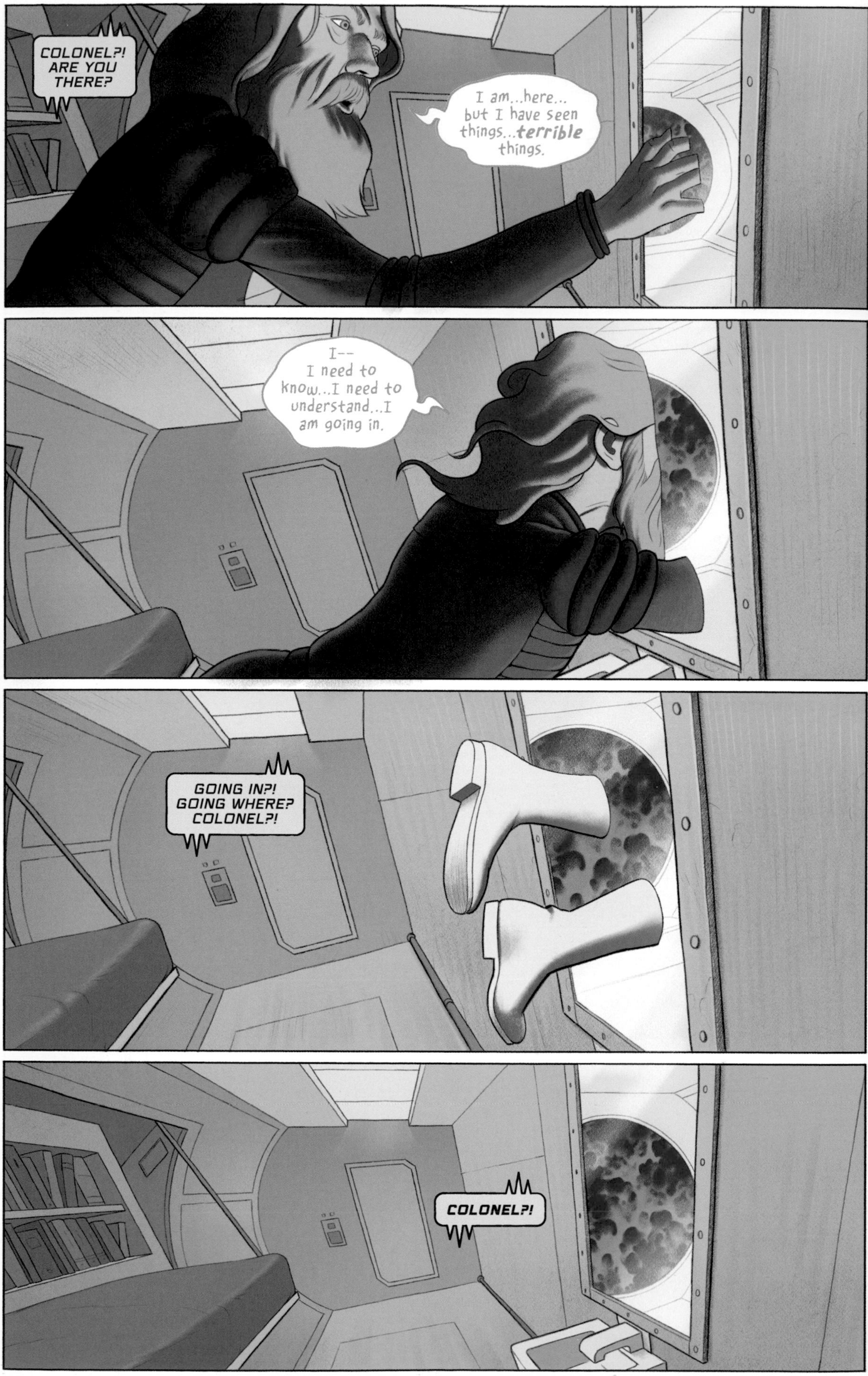
COLONEL?! ARE YOU THERE?
I am...here... but I have seen things...terrible things.
I-- I need to know...I need to understand...I am going in.
GOING IN?! GOING WHERE? COLONEL?!
COLONEL?!

Talky-Walky...I don't know if you can hear me...but I have...found something.
And I think it may be...very important.

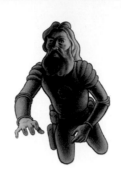

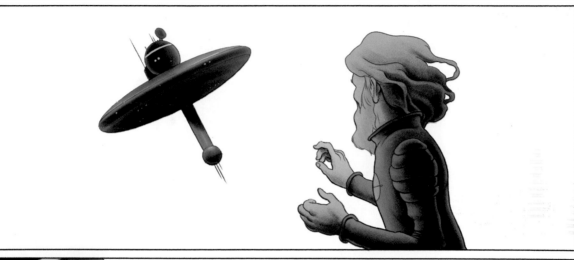

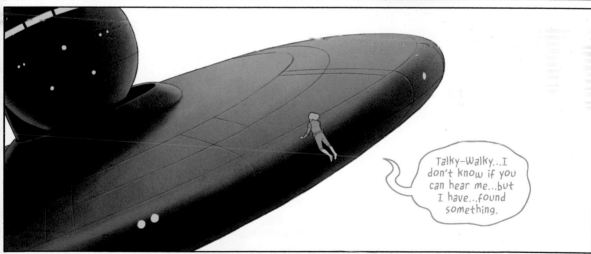

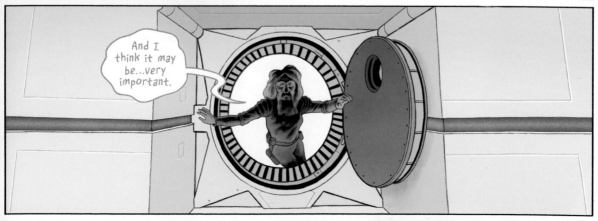

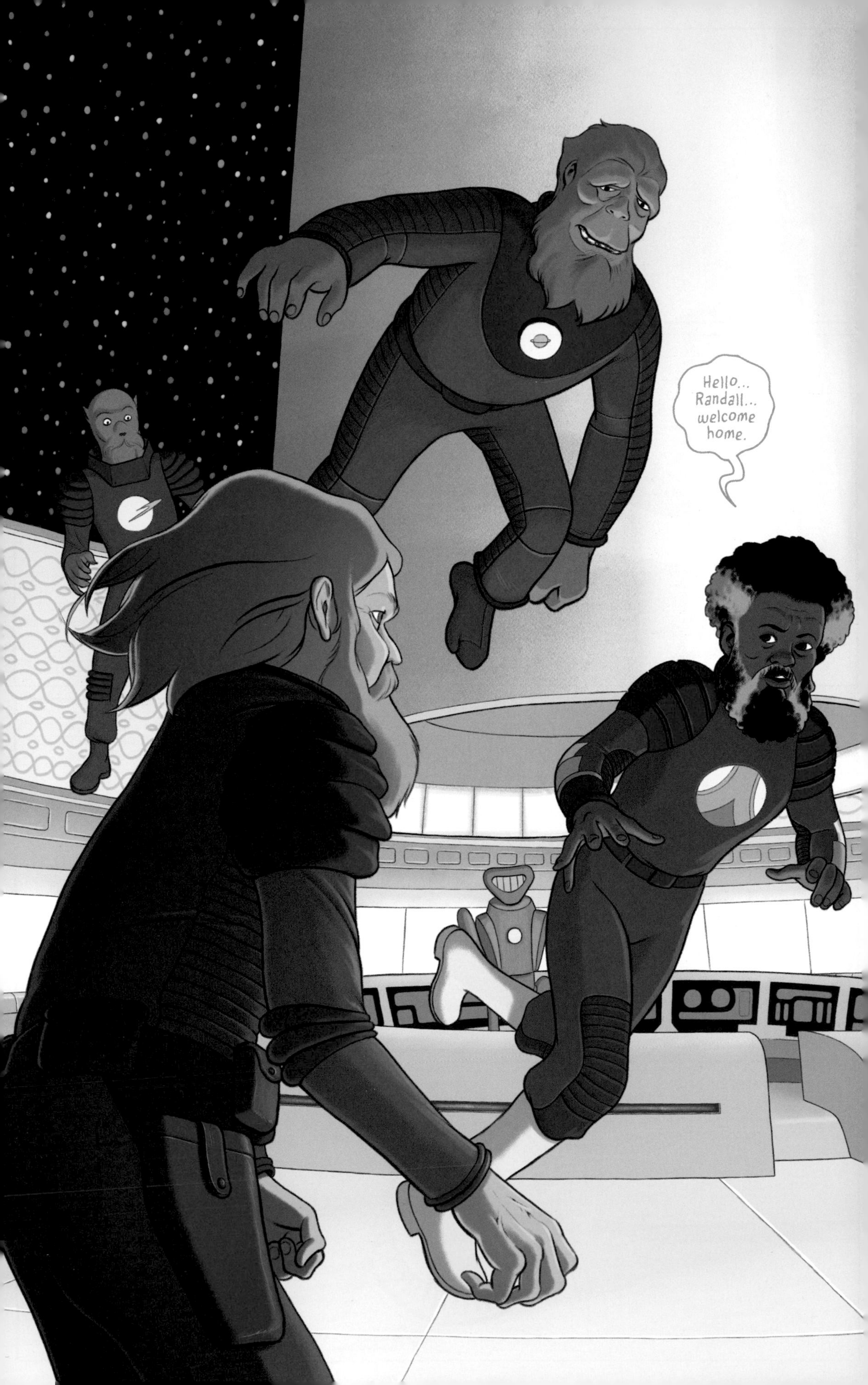
Hello... Randall... welcome home.

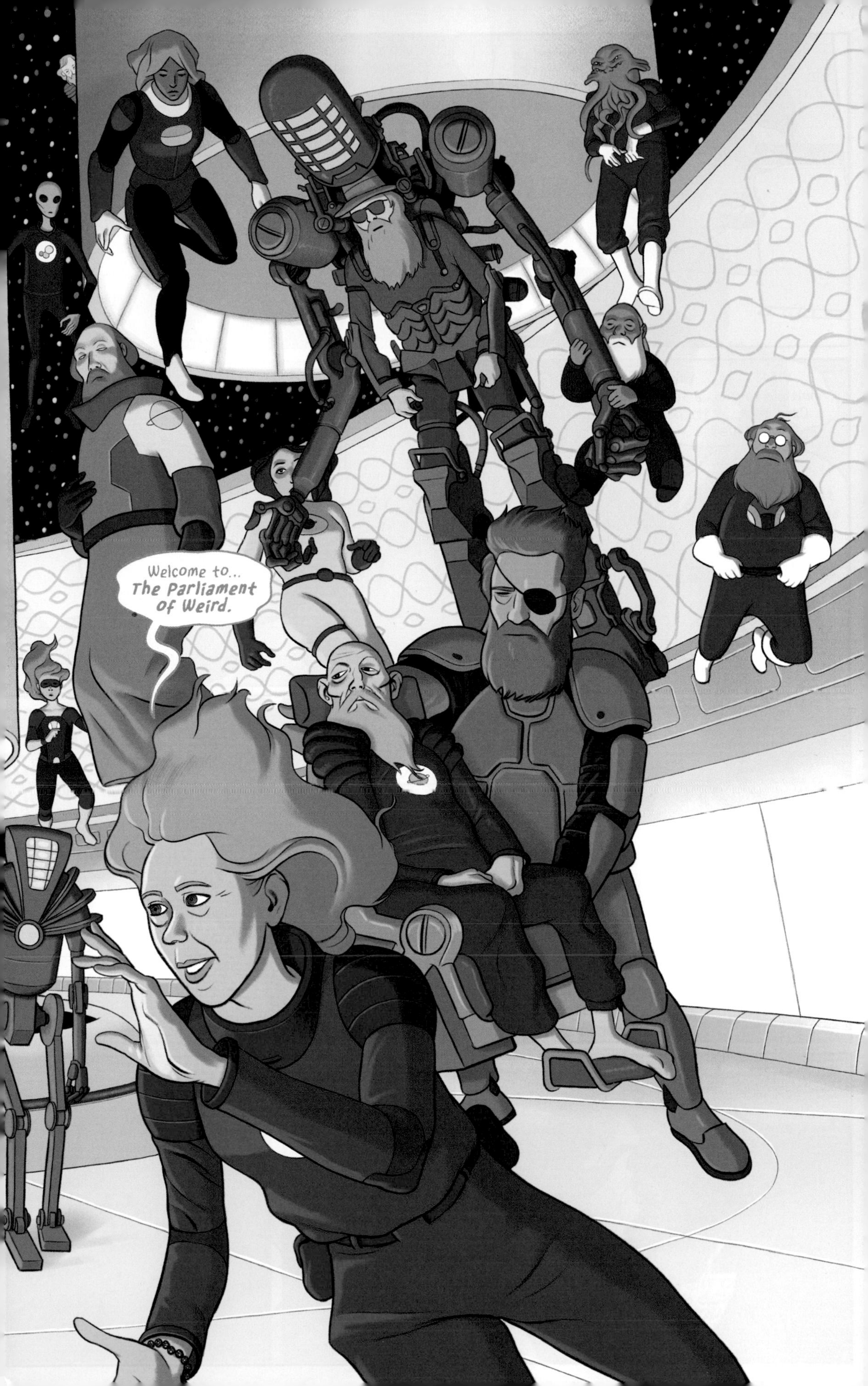
Welcome to... The Parliament of Weird.

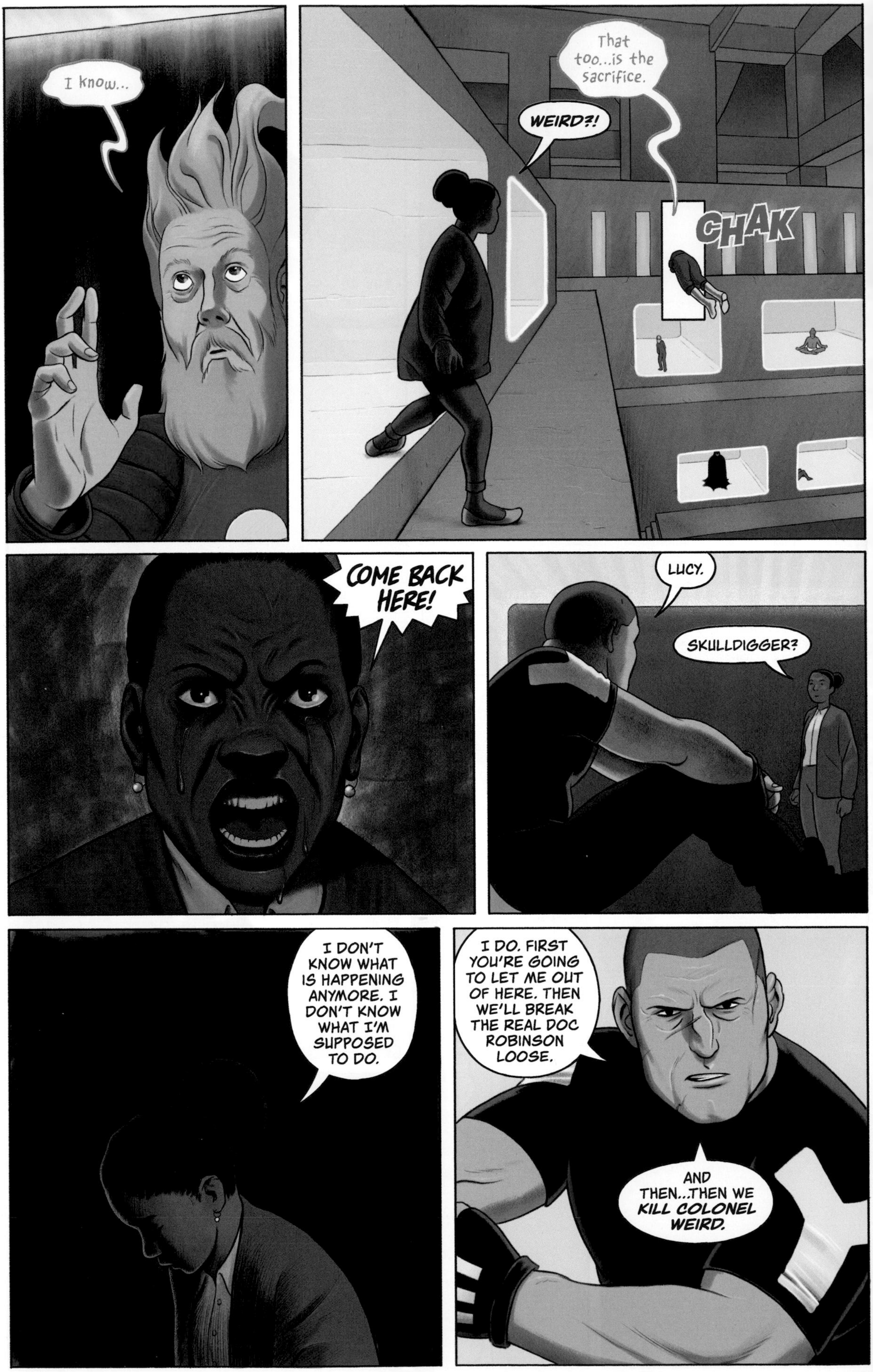
I know...
That too...is the sacrifice.
WEIRD?!
CHAK
COME BACK HERE!
LUCY.
SKULLDIGGER?
I DON'T KNOW WHAT IS HAPPENING ANYMORE. I DON'T KNOW WHAT I'M SUPPOSED TO DO.
I DO. FIRST YOU'RE GOING TO LET ME OUT OF HERE. THEN WE'LL BREAK THE REAL DOC ROBINSON LOOSE.
AND THEN...THEN WE KILL COLONEL WEIRD.

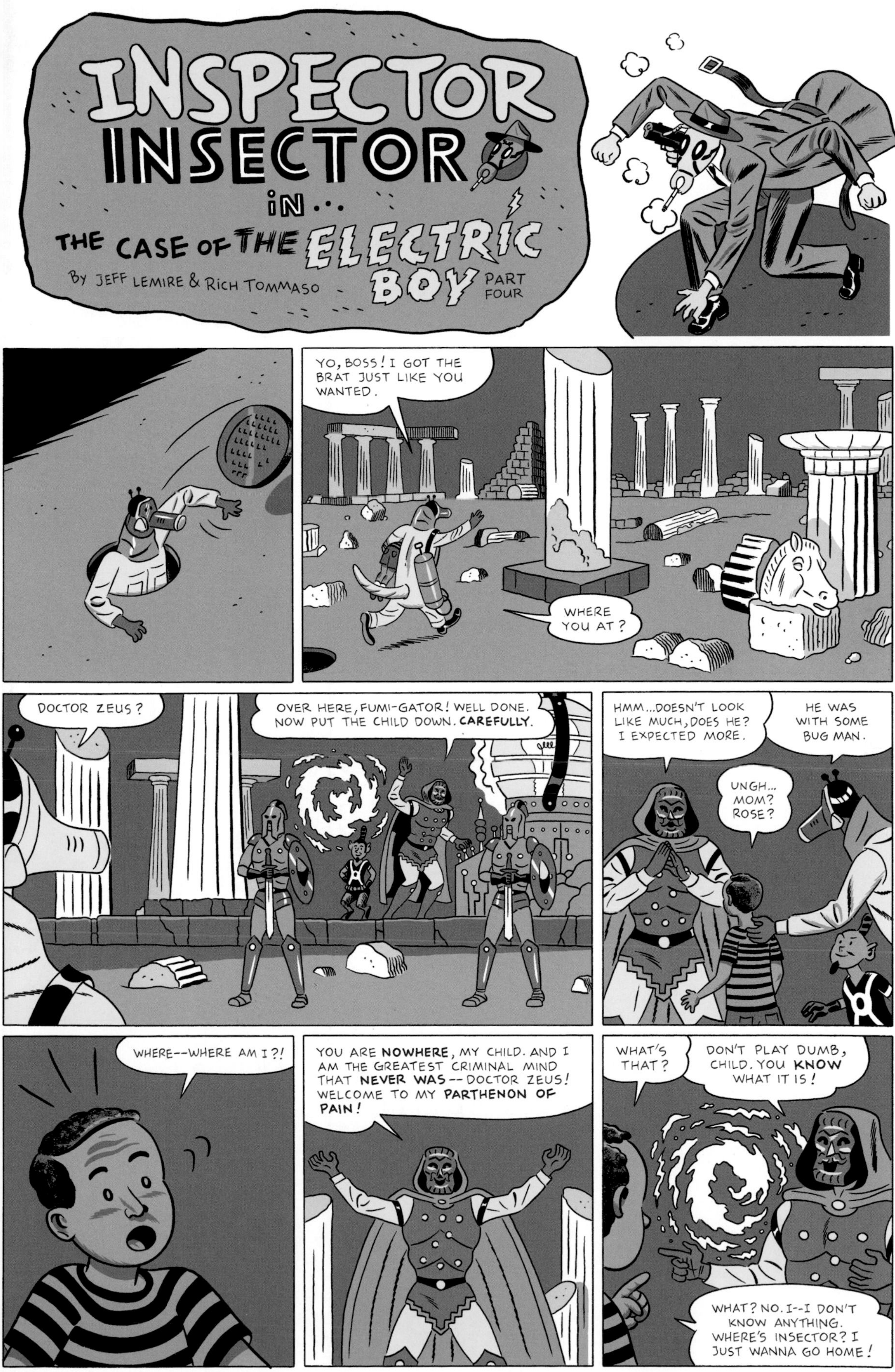
INSPECTOR INSECTOR
in...
THE CASE OF THE ELECTRIC BOY
PART FOUR
By JEFF LEMIRE & RICH TOMMASO
YO, BOSS! I GOT THE BRAT JUST LIKE YOU WANTED.
WHERE YOU AT?
DOCTOR ZEUS?
OVER HERE, FUMI-GATOR! WELL DONE. NOW PUT THE CHILD DOWN. CAREFULLY.
HMM...DOESN'T LOOK LIKE MUCH, DOES HE? I EXPECTED MORE.
HE WAS WITH SOME BUG MAN.
UNGH... MOM? ROSE?
WHERE--WHERE AM I?!
YOU ARE NOWHERE, MY CHILD. AND I AM THE GREATEST CRIMINAL MIND THAT NEVER WAS--DOCTOR ZEUS! WELCOME TO MY PARTHENON OF PAIN!
WHAT'S THAT?
DON'T PLAY DUMB, CHILD. YOU KNOW WHAT IT IS!
WHAT? NO. I--I DON'T KNOW ANYTHING. WHERE'S INSECTOR? I JUST WANNA GO HOME!

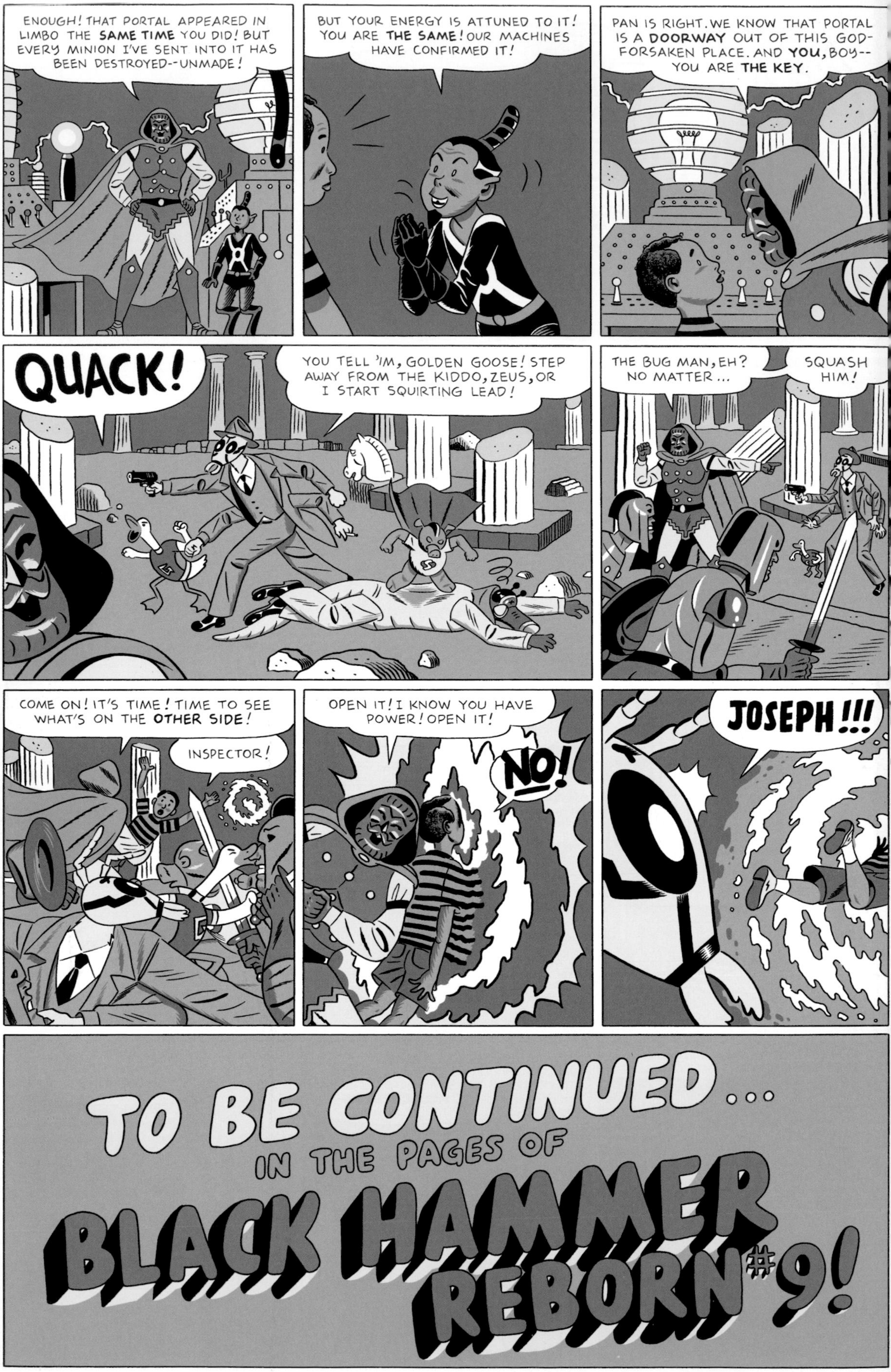
ENOUGH! THAT PORTAL APPEARED IN LIMBO THE SAME TIME YOU DID! BUT EVERY MINION I'VE SENT INTO IT HAS BEEN DESTROYED--UNMADE!
BUT YOUR ENERGY IS ATTUNED TO IT! YOU ARE THE SAME! OUR MACHINES HAVE CONFIRMED IT!
PAN IS RIGHT. WE KNOW THAT PORTAL IS A DOORWAY OUT OF THIS GOD-FORSAKEN PLACE. AND YOU, BOY-- YOU ARE THE KEY.
QUACK!
YOU TELL 'IM, GOLDEN GOOSE! STEP AWAY FROM THE KIDDO, ZEUS, OR I START SQUIRTING LEAD!
THE BUG MAN, EH? NO MATTER...
SQUASH HIM!
COME ON! IT'S TIME! TIME TO SEE WHAT'S ON THE OTHER SIDE!
INSPECTOR!
OPEN IT! I KNOW YOU HAVE POWER! OPEN IT!
NO!
JOSEPH!!!
TO BE CONTINUED...
IN THE PAGES OF
BLACK HAMMER REBORN #9!

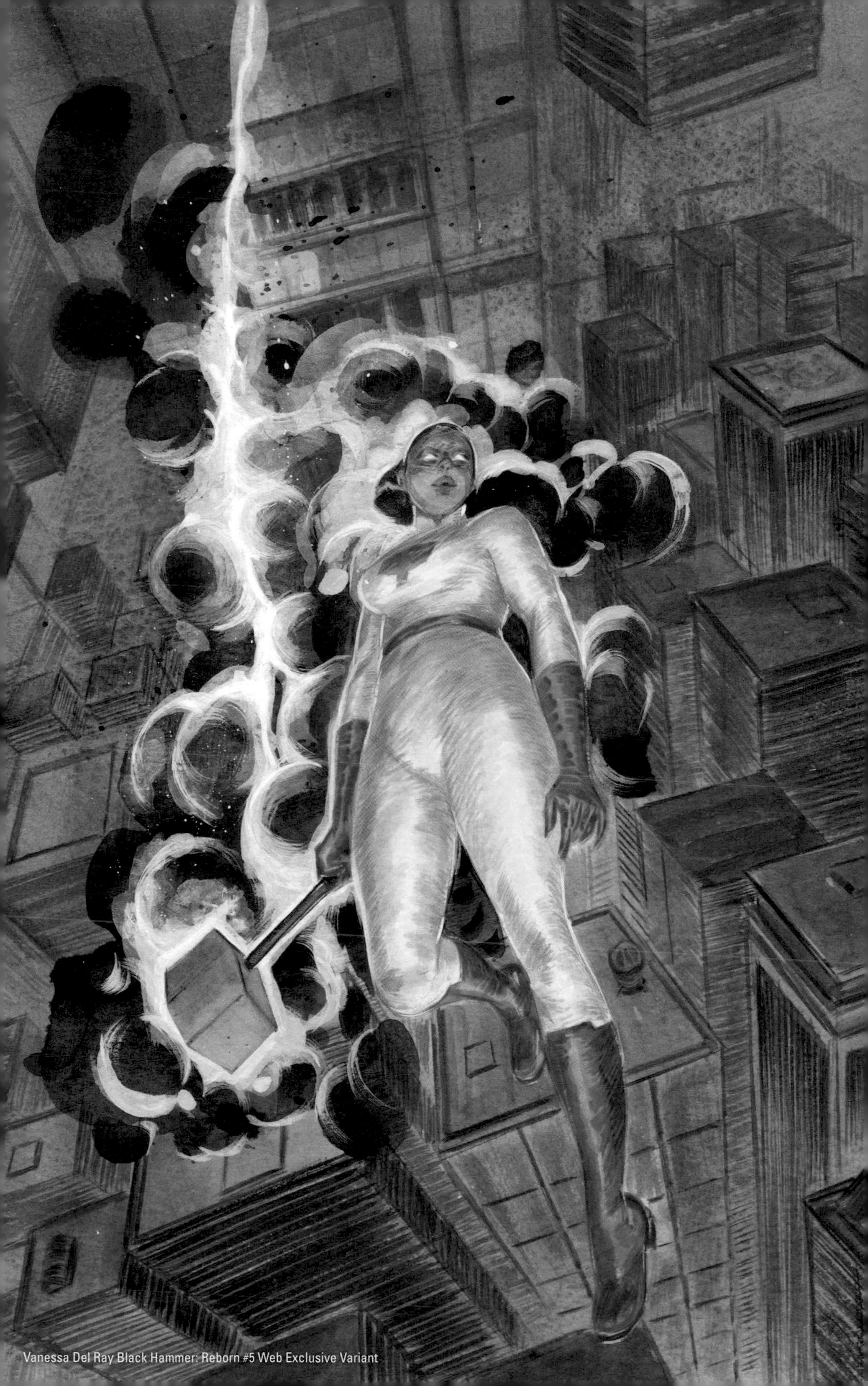

Vanessa Del Ray Black Hammer: Reborn #5 Web Exclusive Variant

BLACK HAMMER™ REBORN SKETCHBOOK

NOTES BY MALACHI WARD AND MATTHEW SHEEAN

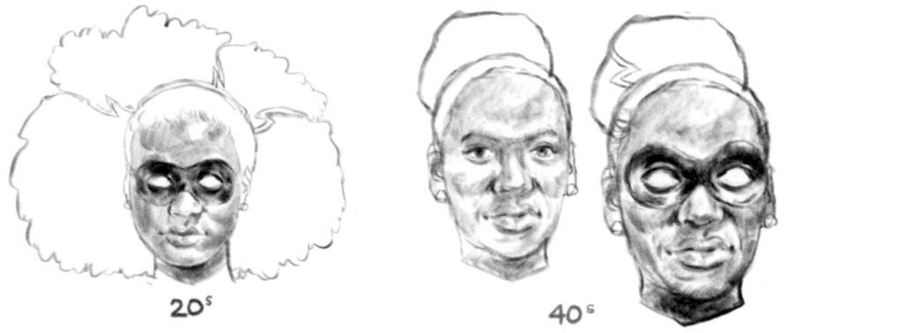

20s
40s

One aspect of cartooning that's notoriously difficult is drawing a character at different ages without just resorting to a gray streak in the hair and a few extra lines on the face. Matt and I made sure to work out Lucy's aging before starting.

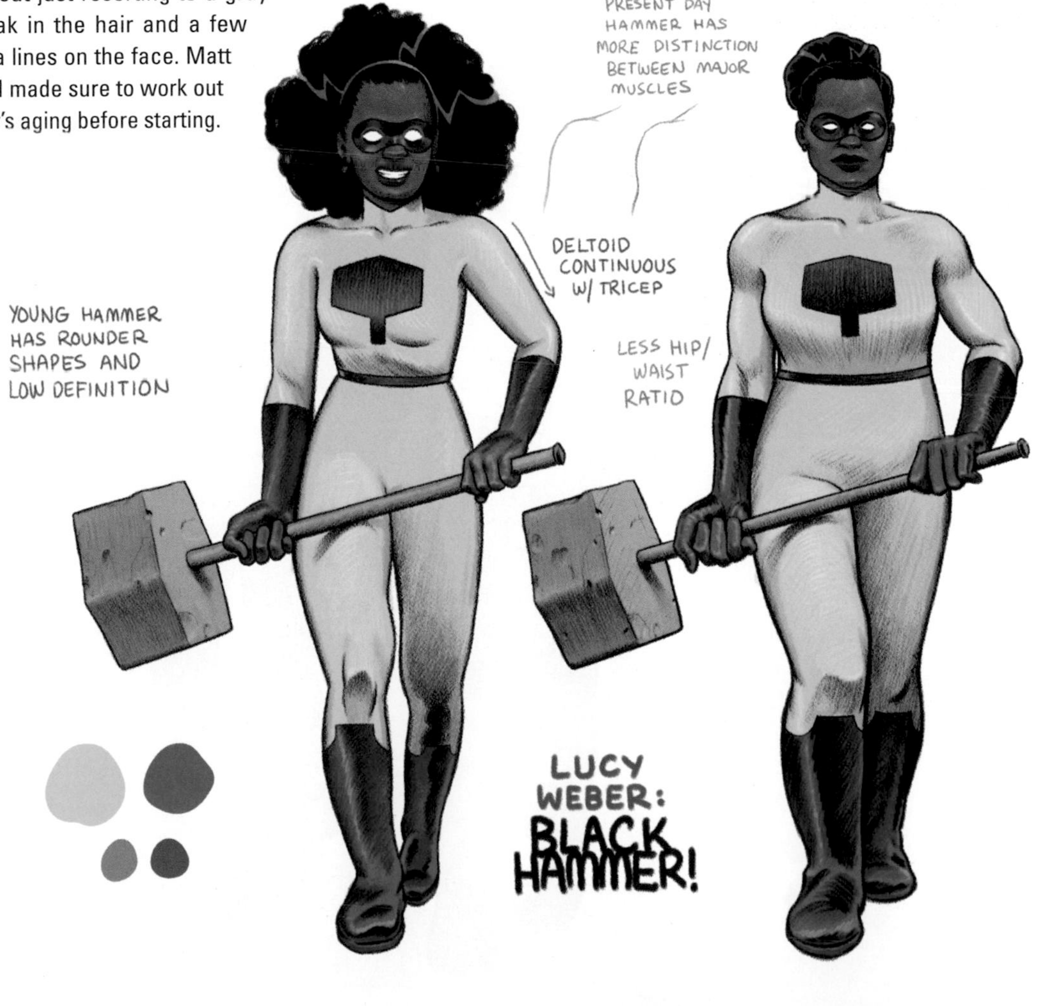

PRESENT DAY HAMMER HAS MORE DISTINCTION BETWEEN MAJOR MUSCLES
DELTOID CONTINUOUS W/ TRICEP
YOUNG HAMMER HAS ROUNDER SHAPES AND LOW DEFINITION
LESS HIP/ WAIST RATIO
LUCY WEBER: BLACK HAMMER!

T.R.I.D.E.N.T.

DESIGNS BY
MATT & MALACHI

LOGOS

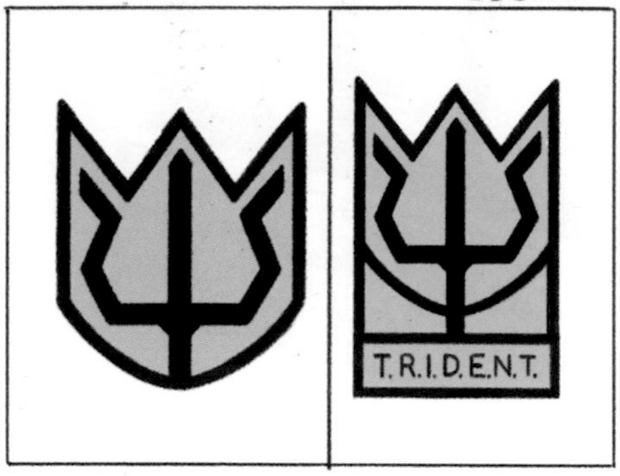
T.R.I.D.E.N.T.

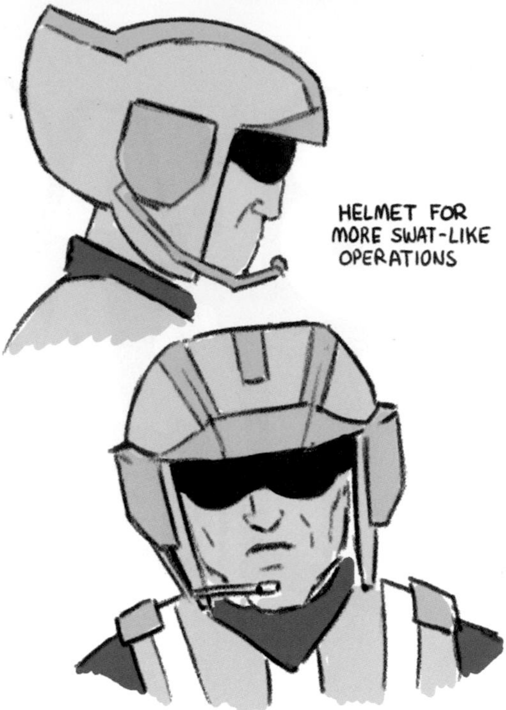
HELMET FOR MORE SWAT-LIKE OPERATIONS

We actually started our run before Caitlin had begun the first issue, so we got a chance to design TRIDENT. We tried to pull in equal parts Steranko and GI Joe.

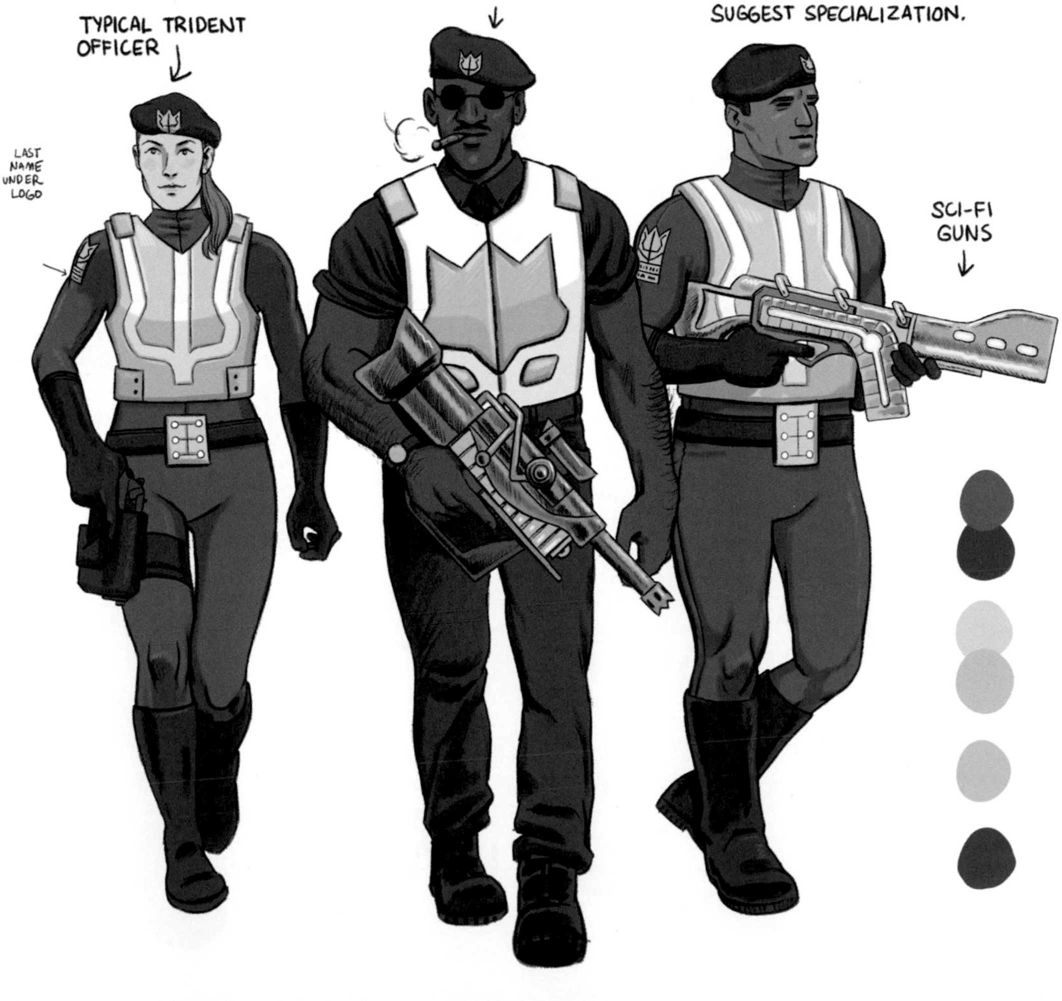
"AGENT 1" COMMAND LEVEL GUY THAT ONLY TURNS UP FOR CRITICAL MISSIONS (PROB. NOT 'TIL #5?)
GIVE AGENTS UNIQUE TECH/WEAPONS MODIFICATIONS TO SUGGEST SPECIALIZATION.
TYPICAL TRIDENT OFFICER
LAST NAME UNDER LOGO
SCI-FI GUNS

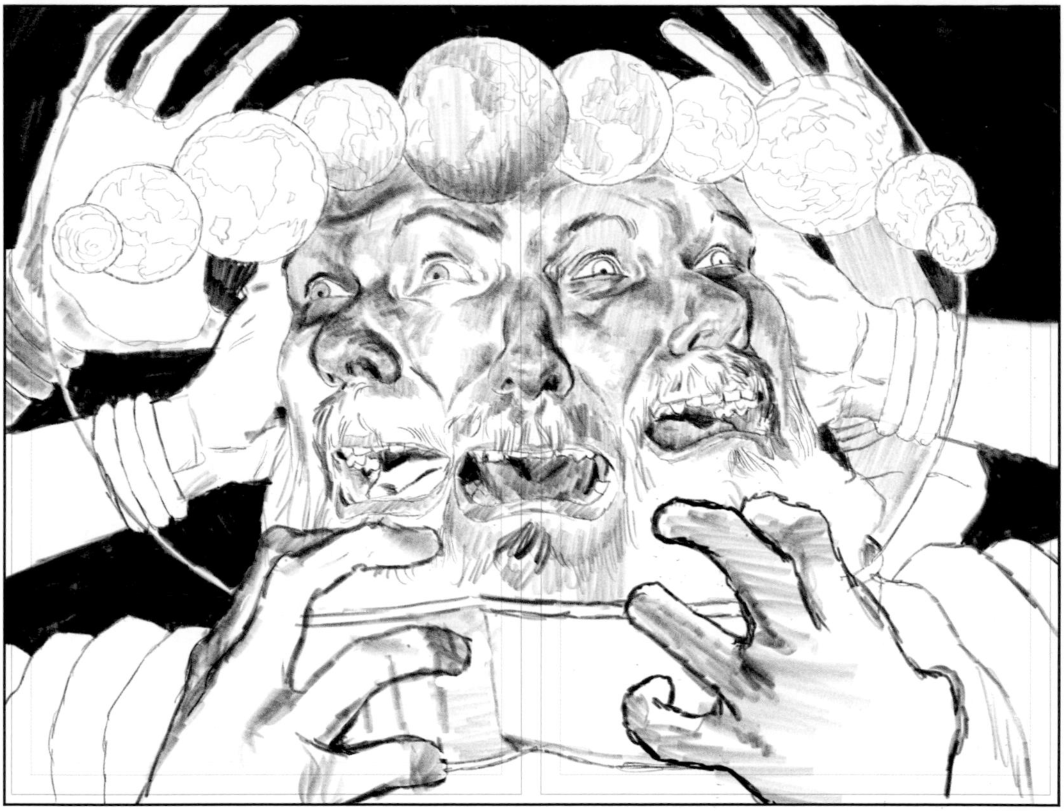

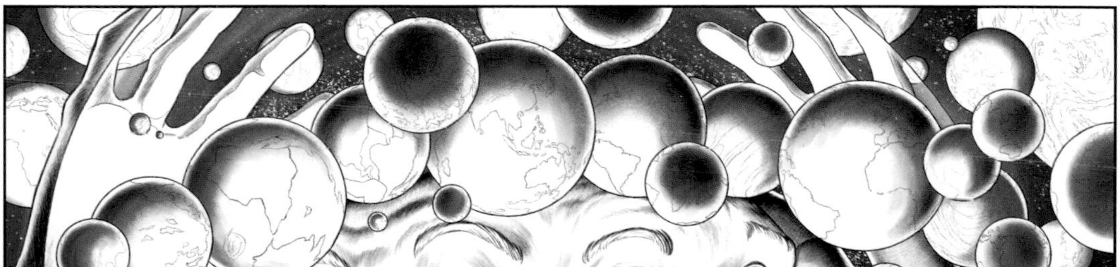

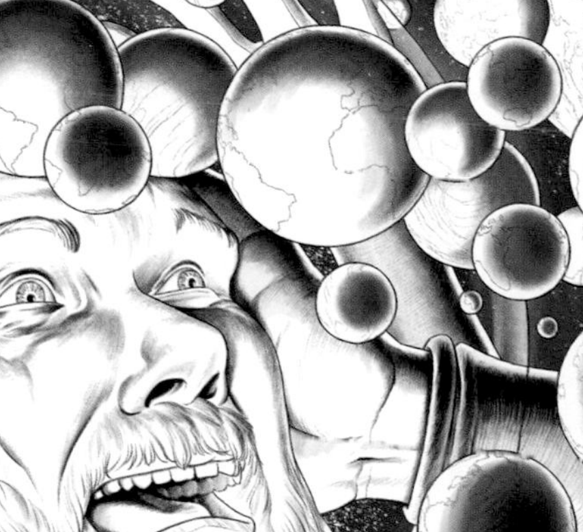

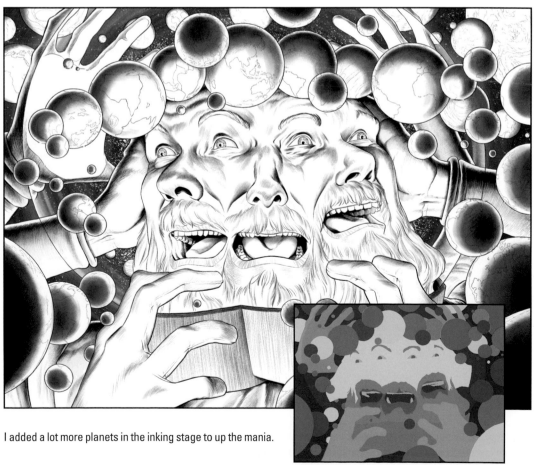

I added a lot more planets in the inking stage to up the mania.

13
Black Hammer Reborn #5 – Lemire & Zarcone

PAGE 14.

1.
BIG PANEL.

They watch as Lucy flies off the rooftop and upwards.

LUCY: But I'm going to find out.

LUCY CAPTION: I'm just on autopilot now. Not even really thinking about what I'm doing or why. It's all like a dream. Surreal.

2.
Lucy flies straight up, Spiral Below her.

LUCY CAPTION: I just keep going, let old muscle memory take over. Because if I stop—if I stop I'll have to *think.* And if I have to think, I'll have to face what just *happened to them.*

14
Black Hammer Reborn #5 – Lemire & Zarcone

PAGE 15.

1.
This is almost a mirror of the last panel on the previous page, except now Lucy is flying straight down towards the Other Spiral.

LUCY CAPTION: So I fly up and then suddenly I'm actually *flying down.*

SFX: -EEP! EEP!

2.
Lucy now flies downwards towards another rooftop very similar to the one she left.

LUCY CAPTION: All I know is this thing was in Rosie's room.

SFX: EEP –EEP –EEP! (getting louder)

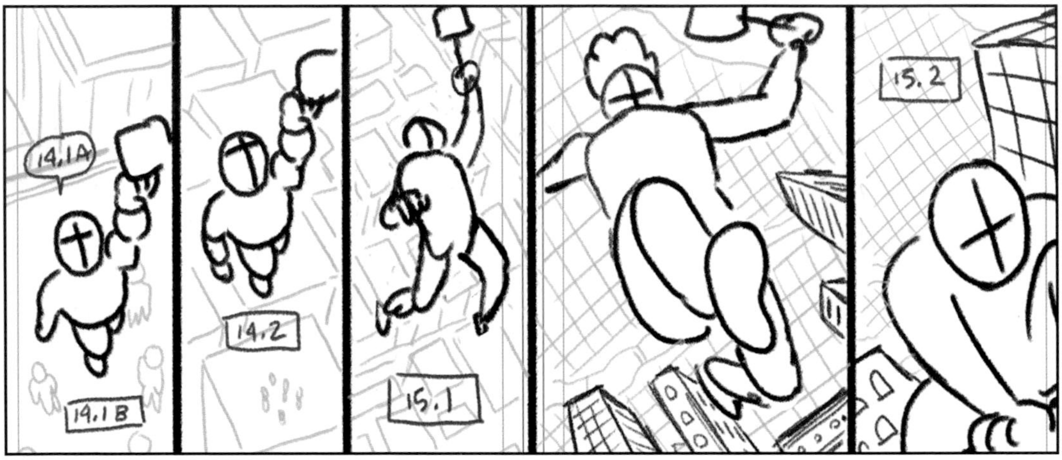
14.1A
14.1B
14.2
15.1
15.2

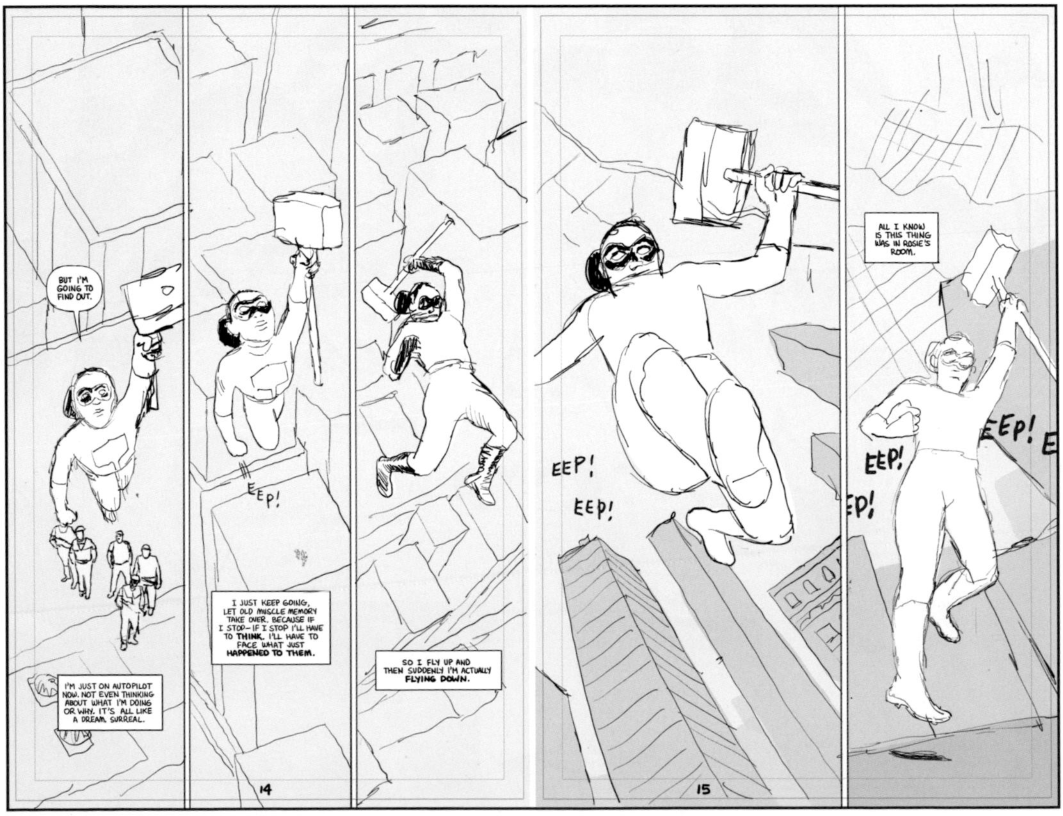
BUT I'M GOING TO FIND OUT.
I'M JUST ON AUTOPILOT NOW. NOT EVEN THINKING ABOUT WHAT I'M DOING OR WHY. IT'S ALL LIKE A DREAM. SURREAL.
EEP!
I JUST KEEP GOING, LET OLD MUSCLE MEMORY TAKE OVER. BECAUSE IF I STOP– IF I STOP I'LL HAVE TO THINK. I'LL HAVE TO FACE WHAT JUST HAPPENED TO THEM.
SO I FLY UP AND THEN SUDDENLY I'M ACTUALLY FLYING DOWN.
14
EEP!
EEP!
ALL I KNOW IS THIS THING WAS IN ROSIE'S ROOM.
EEP!
EEP!
EEP!
15

The script, my layout, then Matt's layout. I really wanted to capture the disorientation of Lucy flying from one rooftop onto an upside-down rooftop. Lots of adjustments to get it just right.

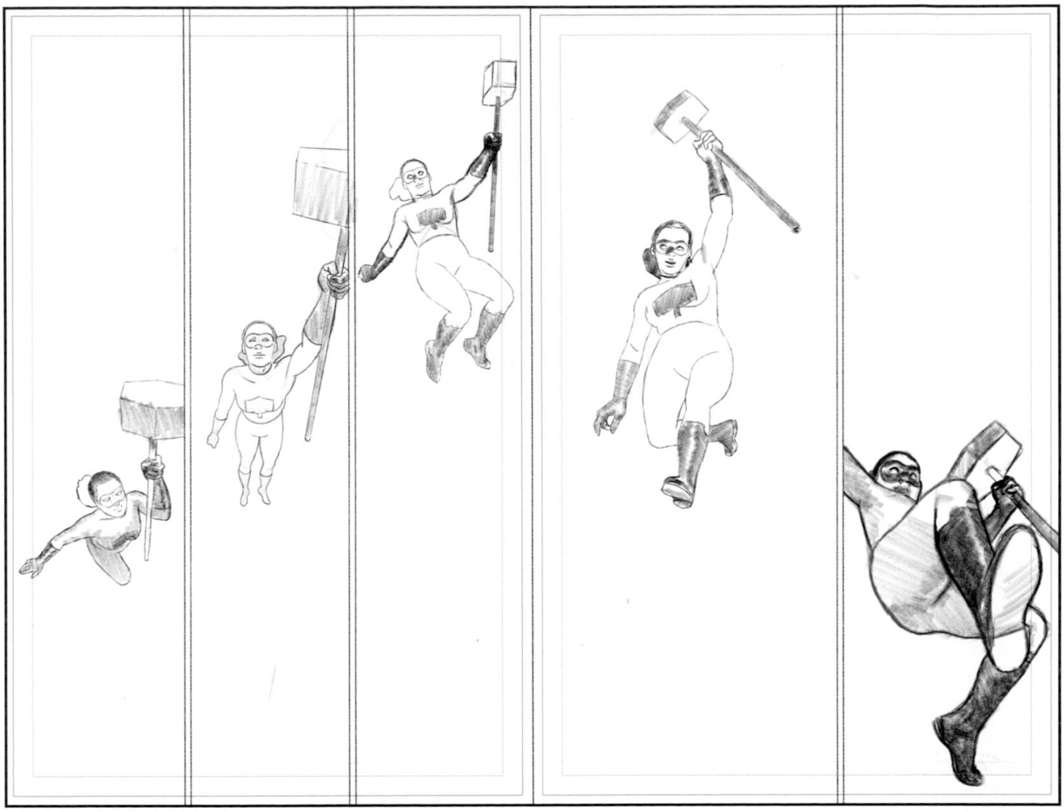

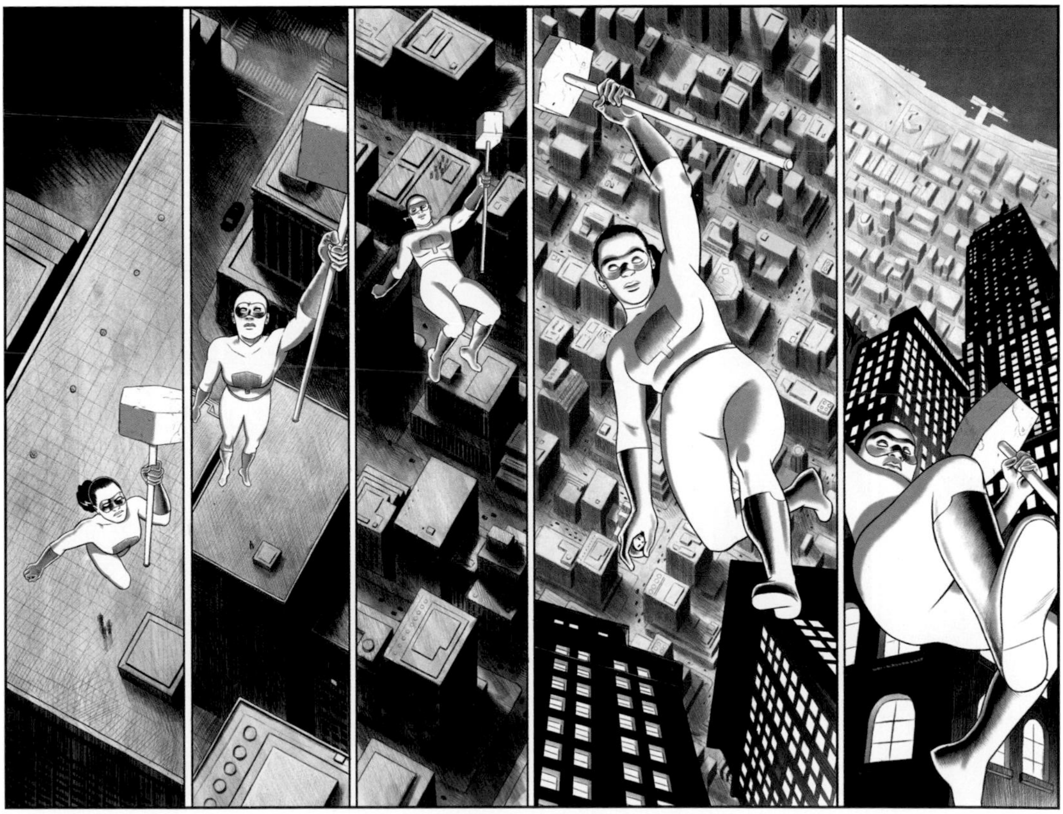

This is the only time where Matt drew the figures and I drew the backgrounds. We also adjusted the angle and size of the fourth Lucy for a cleaner flow across the spread.

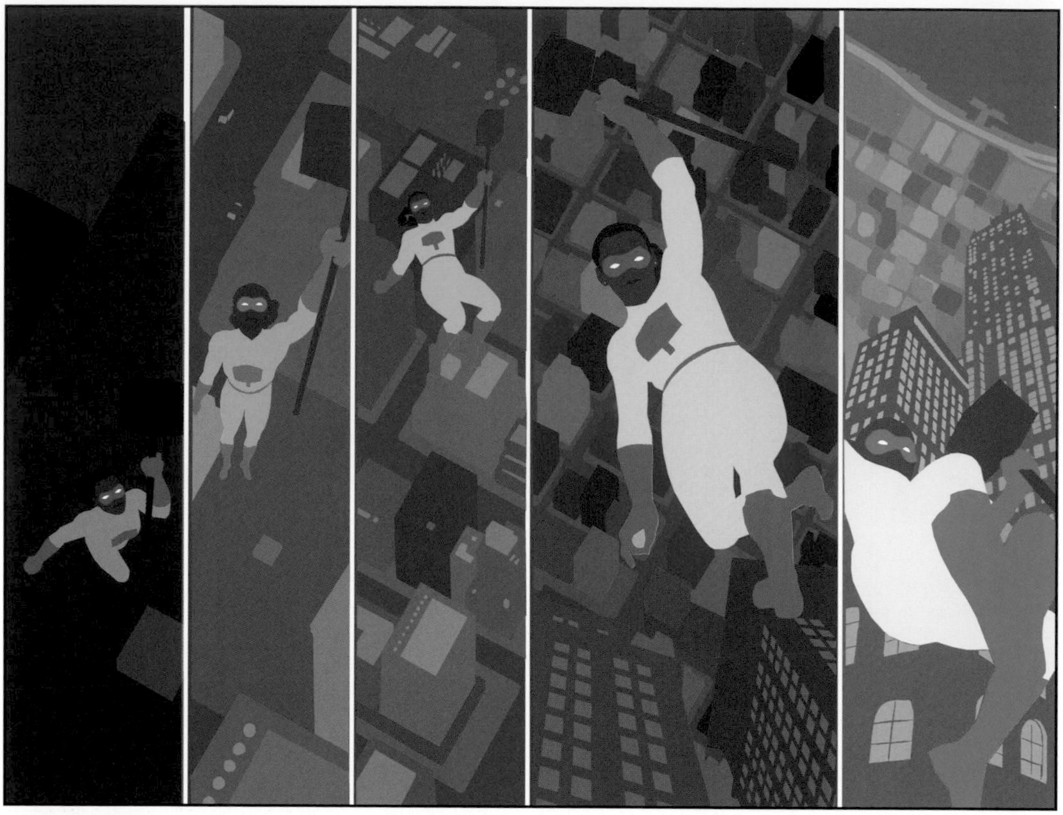

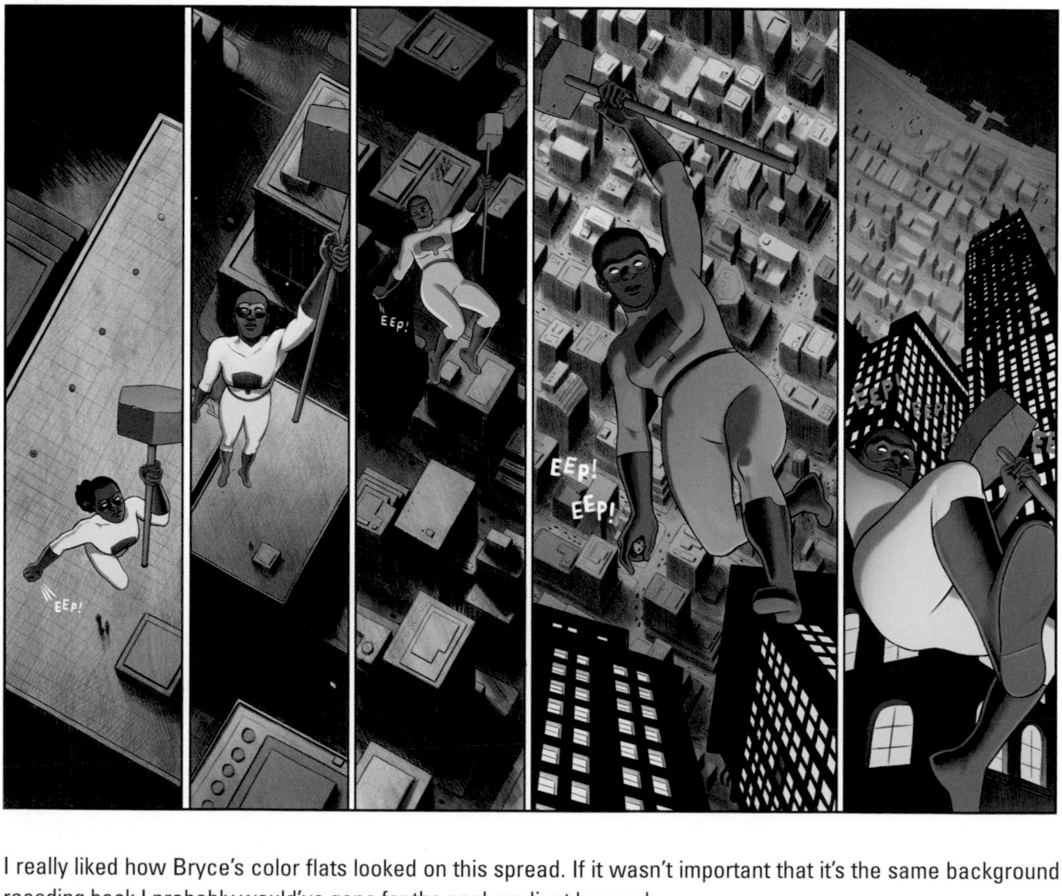
EEP!
EEP!
EEP!
EEP!

I really liked how Bryce's color flats looked on this spread. If it wasn't important that it's the same background receding back I probably would've gone for the cool gradient he used.

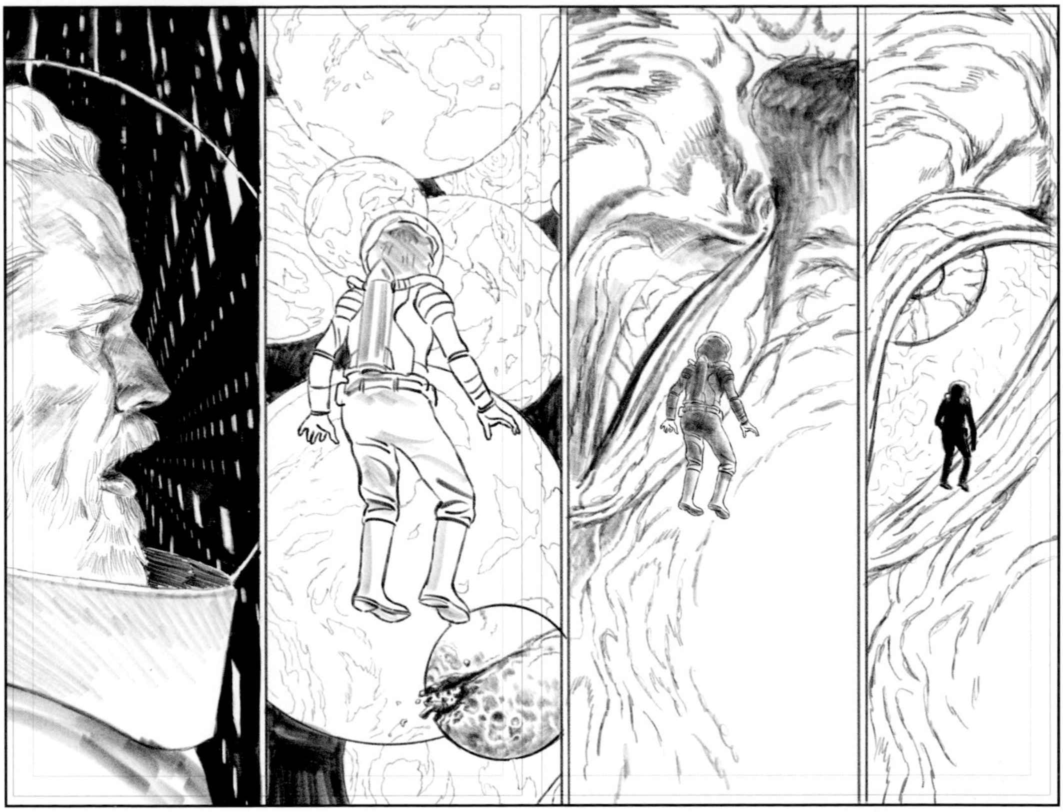

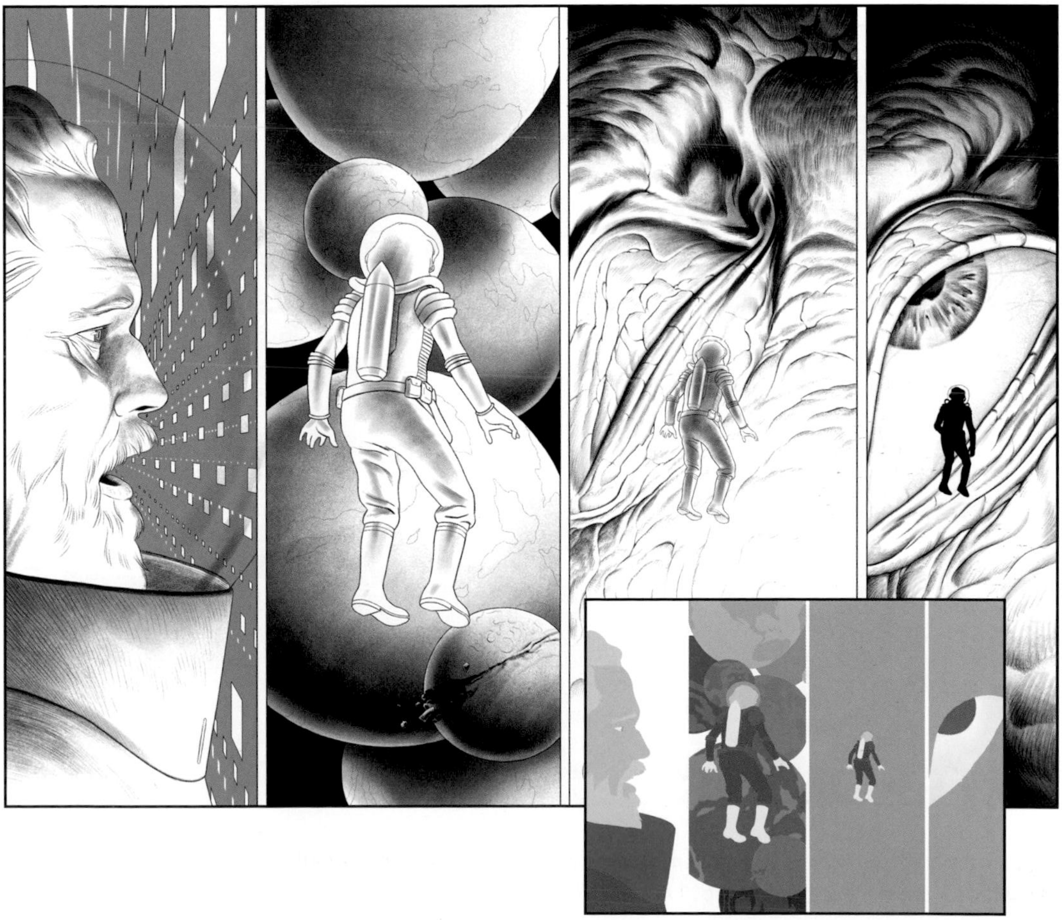

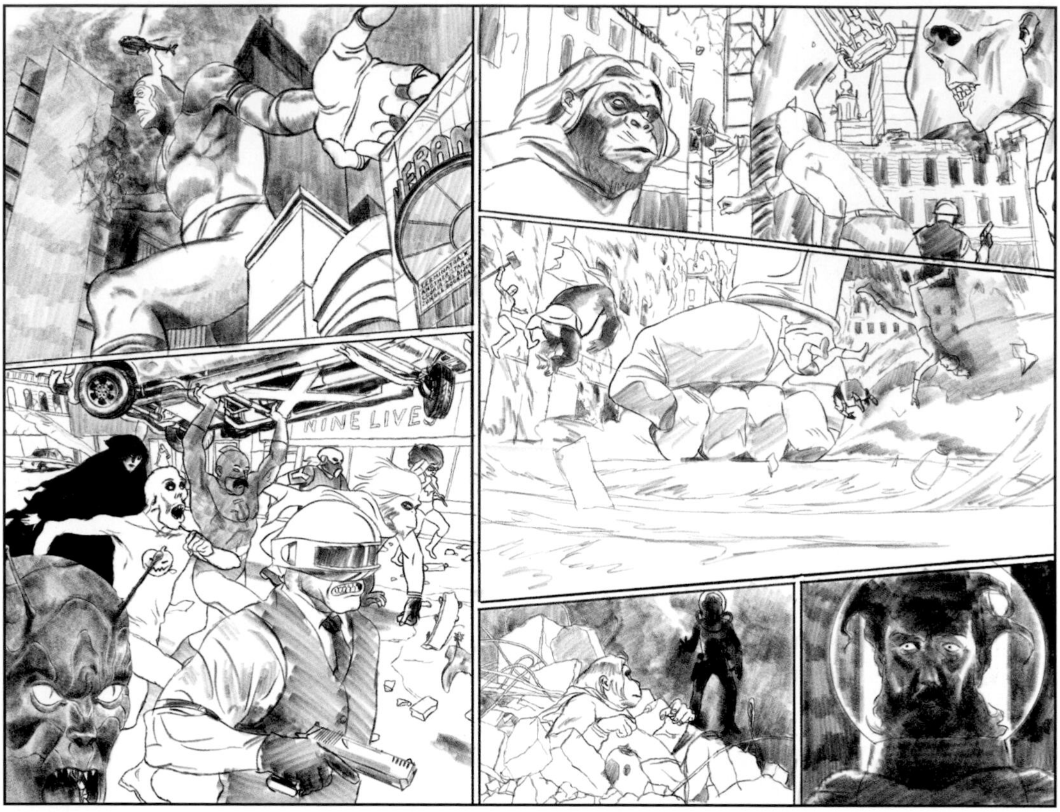
NINE LIVES

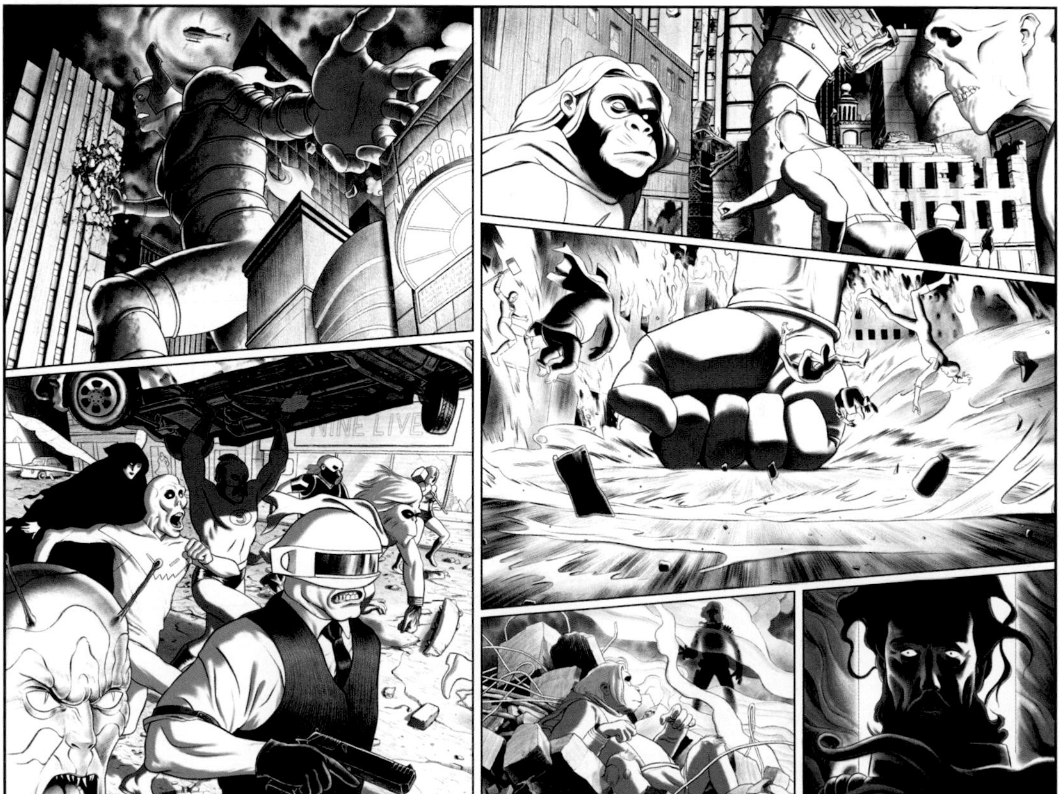

We had basically one spread to go full crisis mode. It's both a pain and fun to do these destroyed-city sequences. Might have more of those in the future . . .

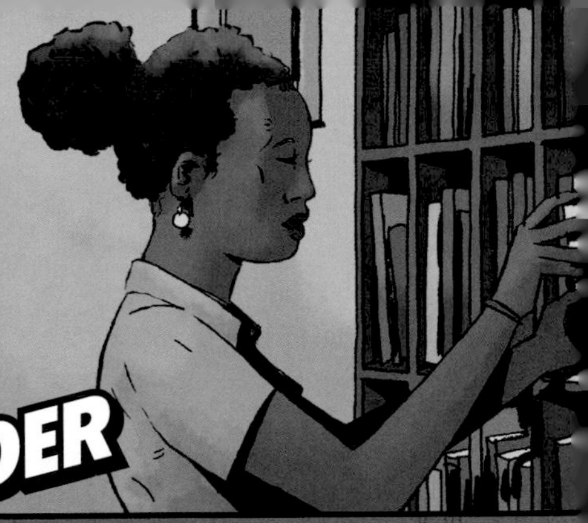

BLACK HAMMER™
RECOMMENDED READING ORDER

TRADES

1. **BLACK HAMMER VOL. 1: SECRET ORIGINS TPB**
   Collects *Black Hammer* #1–#6
   ISBN 978-1-61655-786-7 | **$14.99**

2. **BLACK HAMMER VOL. 2: THE EVENT TPB**
   Collects *Black Hammer* #7–#11, #13
   ISBN 978-1-50670-198-1 | **$19.99**

3. **SHERLOCK FRANKENSTEIN AND THE LEGION OF EVIL TPB**
   Collects *Black Hammer* #12 and *Sherlock Frankenstein and the Legion of Evil* #1–#4
   ISBN 978-1-50670-526-2 | **$17.99**

4. **DOCTOR ANDROMEDA AND THE KINGDOM OF LOST TOMORROWS TPB**
   ISBN 978-1-50670-[illegible]-7 | **$19.99**

5. **BLACK HAMMER VOL. 3: AGE OF DOOM PART 1 TPB**
   Collects *Black Hammer: Age of Doom* #1–#5
   ISBN 978-1-50670-389-3 | **$19.99**

6. **BLACK HAMMER VOL. 4: AGE OF DOOM PART 2 TPB**
   Collects *Black Hammer: Age of Doom* #6–#12
   ISBN 978-1-50670-816-4 | **$19.99**

7. **THE QUANTUM AGE TPB**
   Collects "The Quantum Age" from *Free Comic Book Day 2018* and *The Quantum Age* #1–#6
   ISBN 978-1-50670-841-6 | **$19.99**

8. **BLACK HAMMER '45 TPB**
   Collects *Black Hammer '45* #1–#4
   ISBN 978-1-50670-850-8 | **$17.99**

9. **BLACK HAMMER: STREETS OF SPIRAL TPB**
   Collects *Black Hammer: Giant-Sized Annual*, *Black Hammer: Cthu-Louise*, *The World of Black Hammer Encyclopedia*, and "Horrors to Come" from *Free Comic Book Day 2019*
   ISBN 978-1-50670-941-3 | **$19.99**

10. **BLACK HAMMER/ JUSTICE LEAGUE HC**
    Collects *Black Hammer/Justice League: Hammer of Justice!* #1–#5
    ISBN 978-1-50671-099-0 | **$19.99**

11. **SKULLDIGGER AND SKELETON BOY TPB**
    Collects *Skulldigger and Skeleton Boy* #1–#6
    ISBN 978-1-50671-033-4 | **$19.99**

12. **COLONEL WEIRD: COSMAGOG TPB**
    Collects *Colonel Weird: Cosmagog* #1–#4
    ISBN 978-1-50671-516-2 | **$19.99**

13. **BARBALIEN: RED PLANET TPB**
    Collects *Barbalien: Red Planet* #1–#5
    ISBN 978-1-50671-580-3 | **$19.99**

LIBRARY EDITIONS

1. **BLACK HAMMER LIBRARY EDITION VOL. 1**
   Collects *Black Hammer* #1–#13 and *Black Hammer: Giant-Sized Annual*
   ISBN 978-1-50671-073-0 | **$49.99**

2. **THE WORLD OF BLACK HAMMER LIBRARY EDITION VOL. 1**
   Collects *Sherlock Frankenstein and the Legion of Evil* and *Doctor Andromeda and the Kingdom of Lost Tomorrows*
   ISBN 978-1-50671-995-5 | **$49.99**

3. **BLACK HAMMER LIBRARY EDITION VOL. 2**
   Collects *Black Hammer: Age of Doom* #1–#12, *Black Hammer: Cthu-Louise*, and *The World of Black Hammer Encyclopedia*
   ISBN 978-1-50671-185-0 | **$49.99**

4. **THE WORLD OF BLACK HAMMER LIBRARY EDITION VOL. 2**
   Collects *The Quantum Age* and *Black Hammer '45*
   ISBN 978-1-50671-996-2 | **$49.99**

BLACK HAMMER SECRET ORIGINS
BLACK HAMMER THE EVENT
JEFF LEMIRE DEAN ORMSTON DAVID RUBIN DAVE STEWART
SHERLOCK FRANKENSTEIN
JEFF LEMIRE DAVID RUBIN
DOCTOR ANDROMEDA
JEFF LEMIRE MAX FIUMARA
BLACK HAMMER AGE OF DOOM
BLACK HAMMER AGE OF DOOM
THE QUANTUM AGE
BLACK HAMMER '45
BLACK HAMMER STREETS OF SPIRAL
BLACK HAMMER JUSTICE LEAGUE
HAMMER OF JUSTICE!
SKULLDIGGER SKELETON BOY
COLONEL WEIRD COSMAGOG
BARBALIEN RED PLANET
BLACK HAMMER
BLACK HAMMER
BLACK HAMMER
BLACK HAMMER

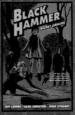

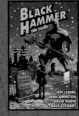

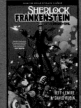

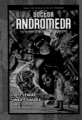

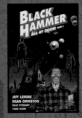

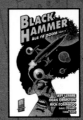

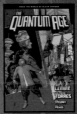

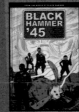

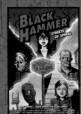

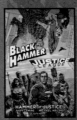

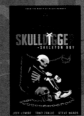

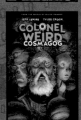

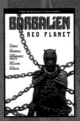

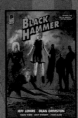

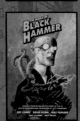

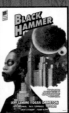

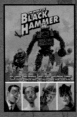

"If you think there's no room left in your life for another superhero comic, *Black Hammer* might just prove you wrong."—IGN

BLACK HAMMER

ONCE THEY WERE HEROES, but the age of heroes has long since passed. Banished from existence by a multiversal crisis, the old champions of Spiral City—Abraham Slam, Golden Gail, Colonel Weird, Madame Dragonfly, and Barbalien—now lead simple lives in an idyllic, timeless farming village from which there is no escape! And yet, the universe isn't done with them—it's time for one last grand adventure.

BLACK HAMMER
Written by Jeff Lemire • Art by Dean Ormston

LIBRARY EDITION VOLUME 1
978-1-50671-073-0 • $49.99

LIBRARY EDITION VOLUME 2
978-1-50671-185-0 • $49.99

THE WORLD OF BLACK HAMMER
LIBRARY EDITION VOLUME 1
978-1-50671-995-5 • $49.99

LIBRARY EDITION VOLUME 2
978-1-50671-996-2 • $49.99

VOLUME 1: SECRET ORIGINS
978-1-61655-786-7 • $14.99

VOLUME 2: THE EVENT
978-1-50670-198-1 • $19.99

VOLUME 3: AGE OF DOOM
PART ONE
978-1-50670-389-3 • $19.99

VOLUME 4: AGE OF DOOM
PART TWO
978-1-50670-816-4 • $19.99

VOLUME 5:
BLACK HAMMER REBORN
PART ONE
Art by Caitlin Yarsky
978-1-50671-426-4 • $19.99

VOLUME 6:
BLACK HAMMER REBORN
PART TWO
Written by Jeff Lemire
Art by Malachi Ward
and Matthew Sheean
978-1-50671-515-5 • $19.99

SHERLOCK FRANKENSTEIN & THE LEGION OF EVIL
Written by Jeff Lemire
Art by David Rubín
978-1-50670-526-2 • $17.99

DOCTOR ANDROMEDA & THE KINGDOM OF LOST TOMORROWS
Written by Jeff Lemire
Art by Max Fiumara
978-1-50672-329-7 • $19.99

THE UNBELIEVABLE UNTEENS: FROM THE WORLD OF BLACK HAMMER
VOLUME 1
Written by Jeff Lemire
Art by Tyler Crook, Tonci Zonjic,
Ray Fawkes, and others
978-1-50672-436-2 • $19.99

THE QUANTUM AGE: FROM THE WORLD OF BLACK HAMMER
VOLUME 1
Written by Jeff Lemire
Art by Wilfredo Torres
978-1-50670-841-6 • $19.99

BLACK HAMMER '45: FROM THE WORLD OF BLACK HAMMER
Written by Jeff Lemire and Ray Fawkes
Art by Matt Kindt and Sharlene Kindt
978-1-50670-850-8 • $17.99

COLONEL WEIRD— COSMAGOG: FROM THE WORLD OF BLACK HAMMER
Written by Jeff Lemire
Art by Tyler Crook
978-1-50671-516-2 • $19.99

BLACK HAMMER: STREETS OF SPIRAL
Written by Jeff Lemire, Tate Brombal, and Ray Fawkes
Art by Dean Ormston, Matt Kindt, Tyler Crook, and others
978-1-50670-941-3 • $19.99

BLACK HAMMER/ JUSTICE LEAGUE: HAMMER OF JUSTICE!
Written by Jeff Lemire
Art by Michael Walsh
978-1-50671-099-0 • $29.99

BARBALIEN: RED PLANET
Written by Jeff Lemire and Tate Brombal
Art by Gabriel Hernández Walta and Jordie Bellaire
978-1-50671-580-3 • $19.99

SKULLDIGGER AND SKELETON BOY
Written by Jeff Lemire
Art by Tonci Zonjic
978-1-50671-033-4 • $19.99

BLACK HAMMER VISIONS
VOLUME 1
Written by Patton Oswalt, Geoff Johns, Chip Zdarsky, and Mariko Tamaki
Art by Johnnie Christmas, Scott Kollins, and Diego Olortegui
978-1-50672-326-6 • $24.99

VOLUME 2
Written by Kelly Thompson, Scott Snyder, Cecil Castelluci, and Cullen Bunn
Art by David Rubín, Matthew Sheean, Melissa Duffy, and others
978-1-50672-551-2 • $24.99

AVAILABLE AT YOUR LOCAL COMICS SHOP OR BOOKSTORE
TO FIND A COMICS SHOP IN YOUR AREA, VISIT COMICSHOPLOCATOR.COM.
For more information or to order direct, visit darkhorse.com.

Black Hammer™, Sherlock Frankenstein™, Doctor Andromeda™, Colonel Weird™, Quantum Age™, Skulldigger and Skeleton Boy™, and Barbalien™ © 171 Studios, Inc., and Dean Ormston. Justice League, DC logo, and all related characters and elements are © and ™ DC Comics. Dark Horse Books and the Dark Horse logo are registered trademarks of Dark Horse Comics LLC. All rights reserved. (BL 6098)

DARK HORSE BOOKS